Langland's Vision
of
Piers Plowman.

The Vernon Text; or Text A.

The Vision of William

concerning

Piers Plowman,

TOGETHER WITH

Vita de Dowel, Dobet, et Dobest,

Secundum Wit et Resoun,

BY WILLIAM LANGLAND.
(1362 A.D.)

EDITED FROM THE "VERNON" MS., COLLATED WITH MS. R. 3. 14. IN THE
LIBRARY OF TRINITY COLLEGE, CAMBRIDGE, MSS. HARL. 875 & 6041,
THE MS. IN UNIVERSITY COLLEGE, OXFORD, MS. DOUCE 323, &c.

BY THE
REV. WALTER W. SKEAT, M.A.,
LATE FELLOW OF CHRIST'S COLLEGE, CAMBRIDGE.

THE "VERNON" TEXT; OR TEXT A.

Published for
THE EARLY ENGLISH TEXT SOCIETY
by the
OXFORD UNIVERSITY PRESS
LONDON   NEW YORK   TORONTO

OXFORD
UNIVERSITY PRESS

Great Clarendon Street, Oxford OX2 6DP
United Kingdom

Oxford University Press is a department of the University of Oxford.
It furthers the University's objective of excellence in research, scholarship,
and education by publishing worldwide. Oxford is a registered trade mark of
Oxford University Press in the UK and in certain other countries

© The Early English Text Society 1867

The moral rights of the authors have been asserted

Database right Oxford University Press (maker)

First Edition published in 1867

All rights reserved. No part of this publication may be reproduced,
stored in a retrieval system, or transmitted, in any form or by any means,
without the prior permission in writing of Oxford University Press,
or as expressly permitted by law, or under terms agreed with the appropriate
reprographics rights organization. Enquiries concerning reproduction
outside the scope of the above should be sent to the Rights Department,
Oxford University Press, at the address above

You must not circulate this book in any other form
and you must impose this same condition on any acquirer

Published in the United States of America by Oxford University Press
198 Madison Avenue, New York, NY 10016, United States of America

British Library Cataloguing in Publication Data
Data available

Library of Congress Cataloging in Publication Data
Data available

Original Series, 28

ISBN 978-0-85-991815-2

CONTENTS

	PAGE
INTRODUCTION	iii

PREFACE I. § 1. Numerous MSS. of "Piers Plowman." § 2. The three forms of it. § 3. The earliest form. § 4. Description of MSS.: I. MS. V; II. MS. H; III. MS. T; IV. MS. U; V. MS. H₂; VI. MS. D; VII. MS. A; VIII. Lincoln's Inn MS.; IX. Harl. 3954; X. Digby 145. § 5. Discussion of the extent of the early MSS. § 6. The exact point of their termination. § 7. *Unique* lines found in MS. U. § 8. Method of printing the text. § 9. The foot-notes. § 10. Alliterative Verse. § 11. Date of the poem. § 12. Author's name and life. § 13. Argument of the poem xii

PROLOGUE TO PIERS PLOWMAN (109 lines)	1
PASSUS I. (185 lines)	7
PASSUS II. (212 lines)	17
PASSUS III. (282 lines)	28
PASSUS IV. (158 lines)	43
PASSUS V. (263 lines)	52
PASSUS VI. (126 lines)	67
PASSUS VII. (311 lines)	74
PASSUS VIII. (187 lines)	92
PASSUS IX., OR PROLOGUE TO DOWEL (118 lines)	103
PASSUS X., OR PASSUS I. OF DOWEL (213 lines)	110
PASSUS XI., OR PASSUS II. OF DOWEL (303 lines)	122
CRITICAL NOTES	137
GENERAL COMPARISON OF TEXTS A AND B	156

INTRODUCTION.

HAVING more than once been asked the question—"What *is* Piers Plowman?"—it occurs to me that it will be useful to many readers to have this question answered for them in a few words. Many persons, even scholars and antiquaries, have loosely used the title *Piers Plowman* as though it were the *name of an author*, instead of remembering that it is the name or subject of a poem; it would be a mistake exactly similar to this, to attribute the "Pilgrim's Progress" to *Christian*. But the author's name is Langland, probably William Langland, and the name of his poem is—The Vision of William concerning Piers Plowman, which has been more briefly expressed as—The Vision of Piers Plowman. But this shorter title is most misleading; so few apprehend the fact that the word *of* in this case is a translation of the Latin *de*, and not the sign of the genitive case; and the confusion has been made far worse by the circumstance that there is another and distinct poem, by another author, the name of which is "Pierce Ploughman's Crede," or "The Crede of Pierce Ploughman," in which the word "of" *is* the sign of the genitive case. If the reader will only bear in mind these two uses of the word *of*, he need never go wrong in this matter. Having thus cleared the way by this preliminary explanation, the whole matter may be briefly stated thus. A poet of the reign of Edward the Third, of whom scarcely anything is known but the name (and even that is uncertain), wrote a poem in alliterative verse which he threw into the form of several successive visions; in *one* of these he describes his favourite ideal character—Piers [1]—and in course of time

---

[1] The character of Piers, in its highest form of development, is identified by Langland with that of Christ the Saviour—"Petrus est Christus."

the name was used as a common title for the whole series of them. His vivid descriptions and earnest language caused the poem to be very popular, and the fertile imagination of the author induced him to rewrite the whole poem twice over, so that what may fairly be called three editions of it still exist in manuscript. The first or earliest of these is given in this volume, and is of great interest.[1] It is the scarcest of the three, and yet sufficiently common; the whole number of MSS. of the poem being very large. The poem—in all its shapes—abounds with passages which we could ill afford to lose; the vivid truthfulness of its delineations of the life and manners of our forefathers has been often praised, and it is difficult to praise it too highly. "Everywhere it gives flesh and blood to its abstractions by the most vigorous directness of familiar detail, so that every truth might, if possible, go home, even by the cold hearth-stone of the hungriest and most desolate of the poor, to whom its words of a wise sympathy might be recited."[2] As indicating the true temper and feelings of the English mind in the fourteenth century, it is worth volumes of history; and the student who is desirous of understanding this period aright cannot possibly neglect Langland and Chaucer. Strangely too, and fortunately, these two authors are, in a great measure, each the supplement of the other. Chaucer describes the rich much more fully than the poor, and shews the holiday-making, cheerful, genial phase of English life; but Langland pictures the homely poor in their ill-fed, hard-working condition, battling against hunger, famine, injustice, oppression, and all the stern realities and hardships that tried them as gold is tried in the fire. Chaucer's satire often raises a good-humoured laugh; but Langland's is that of a man who is constrained to speak out all the bitter truth, and it is as earnest as is the cry of an injured man who appeals to heaven for vengeance. Each, in his own way, is equally admirable, and worthy to be honoured by all who prize highly the English character and our own dear native land. There is a danger that some who take up "Piers Plow-

[1] In particular, Passus X. and XI. contain much that has *never been printed before*.
[2] Professor Morley, English Writers, vol. 1, p. 758; see also p. 775. The reader will also find some most valuable remarks upon Langland's poem in **Dean Milman's** History of Latin Christianity.

man" may be at first somewhat repelled by the allegorical form of it, or by an apparent archaism of language,[1] and some passages are sufficiently abstruse to require a little thought and care to be taken before one can seize their full meaning; but there are few books that so thoroughly repay a little painstaking consideration, and, when once the spirit of the poem is fully entered into, it is found to be replete with interest and instruction. The reader who does not throw it aside *at first* will hardly do so afterwards; and so it must ever be with the works of a true poet, when once the mind is attuned to his thoughts and feelings. Such, then, is "Piers Plowman," a poem written with as intense an earnestness and as untiring a search after truth—which is the ever-recurring burden of it—as any in the English language.

The extreme earnestness of the author and the obvious truthfulness and blunt honesty of his character are in themselves attractive and lend a value to all he utters, even when he is evolving a theory or wanders into abstract questions of theological speculation. But we are the more pleased when we perceive, as we very soon do, that he is evidently of a *practical* turn of mind, and loves best to exercise his shrewd English common sense upon topics of every-day interest. How often does the student of history grow weary of mere accounts of battles and sieges and the long series of plunders and outrages revenged by other plunders and outrages which require to be again revenged in their turn, and so on without end, and long to get an insight into the inner every-day life of the people, their dress, their diet, their wages, their strikes, and all the minor details which picture to us what manner of men they really were! And it is in such a poem as the present that we find all this, and find it, too, not

---

[1] To acquire a *thorough* knowledge of old English is, indeed, almost the work of a lifetime. But *some* familiarity with it, enough to enable one to understand a large portion of our early literature, may be picked up in a few weeks—almost in a few days. It is amazing to find what a bugbear "old English" is to many Englishmen; they look upon it as harder to learn than Chinese. Yet any one who will take the trouble to master one or two of the Canterbury Tales has the key to much of the wealth of our early English literature; and the man who will *not* take the trouble to do this deserves to be guided by guesswork rather than by evidence in his notions of English grammar; as he probably will be.

vi   INTRODUCTION.

merely hinted at or presupposed, but sketched out vividly and to the life by a master-hand. That this is really the case might be shewn by numberless quotations, but the reader will probably prefer to see a few good instances of it only, that he may be tempted to find out more for himself.

To plunge at once *in medias res.* Here is the interior of a beerhouse in the time of Edward the Third, and a description of the company therein.[1]

" Cisse the sutor's[2] wife · sat on the bench,
Wat the warrener · and his wife both,
Tomkin the tinker · and twain of his knaves,
Hick the hackney-man · and Hogg the neelder,[3]
Clarice of Cook's lane · and the clerk of the church,
Sir Piers of Pridie · and Pernel of Flanders,
Daw the ditcher · and a dozen other.
A ribibour,[4] a rattoner[5] · a raker of chepe,[6]
A roper, a reding-king[7] · and Rose the disher,
Godfrey of Garlickshire · and Griffin the Welsh,
And of upholders a heap · early by the morrow
Give the Glutton with good will · good ale to hansel.
Then Clement the Cobbler · cast off his cloak,
And at the new fair · he laid it to sell;
And Hick the ostler · hit[8] his hood after,
And bade Bet the butcher · be on his *side.*
There were chapmen chosen · the *ware to appraise;*
Whoso had the hood · should have [some] amends.
They rise up rapely[9] · and rowned[10] together,
Appraising the pennyworths · and parted [them] by themselves.
There were oaths a heap · *whoever them* heard !
They could not, *for* their conscience · accord to-gether,

In these extracts, I have modernized the spelling, and where words are printed in italics, have slightly altered the language. Words between brackets are insertions of my own. With such slight changes how easy the language becomes ! The *first* extract is a passage of *unusual* difficulty.   [2] cobbler's.
[3] Needle-seller.   [4] ribibe-player.   [5] rat-catcher.   [6] a vagrant chapman.
[7] one of a certain class of feudal retainers.   [8] Here used in the sense of " cast."
[9] rapidly, in a hurry.   [10] whispered, buzzed.

Till Robin the roper · was red¹ to arise,
And named for a numpire · that no debate *were*.
Then Hick the ostler · had the cloak,
In covenant that Clement · should the cup fill
And have Hick's hood—the ostler's · and hold himself *paid* ;
And he that repented rathest² · should arise thereafter,
And greet Sir glutton · with a gallon of ale.
There was laughing and lotering³ · and 'let go the cup ;'
Bargains and beverages · began to arise,
And [they] sat so till evensong · and sung some while,
Till Glutton had gulpèd · a gallon and a gill," &c.—V. 158—191.

Not so unlike modern English common life—these " bargains and beverages," and the " oaths a heap !"

Mark, on the other hand, how our author praises temperance.

" Eat not, I hote⁴ thee · till hunger thee take,
And send thee some of his sauce · to savour thee the better.
Keep some till supper time · and sit thou not too long ;
Arise up ere appetite · hath eaten his fill ;
Let not Sir Surfeit · sit at thy board.
And if thou diet thee thus · I dare lay both my ears,
That Physic shall his furred hood · for his food sell,
And eke his cloak of Calabre · with knobs of gold,
And be fain, by my faith ! his physic to *leave*,
And learn to labour with land · lest livelihood fail."
VII. 248—259.

That is, if men were only temperate and consented to diet themselves, doctors would have to turn farm-labourers to get a living ! A lesson as valuable as it is true, and men are nearly as far off as ever from learning it.

Or suppose, again, that we would know somewhat as to the diet of the poor. Here is the explicit statement of it.

" ' I have no penny,' quoth Piers · ' pullets to buy,
Neither geese nor grice⁵ · but two green cheeses,

---

¹ told, bidden.   ² soonest.   ³ badinage, " chaffing."
⁴ bid.   ⁵ pigs.

And a few curds and cream · and a therf[1] cake,
And a loaf of beans and bran · baked for my children.
And I say, by my soul ! · I have no salt bacon,
Nor no cokeneys,[2] by Christ · collops to make.
But I have porets [3] and parsley · and many cole[4]-plants,
And eke a cow, and a calf · and a cart-mare
To draw afield the dung · while the drought lasteth.
By this livelihood must I live · till Lammas time,
By that, I hope to have · harvest in my croft,
Then may I dight thy dinner · as thee *best* liketh.'
All the poor people · peas-cods fetched,
Baked beans in bread · they brought in their laps,
Chibolles, chief meat [5] (?) · and ripe cherries many,
And proffered Piers this present · *therewith* to please Hunger."
VII. 267—282.

This bread made of beans is the same, I suppose, as the horses and dogs ate :—

" With hounds' bread and horse-bread · hold up their hearts ! "
VII. 203.

This was all very palatable when wages were low, but as soon as the poor got higher wages, as they did at harvest time, nothing would serve them but the finest wheat-bread, and the best and brownest ale ; none of your " half-penny ale " then, or " penny ale " either.

" Labourers that have no land · to live on but their hands,
Deign not to dine a-day · [on] a-night-old worts,
May no penny-ale them *please* · nor no piece of bacon,
But only fresh flesh · or else fried fish,
Both " chaud " and " plus-chaud " · *against* chilling of their maw !
Except he be highly hired · else will he chide,
That he was a workman wrought · [he will] warie the time,[6]
And curse *deeply* the king · and all his council after,
Such laws to *make* · labourers to chasten."—VII. 295—302.

[1] unleavened. [2] lean fowls. [3] a kind of leek. [4] cabbage.
[5] What is " cheef mete " ? Another reading is " kernels," or else " chervils " (Wright), and another " chest-nuts." *Chibolles* are leeks. [6] curse the hour.

Langland is peculiarly at home when he adopts a satirical vein, and I select the following among many instances of it. He describes how the king made up his mind to punish Falsehood, Guile, and Liar, if he could possibly catch hold of them, whereon the three delinquents made off as fast as they could, and could meet with no kindly reception but with the friars, the pardoners, and cheating tradesmen. No one else would have anything to do with them!

"Then Falsehood for fear · fled to the friars;
And Guile doth him to go [1] · aghast for to die,
But merchants met with him · and made him abide,
Besought him in their shops · to sell their ware,
Apparelled him as a 'prentice · the people to serve.
Lightly Liar · leapt away thence,
Lurking through lanes · to-lugged [2] *by* many.
He *was* nowhere welcome · for his many tales,
But *everywhere* hunted · and hote to truss.[3]
Pardoners had pity · and put him to house,
Washed him and wrung him · and wound him in clouts,
And sent him on Sundays · with seals to churches,
And [he] gave pardon for pence · pound-mele [4] aboute," &c.
II. 186—198.

Not that the pardoners were quite allowed to monopolize Liar; the quack-doctors and grocers wanted to press him into their service just as much.

Still better is the poet's indignant reproof of the pert boys who think to shew off their cleverness by scoffing at God and His just ways.

"Now is each boy bold · brothels [5] and others,
To talk of the Trinity · to be holden a sire,
And findeth forth fancies · our faith to impair,
And eke defameth the Father · that us all made,
And *talks* against the clergy · crabbed words.
'Why would God our Saviour · suffer such a worm
In such a wrong wise · the woman to beguile?

---

[1] prepares himself to depart. [2] lugged about, teased.
[3] bidden to pack. [4] by whole pounds at a time. [5] reprobates.

Both hir husband and she · to hell through him went,
And their seed for that sin · the same woe *suffer ?*'
Such motives they move · these masters in their glory,
And make men misbelieve · that muse on their words."

XI. 61—69.

But to pick out all the interesting passages would be to transcribe half the poem; and I may refer the reader to the Preface following—pp. xxxiii., xxxiv., and xxxviii.—for further remarks on the character of the work and of its author, and to pp. xxxix.—xliii. for an "argument" of the whole of the earliest version. I now merely add one more extract, in quite a different strain, which is especially interesting as indicating the dawn of the Reformation, and which (towards the end) is hardly less distinctly and vigorously put than it would have been by Luther himself.

" Now hath the pope power · pardon to grant,
  For people without penance · to pass *into* joy.
  This is a leaf of our belief · as lettered men *teach us,*
      Quodcunque ligaveris super terram, erit ligatum et in cœlis.
And so I believe leally · (our Lord forbid it else !)
That pardon and penance · and prayers do save
Souls that have sinned · seven *times* deadly.
But to trust to Triennials · truly, me thinketh,
Is *not* so *sure* for the soul · certes, as Do-well.
Wherefore I rede [1] you, rinks [2] · that rich be on earth,
Upon trust of your treasure · triennials to have,
Be ye never the bolder · to break the ten hests ;
And, namely, ye mayors · and ye master judges,
(That have the wealth of the world · *and* wise men are holden),
To purchase *you* pardons · and the pope's bulls !
At the dreadful day of doom · *when the* dead shall arise,
And come all before Christ · and accounts yield [Him],
How thou leddest thy life · and His law keptest,
What thou diddest day by day · the doom will[3] rehearse.

      [1] advise.   [2] men.
    [3] Here I have omitted "þe" = for thee, as relates to thee.

A pack full of pardon there · with Provincials' letters,
Though thou be found in Fraternity · among the Four Orders,
And have indulgence doubled · but [1] Do-well thee help.
I *would* give for thy pardon · *not* one pie's [2] heel !
Wherefore I counsel all Christians · to cry Christ mercy,
And Mary his mother · to be mean [3] between,
That God give us grace · ere we go hence,
Such works to work · while that we are here,
That, after our death-day · Do-well [may] rehearse
That at the Day of Doom · we did as He hight [4]."

          Passus VIII., ll. 160—187.

[1] unless.   [2] magpie's ?
[3] mediator.   [4] commanded; omitting "us," as in MS. T.

PREFACE I.

TEXT A.

§ 1. THE MSS. of "Piers Plowman" are indeed numerous. Extracts from *twenty-nine* have already been exhibited in my tract published for the E. E. T. S. in 1866. Besides these, I have seen or heard of several others, viz. a second MS. at Dublin, two belonging to Lord Ashburnham,[1] one in the library of Lincoln's Inn, two among the Douce MSS. at Oxford (numbered 104 and 323), MS. Ashmol. No. 1468, one in the possession of H. Yates Thompson, Esq., of Liverpool, and a fragment of four leaves only (but of a fair text), in MS. Lansdowne 398, fol. 77.[2] In MSS. Additional (B. M.), 6399, there is a piece called "Langland, commentary on his Piers Plowman," but it is only a fragment of about three leaves in a modern hand. I feel sure there are yet more in various parts of the country, many probably in private hands, and I should be much obliged for any information concerning them. I have to thank Lord Ashburnham and H. Yates Thompson, Esq., for the kind way in which they have assisted me, by sending me transcripts of the passage printed in the "Extracts," and for further information concerning their MSS.

§ 2. The poem takes no less than *five* different shapes, but *two* of these are merely owing to differences of arrangement made by the scribes; and there are really no more than *three* forms of it. Before discussing these, I shall give to them the following names, for distinct-

---

[1] One of these seems to have belonged to Dr Adam Clarke; but Dr Clarke had *two*. Where is the other?

[2] I think Sir Thos. Phillipps has two other MSS., besides the one from which Whitaker printed his edition.

ness' sake. Those of the *first* or *earliest* form I shall speak of as being of Type A, or of the "Vernon" type, because the best example of it is furnished by the *Vernon* MS. at Oxford; those of the *second* or *next earliest* form belong to Type B, or the "Crowley" type, so named because the earliest printed edition was taken from one of these, and was printed by *Robert Crowley* in 1550;[1] those of the *latest* form belong to Type C, or the "Whitaker" type, of which only one has ever been printed, viz. by Dr Whitaker, in 1813. It will also be convenient to speak of *Text* A, *Text* B, and *Text* C, meaning by these the texts which I am now editing; thus Text A means the text given in the present volume, the text of the best MS. of the *Vernon* type. The present preface, for the most part, concerns MSS. of this type only.

§ 3. Of this earliest and most interesting form of the poem very little seems to have been hitherto known. The only reference to it in Mr Wright's preface to his edition is where he tells us that "a few readings are added from a second MS. in Trinity College Library (R. 3. 14)," of which more presently; and he speaks of only "two classes" of MSS. But in Warton's Hist. of Engl. Poetry, vol. 2, appendix, p. 482, is the following noteworthy passage. "Among the Harley MSS. there is a fragment of this poem written upon vellum (No. 875),[2] of an equally early date with Vespasian B. xvi.,[3] and in a character nearly resembling it. Unhappily this fragment extends only to the 151st line of the 8th passus, nor is it free from lacunæ even thus far.[4] Our loss is however in some measure repaired—perhaps wholly so[5]—by the preservation of a transcript on paper, in the same collection (No. 6041), which, though considerably younger, and somewhat modernized in its orthography, exhibits a much more correct[6]

---

[1] The excellent edition by Mr Wright exhibits this form of the poem.
[2] Described below; see description of MS. No. III.
[3] This MS. is very old and very good; but it belongs to Type C; I can find nothing better of its kind, and shall therefore probably use it to form Text C.
[4] Some leaves are lost; but there are no other lacunæ, except such as it has in common with Harl. 6041 and all the MSS. of the earliest type.
[5] What would Warton have said had he seen some of the MSS. described below! In particular, MS. T closely resembles the one he is here speaking of, but is *far better*.
[6] It is sometimes *less* correct; as the reader may see for himself.

and intelligible text. *From this manuscript it is evident, that another and a third version was once in circulation; and if the first draught of the poem be still in existence, it is here perhaps that we must look for it.* For in this, the narrative is considerably *shortened*, many passages of a decidedly *episodic cast*—such as the tale of the cat and the ratons, and the character of Wrath—are wholly *omitted;* others, which in the later versions are given with *considerable detail* of circumstance, are here but *slightly sketched;* and though *evidently the text-book* of Dr Whitaker's and Crowley's versions, it may be said to agree with *neither*, but to alternate between the ancient and modern printed copies."[1] The italics are mine, intended to draw attention to the truth and importance of the above note, in which most of the characteristics of the early MSS. are so well hit off. I would add further that (as the reader will soon see), we now know of many more MSS. of this type; that we have abundant evidence of its being really the first and original draught of the poem, that Type B is obviously derived from it almost wholly by amplification and addition, and preserves nearly the same order in the narrative, even where C wanders away from both; and that (which greatly helps the argument) the Latin quotations occurring in A are much fewer than those found in the corresponding parts of B and C, even when all allowance is made for the amplification of the story. More than this, such Latin quotations as *do* occur in A are nearly all from the Bible, and chiefly from the more familiar parts of it, the Psalms and the Gospels; in the later texts, they have a wider range. It is also to be noted that the oldest and best MS. yet found, the Vernon MS., belongs to the earliest type. But the great feature of MSS. of the A type is this, that they do not extend beyond eleven passus. They contain considerably less than *one half*, perhaps not much more than *a third* of the whole poem. As there is, in the case of three of them, an apparent contradiction to this, this point will be best discussed after the MSS. have been fully described; and, to make the matter clear as briefly as possible, I here at once enter on the description of all the MSS. of this class with which I am acquainted.

[1] He means, between Crowley's and Whitaker's copies. To "alternate" is scarcely the right word; it is *far* closer to the former of these than the latter. Still, it sometimes comes closer to the latter in a few points.

§ 4. DESCRIPTION OF THE MSS.

I. Vernon MS. ; denoted throughout this volume by the letter V, and used to form Text A.[1] Its date is about 1370—1380. This MS. is indeed a noble and an admirable one. Its immense size, and the beauty of the vellum, of the writing, and of the illuminated letters have long since attracted notice, and it has already been made considerable use of by editors, and several extracts from it are in print. It would be a good deed to print it all, and it will receive considerable attention from our Society. It has received the name of "Sowlehele," as containing things useful for the *soul's health ;* and the name is a good one : the poems and treatises in it, which are very numerous, being chiefly of a religious cast. On a square slip, pasted inside the cover, are the words, somewhat defaced, "Bibliothecæ Bodleianæ Dono dedit Edvardus Vernon Armiger olim ex col. Trin. in hac universitate Superioris ordinis Commensalis in nupero bello civili a partibus regijs strenue propugnabat Militum tribu[nus]." It contains considerably more than 400 large leaves, each containing two columns, and each column, when written without breaks, contains about 80 lines.[2] The "Piers Plowman" occupies but a small space in it, beginning at fol. 394 *b*, col. 2, and ending with fol. 401 *b*, taking up just 28 columns and a half. The initial letters, denoted in this volume by large capitals, are illuminated in gold and colours. The Passus are not numbered, but are denoted by leaving a blank line above them, and these divisions exactly agree with those of the other MSS. of the same type. The poem is written in long lines, as here printed, and each line is divided into two by a metrical dot, here denoted by an inverted full stop, indicating a pause of the voice, such as is often equivalent to a comma in punctuation, but which must sometimes be disregarded as a punctuating mark, just as we sometimes so disregard a colon in the Prayer-book version of the Psalms. Besides these dots, it has others occasionally inserted, as, for instance, after *me* in l. 2, after *beo-heold* in l. 13, *dich* (l. 16), *feld* (l. 17), *worchinge* (l. 18), &c. These also have reference to the pauses in

---

[1] In the "Parallel Extracts" it is numbered 1.
[2] For some account of the MS. see the description of it by J. O. Halliwell, Esq., published by J. R. Smith, 1848.

recitation, and subdivide the half-verses into quarter-verses; but they are introduced so sparingly, upon the whole, that I have omitted them, as only tending to confuse. The word *I* is always followed by a point, as (I.), and the word *and* (.and.) has a point both before and after it; these slight peculiarities I have not preserved. In other respects, however, it has been very faithfully followed, its capital letters preserved, and all expansions of contractions marked by the use of *italics*.[1] The paragraph marks (¶) are, in the MS., painted red and blue alternately. Among the illuminated letters we often meet with the *thorn-letter* (þ), but never a capital ȝ. This is owing to the illuminator, who has made a capital Y more than once where a small ȝ can be detected as having been written to tell him what to do.

This MS. was taken for the *text*, not solely because it is the oldest and best written, but also because a careful collation of it with the rest has shewn that its readings are, on the whole, better than those of any other. It seems to me to be the best known MS. of "Piers Plowman" *in every respect*. Still, it is not perfect. It is a peculiar difficulty, in writing out alliterative poems, to avoid missing a line. This is easily ascertained by mere practice in transcription, and I have especially noticed that hardly any MS. of "Piers Plowman" is free from this defect. It very frequently happens that the missing lines are most obviously needed to complete the sense. On this account, and also because it is best to shew *every* line that can be found in the early MSS., lines have been inserted from other MSS. wherever they occur. Only one or two bad ones have been relegated to the foot-notes. The reader will observe how very few of these extra lines there are, after all, and how *very closely* all the MSS. of

---

[1] Much trouble has been saved me by the extreme correctness of the transcript made for me by Mr Geo. Parker, of Rose Hill, Oxford, to whom I am much indebted; as also to Mr E. Brock, who assisted me in the collation of the Text with the Harleian MSS. But I have not omitted to compare either the transcript or the proof-sheets with the MS. throughout, and both of these again with the extracts from this poem so lately printed in Mr Morris's "Specimens of Early English Poetry." That there are a few (unimportant) variations of spelling between his text and mine I am aware; and I have ascertained that mine is, in such instances, correct. Much pains has been bestowed upon the present text, and I think the printer's errors in it cannot but be very few. That whatever do occur are utterly unimportant, I am most **fully confident.**

Type A agree together in their general contents, their differences being chiefly verbal. The text has also been emended by help of the other MSS. where it seemed to need it; the amended word being inserted between square brackets, and account of it rendered in the foot-notes. In a *very* few cases, a word occurring in MS. V has been suppressed in the text, notice being of course given of this in the foot-notes.

The MS. has but one great defect. It is, that a single leaf has been cut out of it with a sharp knife, the extreme inner edge of the leaf being still visible. Most unfortunately, this leaf is the *very one* which contains the concluding portion of the last Passus; so that we cannot certainly say how it ended. At the same time, it is very evident that it never contained much *beyond* these eleven Passus, for a leaf can only contain 320 lines at most, and there are about 140 lines lost from the eleventh Passus, which would very nearly fill up the one side of the leaf. But the poem which follows "Piers Plowman" has lost its beginning, so that the contents of this leaf can be nearly accounted for.[1] The abundance of my materials has enabled me to remedy this defect in a great measure, by giving the missing portion of the poem from MS. T, with collations from four others.

II. MS. Harl. 875, denoted in this volume by the letter H; of early date, about 1400.[2]

This valuable MS. is the one alluded to by Warton. It is of vellum, and consists of 21 leaves only (size, about 10 inches by 6½), with about 40 lines to the page. One leaf, the 17th, is lost, and it is imperfect at the end, terminating at l. 144 of Passus VIII. I greatly doubt if it ever went further than the end of this Passus, as will be shewn presently, in discussing the probable point of termination of the

---

[1] I have not succeeded in finding out *how much* of the succeeding poem is lost. It seems to be on the subject of Joseph (of Arimathea?) and is written in alliterative verse; but the verses are run together, so that the folio begins in the middle of a line, thus:

. . . . sire, he seis · and sone*n*day is nowe;
And þei lenden of þe toun · and leuen hit þere."

Mr Halliwell's description is here wrong; he calls the piece succeeding "Piers Plowman," *Judas and Pilate;* but the beginning of this poem—"Judas was a luþer brid"—is on fol. 404 *verso.* β, not, as he says, on fol. 403 *recto.* α.

[2] Numbered 7 in the " Parallel Extracts."

MSS. of this type. This MS. is, in general, very close to the "Vernon," and pairs off with it better than any other does, as will soon appear by studying the foot-notes. It contains additional lines occasionally, and seems to be the *fullest* of the series. It is therefore very useful for completing the sense, in passages that seem incomplete. It may be, however, that a few of these extra lines are spurious; at any rate, the two long parentheses, Pass. II. ll. 136—139, and ll. 141—143, are very awkward, and seem peculiar to this MS. It has been collated with the text throughout as far as it goes, and all its important variations of reading will be found in the foot-notes, and the proof-sheets have been compared with the MS.

III. MS. in Trinity College, Cambridge, marked R. 3. 14, denoted in this volume by T; date, near the beginning of the fifteenth century.[1]

This is a very remarkable and valuable MS., and has been used to complete the text, at the end of Passus XI. It contains 72 written leaves of vellum, containing about 42 to 46 lines on a page; the size of each page being 11½ by 6½ inches. On the fly-leaf preceding the poem is a coloured drawing, with the motto "God spede þe plouȝ & sende us korne I-now." A copy of this drawing is given, as a frontispiece, in Mr Wright's edition of the poem. The volume contains the *whole* of "Piers Plowman," but this has only been achieved by fitting on a part of a MS. of Type C to the earlier text. There would be nothing remarkable in this were it not that the same peculiarity occurs in two other MSS.[2] Hence arises the question—Are the texts A and C merely *joined* in all three MSS.; or is it that Text A was originally completed by what was afterwards the latter part of Text C? The latter supposition is altogether out of the question, as will be seen in the sequel, and hence we are sure that the texts are *joined*; and, indeed, on closer inspection, the signs of junction become obvious. The system of division into Passus and of numbering the Passus is *not the same* in A and C; and this furnishes an easy test; for the former part of this MS. follows the A-text system, the latter the C-text system; and, as a necessary consequence, we find that the

---

[1] Numbered 11 in the "Parallel Extracts."
[2] Both described below, and numbered V and X.

numbering of the *Passus* is all wrong at the point of junction. At this point we find written *Passus tercius de dowel*,[1] and *only eighteen lines* below comes the title *Passus secundus de dobet*;[2] the next Passus has no title, but the next after that is *Passus quartus de dowel*; after which the numbering is more consistent and regular. The insertion of the title *Passus tercius de dowel* above what is really the mere end of a *Passus* shews that at this point the junction was made;[3] and it is *at this very point* that the Douce and Ashmolean MSS. (D and A) break off. The texts are, however, joined exactly at the right place, which was easily done merely by looking for the quotation *Brevis oracio penetrat celum*, which forms an excellent catchword. To remove, however, all doubts in the reader's mind, it is proper to add that, though the junction of the two texts has been effected as well perhaps as it could have been effected, there are certain differences of arrangement of the subject-matter in texts A and C, which interfere with the continuousness of the story, so that the patching becomes at once obvious upon comparison. Briefly, *external* evidence *indicates* that two quite different texts are here joined, and the *internal* evidence *proves* it, as I think, beyond a doubt.

This is the best place to note that this MS. abounds with tags at the end of words, which some would consider as equivalent to a final *e*. I am not myself of this opinion (at any rate as regards this MS. in particular); but, that they may not be disregarded, I have printed an italic *e* wherever they occur. Such a spelling as "life" seems, however, inferior to "lif."

The MS. has been collated with the text down to the point where it is itself used to complete the text. Having had ready access to it at all times, the proof-sheets have been compared with it several times over.

IV. MS. belonging to University College, Oxford, denoted in this volume by U; date, the early part of the fifteenth century.[4]

---

[1] The seventeen lines with this title belong to *Passus* II. *of Do-wel*, which, however, the scribe ought to have reckoned as *Passus* I., according to the method he adopts farther on.

[2] *Dobet* is a mere error for *dowel*; this is consistent then with the scribe's subsequent way of numbering, which differs from that in Dr Whitaker's edition.

[3] See description of MS. No. X.

[4] Numbered 10 in the "Parallel Extracts."

Besides "Piers Plowman," it contains many pieces in Latin. The English portion comes first, and consists of 31 vellum leaves, followed by 5 on paper; the size of the page is about 8 inches by 6, and each page contains about 33 lines. The 3rd leaf is missing. It is an important and valuable MS., especially from its evident independence of the rest, agreeing sometimes with one and sometimes with another, sometimes even with none, yet corroborating them in the main. It must have been copied from an older and imperfect one, or still more probably, from *two* others, some of the leaves in which were out of place. Hence some of its text is most absurdly transposed, and takes the following order. From the beginning it is regular down to Passus II. l. 25, which is immediately followed (on the same page) by Passus VII. ll. 71—213, and then returns to l. 182 of Passus I., the last four lines of Passus I. and some twenty lines of Passus II. occurring *twice over*. It then goes on down to Passus VII. l. 70, when the passage which has already occurred is omitted. The vellum portion is better than the paper, and apparently by an earlier hand, though both are of the earliest type. The paper portion begins with "But honysche hym as an hound · & hote hym go þennes" (Passus XI. l. 48), and is of less value, and its readings less to be relied on. Still, it has been collated with the text throughout, and repeatedly compared with the proof-sheets.

V. MS. Harl. 6041; denoted hereafter by the symbol H_2; date, scarcely earlier than 1450.[1] This is the MS. to which Warton has drawn attention in the passage above quoted, and his conjecture, that it belongs to the earliest class, is perfectly right. Yet it is but a poor one, compared with the four already mentioned. It is on paper (size, about 9 inches by 6), and the writing is loose and not very careful; mistakes are not unfrequent. On fol. 96 *b* we find the note, "This boke perteynet to my dAne willi*a*m holyngborne." Several leaves are partly torn out. It is remarkably close to MS. T; and, hence, after collating it closely with the text from the beginning down to l. 146 of Passus II., I ceased doing so; finding that it is, practically, little else than an inferior duplicate of T, and may be neglected without much loss. Yet it has occasionally been consulted in difficult

---

[1] Numbered 15 in the "Parallel Extracts."

passages, and readings from it will be found here and there throughout the book. It was especially useful for collation throughout the last portion of Passus XI. It resembles T also in its being a mixture of types A and C; the point of junction is the same, but the only indication of it is that, seventeen lines lower down, there is a marginal note, "*primus passus* deficit hic," which, seeing that *Passus tercius* is in question, is a mark of confusion as well as of deficiency.

VI. MS. Douce 323; denoted hereafter by D. This is in a comparatively late hand (about 1480?), clearly written upon paper, each leaf about 11 inches by 8, with a very wide margin, about 31 lines to the page. *Contents.* fol. 1—101. A history of England, printed by Wynkyn de Worde, 1515. folio, under the title of "Fructus Temporum." Begins—"In the noble lande of Surrye;" ends—"withoute eny chalange of eny man. Amen. Deo gracias." Fol. 102—140 *a*; "Piers Plowman;" begins—"In A somer sesoun," &c.; ends—

"Percen wi*th* a pate*r* noster þe paleys of heuene
With-oute pena*u*nce at here partyng in-to heye blysse.
Now of þis litel book y haue makyd an ende,
Goddis blessyng mote he haue þat drinke wil me sende.
Explicit liber petri plouman."

Fol. 140 *b*—159 *b*. The Abbey of the Holy Ghost, with a drawing of the Abbey on fol. 159 *b*. Fols. 160—167. Sir Ypotyce, beginning "Alle þat will of wysdom lere;" ending—"And þankeþ god al his wille;" (imperfect?). This MS. follows T rather closely, but is full of gross blunders. On this account, after collating with Passus I.—IV., I desisted, finding that it only tended to choke the foot-notes with inferior readings. But it was useful again for the latter part of Passus XI.

VII. MS. Ashmole 1468; denoted by A. Imperfect, on paper, of no very early date, and has many corrupt readings. It begins at Passus I. l. 142, and ends with the line—

"Wi*th*oute penauns at here p*ar*tyng into þe blisse of heuyn. Amen. Amen. Amen."

A few Latin quotations are scribbled below, which have occurred in Piers Plowman. Very little use has been made of this, as it seems an inferior MS.; yet it furnished a few good readings at the end of Passus XI.

The above are the only MSS. of which I have made use; but there are others of Type A; viz. the following ones:

VIII. MS. in the library of Lincoln's Inn; date, about 1450? It contains—1. Part of Le Beau Desconus; 2. Merlin; 3. Alexander; 4. Bellum Trojanum; 5. Piers Plowman, and is incomplete at the beginning and end. See Hunter's "Three Catalogues," p. 399.

The Piers Plowman is contained in 17 leaves, containing about 52 or 53 lines in a page. It is imperfect, and the last page is much defaced, rubbed, and discoloured; the last words on the page that can be traced are ... bischopis lettres ...; i. e. about 20 lines from the end of Passus VIII., and only some 14 lines beyond the point where H ends; probably neither of them ever went further than the end of this Passus, i. e. than the end of the Vision of Piers Plowman, *properly so called*. On comparing a transcript of a considerable number of lines kindly made for me by Mr Furnivall, I found that the text has been much corrupted by the scribe, and that to collate it would only fill the foot-notes with false readings, except in places where the text is sufficiently ascertained without it. The corruptions are due to an inordinate love of alliteration, so that a new word is often incorrectly put for an old one for the mere sake of getting a *fourth* word in the line beginning with the rime-letter, contrary to the rules of an alliterative verse, which does not *require* this, but on the contrary seeks, *as a rule*, to avoid it.[1] Hence we get such lines as,

"Went wyde into þis worlde wondres to *wayte*," (l. 4);

"Vndur a brod banke by a borne *brymme*," (l. 8);

"I sagh a tour on a tofte treowliche *ytymbred*," (l. 14).

The scribe has made yet one more mistake; he sometimes separates the line into two half-lines, each alliterative in itself; as,

"In abite as an hermyte, vn-worthy of werkes," (l. 3).

"For to seche seynt Iame & rerykes[2] at rome, (l. 47).

---

[1] Of course, *some* lines of this form are genuine; and notably l. 1, in which nearly *all* the MSS. of all types agree.   [2] *Sic*; an error for *relykes*.

Careful examination of the MS. shews, in fact, that it is best dismissed.

There are yet two more MSS., which though not *strictly* agreeing with those of the earliest type, are yet mere modifications of it; they are a little amplified, yet much less full than Text B. I also consider them here, because but little further use will be made of them.

IX. MS. Harl. 3954; date about 1420.[1] The "Piers Plowman" extends from fol. 92 to fol. 123 *b*. The MS. is on vellum; and the pages are of a peculiar shape, about 11 inches long by a little less than 6 inches wide; each page contains about 40 lines. It has some very peculiar spellings, as *qwat* for *what*, and *xal* for *shall*, which are marks of an East-Midland dialect. At the beginning, it follows Type B, giving a long prologue which contains the "story of the rats," but it omits many passages which occur in such MSS., and, towards the end, approaches Type A. I do not consider it of much value, and believe it to be frequently corrupted. The concluding lines are noteworthy, and illustrate the above remark. They should be compared with the concluding lines in this volume.

Ben non rathere I-rauysched fro the ryth beleue
þan arn þose grete clerkys þat know many bokys;
Ben non sonere I-sauyd, non saddere of concyens
þan pore puple as plowmen, & pasturers of bestys,
Sawerys & sowerys & sweche leude Iottys;
For þei leuyn as þei be leryd, & oþer-wyse nouth,
Musyn in no materes but holdyn þe ryth be-leue.
He þat redyth þis book & ryth haue it in mende,
Preyit for pers þe plowmans soule,
With a pater-noster to þe paleys of heuene,
With-outyn gret penans at hys partynge to comyn to blys.

Explicit tractus de perys plowman, q. herū [2] (?); Qui cum patre & spiritu sancto viuit et regnat per omnia secula seculorum. Amen.

These lines are a sad jumble, and the "praying for pers þe plowmans soule" is particularly out of place, as Piers is not the *author* of

---

[1] Numbered 9 in the "Parallel Extracts."
[2] i. e. "quoth herun," I suppose, intimating that Herun was the scribe's name.

the poem, but the *subject* of it; and it is clear that the author had always in his mind the resemblance of his Piers Plowman to Christ. This is shewn, curiously enough, by the Latin colophon, where the *Qui* certainly refers to *perys plowman*, and as certainly means Christ himself and no other. This MS. may be now dismissed without more words.

X. MS. Digby 145; late 15th century, on paper.[1] This is but a poor copy, and is a mixture of texts. The early part of it is, like the last one, an amplification of Text A; the latter part follows Text C. The junction is effected, as in MSS. III. and V., at the quotation *Brevis oracio penetrat celum*; and it is worth noting how the preceding line has been altered about, shewing the scribe's difficulty. This line runs,

"wi*th*out pen*au*nce at her partyng * into hye blisse,"

but is "cooked" in four ways. It has "&" prefixed to it in the margin; it has "passyn" written over it at the mark *; it is followed by "Amen" with a stroke through it; and also by "P. III. de (?) dowell" partly erased, the *dowell* alone being distinctly legible. I have made no use of this MS. and do not think it worth much attention.

§ 5. DISCUSSION OF THE EXTENT OF THE EARLY MSS.

It will now be readily apparent what strong grounds we have for supposing that the early draught of the poem contained no more than *eleven* Passus. For of these 10 MSS., *none* go any further;[2] although an attempt has been made in three of them, Nos. III., V., and X., to supplement them by help of MSS. of Type C; which attempt, however, failed in two respects, viz. through the difficulty of reconciling the two ways of numbering the Passus, and the difficulty of making the story continuous, owing to the different ways in which the subject-matter is arranged in the two types. But one point of great importance must now be noticed. The whole poem is called "Piers Plowman" only by a certain latitude of phrase, and the Passus have been in this volume numbered from I. to XI. merely as a

---

[1] Numbered 16 in the "Parallel Extracts."
[2] With one remarkable exception, discussed in § 7.

matter of convenience. Strictly speaking, this is *incorrect*. There are really *two* poems, each perfectly distinct from the other, with different titles, and separate prologues. The first has for its true title, "The Vision of William concerning Piers the Plowman;" the second is—" Vita de Do-wel, Do-bet, et Do-best."[1] Each poem is complete in itself, and the concluding passages of each are wrought with peculiar care with a view to giving them such completeness, by stating, at the end of each, the result which in each case the author wished to bring out strongly. The only connection between them is that the second is a sort of continuation of the first, and supposes that the dreamer, not being wholly satisfied with the first result of his inquiries, sets out once more to renew and extend them. It is a mark of the later forms of the poems that the distinction between them is less heeded, as though the author had accepted the necessity of their being written and considered as *one*. This is very clearly shewn by the titles of the different Passus in the A-type MSS. In none of them is there any title to the Prologue to the first poem, but the succeeding Passus are numbered from I. to VIII. in MSS. T,H,U,H₂, and D, except where a title is occasionally lost, or where (once only in H) it is miswritten. But the Prologue to "Dowel, &c." has the following titles :

Incipit hic dowel . dobet . and dobest V ;

Explicit hic visio will*el*mi de Petro de Plou3man : Eciam incipit vita de do-wel do-bet *et* do-best, *secundu*m wyt *et* resou*n* T ;

Explicit hic visio will*el*mi de petro plowman, Et hic incipit dowel dobet *et* dobest *secundu*m wit *et* resoun U ;

Explicit hic visio will*el*mi de petro the plou3man ; Eciam incipit uita de dowel and dobest, *secundu*m wit *et* reson H₂ ;

Vita de Dowel Dobet and Dobest secu*ndu*m wyt and resoun D.

The last two Passus are called *Passus primus* (and *secundus*) *de dowel, &c.*, in T and H₂, and the same in U, omitting the *&c.* In D the former of them has the very significant title, *Primus passus in secundo libro*.

Hence it appears that there is here no thought of reckoning in

---

[1] Or, in full, " Vita de dowel, dobet, et dobest, secundum wit et resoun." It is also called, " The Vision of the same concerning Dowel, Dobet, and Dobest."

the *Passus* of Dowel as being any part of Piers Plowman, as was afterwards done in MSS. of the later types, especially in the one printed by Mr Wright, where we find such titles as *Passus Decimus de Visione, et Secundus de Dowel,* and the like.[1] It follows that the numbering of the last three Passus in this volume as IX., X., and XI. is quite incorrect in theory, but of course the advantages of it in practice (especially in constructing a glossarial index) are so obvious as to outweigh all other considerations.

§ 6. Two points then are established: (1.) that our MSS. of this type have but eleven Passus, and (2.) that the first eight of these, with their prologue, belong to Piers Plowman, the last three to the Vita de Dowel. It should further be noted that the exact point of termination is clearly indicated by the Douce and Ashmolean MSS., and by MS. Harl. 3954, and there is every probability that the Vernon MS. terminated here also. But the Lincoln's Inn MS. and Harl. 875 do not go nearly so far, and it is a significant circumstance that they just stop short of the end of "Piers Plowman," properly so called. Considering this, and remembering how often MSS. have just their last leaf wanting, I think it exceedingly likely that they never contained the "Vita de Dowel" at any time; another slight indication of the real distinctness of the two poems.

§ 7. But there is one strange exception. Perhaps the reader may have noticed how careful I have been to say nothing as to where the University College MS. (U, No. IV.) terminates. This is because any previous mention of it would have tended greatly to confusion. If the reader will turn to the end of the "Critical Notes," he will see 18 lines printed *in extenso* which form the beginning of a "Passus *tercius* de dowel," and continue the poem *beyond* the last line of the other texts. These 18 lines are a puzzle; as far as I can ascertain, they are *unique,* and resemble nothing in *any other* MS. *whatsoever.*[2] They do not agree with either Text B or C. What then can be made of them? I can only offer the suggestion, either that they were added by some person not the author of the poem (though they are very

---

[1] Of course, this is yet one more proof that Type A is older than Type B.

[2] Should this statement be wrong, I should be much obliged by having a corresponding passage pointed out to me. The eleventh line seems to answer to the first line of Passus Undecimus in Text B; see Wright's edition, vol. i. p. 202.

much in his manner), who attempted a continuation of it; or else that the author himself began a continuation which he afterwards abandoned, betaking himself first to an expansion of the part already written, and afterwards adding thereto a continuation different to the one he at first contemplated. The latter supposition seems to me very probable; especially as there must have been a little more of this Passus, and yet not much more. The MS. has here lost two leaves, or four pages, so that the utmost that is lost is probably not more than 112 lines, as there are 28 lines to the page. Supposing we were to add 112 to 19, we should get 131 lines, a fair average length for a Passus, thus giving *three* Passus to "Dowel" instead of *two*. And some of these lines may have been used again.

§ 8. METHOD OF PRINTING THE TEXT.

This has been already in a great measure explained in describing the Vernon MS.; see § 4. I. The text is mainly from that MS., but has additional lines and emendations inserted between square brackets. The concluding portion of the last Passus is from MS. T; see § 4. III. On a careful consideration of Mr Wright's arguments for printing the poem in *short* or *half*-lines, I am not convinced by them. There is no MS. authority for any such practice, *all* early English alliterative poems (at any rate after the time of Edward II.) being written in long lines invariably. Certainly, the metre was imitated from the Anglo-Saxon poems of Beowulf and Cædmon, and *those* were written in short lines; but it is a question of chronology, and to recur to the Anglo-Saxon method is an anachronism. For the same reason, the arrangement of the lines in Layamon has little to do with it, as that belongs to the reign of Richard I. or John. The argument that the use of the dots in the middle of the lines by the scribes is a clear indication that each line was really made up of *two*, quite falls through on examination. For the scribes were very careless about the insertion of these dots, and MSS. of "Piers Plowman" in which they are preserved throughout are rare, but those in which they are wholly neglected very numerous. In the 10 MSS. above described, the metrical point is carefully preserved in *only one*, viz. the *Vernon*; and it is some proof of the value of MS. T that it is often *preserved* throughout whole pages, though in other pages it does not appear. In none of the rest does it appear at all, save very rarely. The Latin verses which appear in the prologue of Text B are *not* in short rimed lines, but are *long* lines, or Leonine verses, i. e. hexameters and pentameters, and should be printed,

Sum rex, sum princeps, neutrum fortasse deinceps, &c.

But the discussion of which way is the more correct is not very material; the practical question is, which is the more convenient. Mr Wright did well in adopting the method that suited his purpose best, and for a like reason I have adopted the system of printing in long lines, viz. because it renders the poem uniform with the "Early English Alliterative Poems" and the "Morte Arthur." At the same time, I by all means advocate the retention of the metrical dot, as greatly helping the reader to perceive the rhythm; which was, after all, the real reason for its use.

The lines of each Passus are numbered separately; the great convenience of this will appear hereafter, when the different texts come to be compared. But I have not reckoned in the Latin quotations as counting for lines, except where they are designedly thrown into the shape of alliterative verses. For these quotations are sometimes written in the margin of a MS., or are merely indicated by their first few words, added at the beginning or ending of a line; and a modern poet would print them as foot-notes. If reference to them is to be made, they may be indicated by the number of the line preceding them. When they are not reckoned in, this is pointed out by their being "set back." For the punctuation of the text I am, of course, responsible.

§ 9. METHOD OF PRINTING THE FOOT-NOTES.

The MSS. T, H, and U have been collated throughout as far as they go. MS. D has been collated throughout the Prologue, Pass. I.—IV., and part of Pass. VI. and Pass. XI.; MS. H_2 from the beginning to Pass. II. l. 146 (with *occasional* references to it throughout the poem), and throughout Passus IX., X., and XI. The Ashmolean MS. furnished a couple of good readings in Pass. XI. The foot-notes will be very readily understood; they exhibit in general the variations of the other MSS. from the text. Thus the foot-note at l. 20 of the Prologue—*and pleiden hem*] plei3ede TUD. *hem ful*] but H.—simply shews the substitution in TUD of the *one* word *plei3ede* for the *three* words of the text; and that, in H, the last part of the line is of the form " and pleiden but seldene," though not perhaps with *exactly* that spelling. In quoting from TUD at once, I mean that the spelling of the MS. *first mentioned* (in this case MS. T) is given, and that U and D differ from it but very slightly. The real readings are—*plei3ede* T ; *pleiden* U ; *pleyed*. D. To have given *all* such variations of spelling would have been impossible, and would have caused more trouble and expense than printing all these texts at full length. But I have endeavoured to give *all useful* information by noting down the various spellings of unusual or noteworthy words, even when the differences are but slight; thus, at l. 40 will be found the various spellings of *eoden* = went; at l. 52 those of *lobres* = lubbers or loobies, though even here I did not consider it worth while to note that MS. U uses a *y* for an *i*, and spells the word *lobyes*. Again, a good deal of space has been saved by not noticing the use of *ac* for *but*, and *vice versâ ;* these words are used indiscriminately as equivalent ones in several of the MSS. A few other slight variations of a similar kind have been left unnoticed. Where a reading is obviously absurd, the mark (!) has been appended to it ; and some few absurd readings in the Douce MS. have been passed over with the sole remark, " D *is corrupt*." The expansions of contractions are generally marked by italics ; but in a few common words this has not been done. The metrical dots are inserted in the lines quoted at length in the notes, for the reader's convenience ; they do not, in general, occur in the MSS. It will sometimes happen that the reader, if he tries (by help of the foot-notes) to reproduce the line as it stands in any given MS., as e. g. in MS. T, will find that he produces a line which is obviously absurd. But I cannot help that ; the scribe of MS. T ought to have known better, but he did not. The object, throughout, has been to crowd into the foot-notes as much information as possible, so that the amount of *additional* information which might be gained from a perusal of the MSS. themselves should be the smallest possible, and that they may be found to be well represented in print as far as need be. From a conviction that all such information, if not accurately rendered, is simply valueless, great care has been taken in revising the proof-sheets, which are, I hope, free from material faults.

§ 10. A FEW WORDS ON ALLITERATIVE VERSE.

I hope to give, in a later volume, a tolerably full account of alliterative verse. Meanwhile, I would refer the reader to my note on the metre of "Morte Arthure," prefixed to Mr Perry's edition of that poem, for a brief account of it. It is a metre in which the number of actual syllables is not much regarded, but where all depends on the occurrence of four (or sometimes five) strongly accented syllables in each line. Of these, two should be in the *second* section of the verse, and two (or three) in the *first*. The strongest accent should generally fall on the first strongly-accented syllable in the second section, and the initial letter of that syllable is called the *rime-letter*, and the strongly-accented syllables of the first section should begin with the same letter, or be *alliterated* with it. It is a metre peculiarly fitted for recitation, and addressed, almost more than any other, to the *ear*, and one the *swing* of which is very easily caught. Believing that a plain and easily-understood example of it in modern language is really a better guide to it than precise rules, I quote the following, pointed after the same manner as in "Piers Plowman."

"Lightly down-leaping · he loosens his helmet;
Lightly down-leaping · he lappeth the cool wave:
He feels that his forces · wax faint, as he drinketh;
He slumbers and sleeps · as he sinks on the boulders.
He rests on his rock-bed · naught recking, for ages;
His head, with his hoar locks · still heaves with its breathing.
When flameth and flasheth · the flare of the lightning,
When rustle the rain-drops · and rolleth the thunder,
Lo! Harold the hero · still handles his sword-hilt,
Seeking to seize it · tho' sunk in his slumber."[1]

Any one who can perceive the rhythm of these lines (and it is not

---

[1] See "Songs and Ballads of Uhland," by the Rev. W. W. Skeat, p. 304. I quote this literally *faute de mieux*, not knowing where else to find an example; and I quote

very easy to miss it), has a key to a right scansion of Piers Plowman ; it being remembered that in this poem also, as in Chaucer, many final e'-s, &c., must be pronounced *fully;* which a modern reader is very apt to overlook. The first line is, e. g.

In a somer sesun · whon softe was þe sonnè,

where *sonnè* is a dissyllable. Yet even if this be disregarded, and the language partly modernized, the first four lines of the poem remain very fair lines still, and have a distinct and obvious melody in them ; as thus—

In a summer season · when soft was the sun,
I shop me into a shroud · a sheep [1] as I were,
In habit of an hermit · unholy of works,
Went I wide in this world · wonders to hear.

§ 11. DATE OF THE POEM.

We are indebted to Tyrwhitt for having pointed out that the "Southwestern wind on a Saturday at even" mentioned near the beginning of Passus V. refers to the storm of wind which occurred on Jan. 15, 1362, which day was a Saturday.[2] There may have been more than one Saturday marked by a furious tempest, but the remark is rendered almost certainly true by observing that other indications in the poem point nearly to the same date, especially the allusion to the treaty of Bretigny in 1360, and to Edward's wars in Normandy ;[3] as also the mention of the "pestilence," no doubt that of 1361.[4] These things put together leave no doubt that Tyrwhitt is right, and as the "wind" is spoken of as being something very recent, the true

only these lines, because the preceding ones are, some of them, less regular. I believe that this rhythm, in the hands of a poet of true genius, might be found capable of great things, and far more worthy of cultivation than are "barbarous hexameters."

[1] Mr Morris explains "scheep" by *shepherd;* and "schepherde" is the reading of Text C.

[2] "A.D. M.CCC.LXII.—XV die Januarii, *circa horam vesperarum,* ventus vehemens *notus Australis Africus* tantâ rabie erupit, &c. ;" quoted by Tyrwhitt (in a note to the Advertisement at his Glossary to Chaucer), from the Continuator of Adam Murimuth, p. 115 ; Cf. P. Pl., Pass. V. l. 14.

[3] Pass. III. 182 ; see Fabyan's Chronicles, p. 470.

[4] Pass. V. 13. There were *three* great pestilences, in 1348, 1361-2, and 1369 ; clearly, the *second* one is meant.

date of the poem is doubtless 1362. But *how much* was then written? Not all certainly, possibly only the Vision of Piers Plowman, i. e. only the first eight Passus. The first few lines of the Vita de Dowel seem to imply that there was a *short* interval between the two poems, i. e. if we take them literally, and I can see no reason why we should not. This would assign the early part of 1362 as the date of the former poem, and the end of the same year or the beginning of 1363 as the date of Dowel. In all probability, the expansion of the poem into the form it assumes in Text B was not immediately begun, and it would necessarily take some time and deliberation to render it nearly three times as long as at first, and to multiply the number of Latin quotations by *seven*. The latter fact, in particular, implies some considerable time spent in study. Now such a consideration as this seems to me altogether to remove a chronological difficulty which has hitherto been a puzzle. It is, that the mention of John Chichester as mayor of London [1] contradicts the date 1362, inasmuch as he was not mayor till the year 1369. But observe, that this mention of him does not occur in any MS. of the A-type, so that the contradiction ceases to exist if we suppose the later Passus of the *second* version of the poem not to have been composed till after 1370 ;[2] perhaps, indeed, not till 1375 or 1376, if we observe that

[1] Fabyan says John Chychester, goldsmith, was sheriff of London in 1358-9, and mayor in 1368-9.

[2] Our author seems to be a year wrong; he says,

"A thousand and thre hundred · twies thretty and ten."
MS. Laud 581. Pass. XIII. (Text B.)

Nearly all other MSS. read "twies *twenty* and ten;" which is *not alliterative*. I do not see why Mr Wright is so dissatisfied with this date, and assumes Stowe to be wrong because, in his Survey of London, p. 159, he has the passage—"Moreover, in the 44. of Edward the third, John Chichester being maior of London, I read in the Visions of Pierce Plowman, a book so called, as followeth. There was a careful commune when no cart came to towne with baked bread from Stratford : tho gan beggers weepe, and workemen were agast, a little this will be thought long in the date of our Drite, in a drie Averell, a thousand and three hundred *twise thirtie and ten, &c.*" He thinks Stowe may have altered the date, because the "drye Aprill" must mean the drought of 1351 mentioned by Fabyan, and that Chichester may have been mayor more than once. But the same Fabyan gives a list of mayors, and makes Chichester mayor once only, in 1368-9. I think it more likely that there were two "dry Aprils." Stowe does not stand alone in his reckoning. Bale gives the date 1369 ; so does Wood (Hist. and Antiq. Univ. Oxon. l. ii. p.

the language used in referring to this circumstance is such as we should use in speaking of a thing that happened five or six years ago rather than recently. To this supposition I can see no objection; and I therefore propose the theory that we should refer the first 8 Passus of Text A to the early part of 1362; the Vita de Dowel, in its short and original form, to the end of 1362 or the beginning of 1363; and the revision of the whole poem, and expansion of it into its second shape, to about 1376.[1] The *second* revision of it, and its alteration into the *third* form, may have been four or five years later still. It seems to be in the natural order of things that a poem, originally struck off in perhaps no long time, should afterwards have been elaborated with much care and diligence when its popularity was well established. That most of the additional matter in both the later forms of the poem was by Langland himself I have little doubt; his style is very peculiar, and many of the subsequently interpolated passages are the very best of the whole. It is easy to say that others may have added to it; but the question is, who *could* have done so? There were not two Langlands, surely; and though there are other (anonymous) alliterative poems of considerable merit, such as, for instance, "William of Palerne,"[2] I greatly doubt if they reach the high standard of poetical power which is conspicuous in Piers Plowman. Conspicuous, that is, after some study; for his phraseology is, at first, difficult to follow, and there are some words which are very unfamiliar to all but those who are fairly well versed in the language of the period; and hence it has come to pass, as it would seem, that though this poem has often been very highly praised—more praised, perhaps, than read—the author has still had but scanty justice done to him. At a first perusal, the poem, though often striking, seems

107); and so does Buchanan (De Scriptoribus Scotis. MS. Bibl. Univ. Edin.). Mr Wright's difficulty arose from supposing that the poem was written *all at once*; whereas Langland almost expressly states the contrary (Text B. xiii. 3).

[1] Tyrwhitt says, "Indeed, from the mention of the kitten in the tale of the Rattons, I should suspect that the author wrote at the *very end* of the reign of Edward III., when *Richard was become heir-apparent;*" Chaucer; Essay, &c., note 57. With this I entirely agree.

[2] Otherwise called, "William and the Werwulf," but it is only a translation of *Guillaume de Palerne*. The poem on the "Deposition of Richard II." (Wright's Political Poems, vol. i. p. 368) is the only one in Langland's style.

rather heavy, upon the whole, and somewhat wearisome; but when some insight is gained into it, it becomes more pleasing and attractive, and its *power* and *truth* become more apparent. The astonishing vigour and force of the language begins to dawn upon one, and a greater familiarity with it continually increases our admiration. Continual re-perusal of it proves a constant source of pleasure and of profit, and it is not too much to say that when we speak of the great poets of England, of Chaucer, Spenser, Shakespeare, and Milton, there are few who better deserve to be named together with these than one whose very name we scarcely know, the author of "The Vision of Piers Plowman"—WILLIAM LANGLAND.

§ 12. THE AUTHOR'S NAME AND LIFE.

I have just spoken of the author's name as being probably William Langland. That his surname was Langland, Langelande, Langlond, or Longland (it is spelt all ways) seems to be generally agreed. His Christian name has been given as John, Robert, and William. The first of these seems to have been a mere guess of Stowe's (*Ann.* p. 238), who speaks of John Malverne, Fellow of Oriel College, in Oxford, as having "made and finished his book, entitled, the Visions of Peers Plowman," in 1342; where, besides assigning an obviously wrong date, he seems to attribute the book to the wrong author. Bale has the following passage, containing all that is known of the author's life. "Robertus Langelande, sacerdos, ut apparet,[1] natus in comitatu Salopiæ, in villa vulgò dicta Mortymers Clibery, in terra lutea, octavo à Malvernis montibus milliario fuit. Num tamen eo in loco, incondito et ægresti, in bonis litteris ad maturam ætatem usque informatus fuit, certò adfirmare non possum. Ut neque, an Oxonij aut Cantabrigiæ illis insudaverit; quum apud eorum locorum magistros, studia præcipuè vigerent. Illud veruntamen liquidò constat, eum fuisse ex primis Joannis Wiclevi discipulis unum, atque in spiritus fervore, contra apertas papistarum blasphemias adversus Deum et ejus Christum, sub amœnis coloribus et typis edidisse in sermone Anglico pium opus, ac bonorum virorum lectione

---

[1] I do not think it at all clear that he was a priest; on the contrary, one would glean from the poem that he was a married man, and therefore *not* a priest.

dignum, quod vocabat *Visionem Petri Aratoris, lib.* 1. *In æstivo tempore cum sol caleret.*[1] Nihil aliud ab ipso editum novi. In hoc opere condito, præter similitudines varias et jucundas, propheticè plura prædixit,[2] quæ nostris diebus impleri vidimus. Complevit suum opus anno domini 1369, dum Joannes Cicestrius Londini prætor esset." Balei, Script. Illustr. majoris Britanniæ. Cent. vi. p. 474. Basileæ, apud Oporinum, 1559.

Meagre, indeed, is this account, and obviously gleaned, for the most part, from the poem itself. The same information is repeated in a piece of writing inside the cover of Lord Ashburnham's MS. cxxx. "Robertus Langlande, natus in comitatu Salopie in villa Mortimers Clybery in the Clayland and within viij miles of Malvern hills, scripsit piers ploughman, li. 1. In somer season, &c." This is in the handwriting of John Bale, and is no new testimony. David Buchanan also calls him "Robertus Langland," but claims him as a Scotchman, and a Benedictine monk of Aberdeen, which is out of the question.[3] For all this, I prefer to suppose that his name was really William. Bale's testimony only takes us back to the sixteenth century, but Sir F. Madden found a note in a hand of the fifteenth century in one of the Dublin MSS. to this effect,—" Memorandum, quod Stacy de Rokayle, pater *Willielmi de Langlond*, qui Stacius fuit generosus, et morabatur in Schiptone under Whicwode,[4] tenens domini le Spenser in comitatu Oxon., *qui prædictus Willielmus fecit librum qui vocatur Perys Ploughman.*" Still more to the purpose are the numerous titles found in the MSS. themselves, where the name *Willelmus* or *Willielmus* occurs again and again,[5] in MSS. of every class. Tyrwhitt notes this in the case of MS. Vesp. B xvi., and quotes the line (verse 5 of Pass. 2), "And sayde, *Wille*, slepest thou," &c., where other MSS. have "sone."[6] But I would rely yet more on l. 118 of Pass. IX.,

"Oure *Wille* wolde I-witen · ȝif wit couþe hym techen."

---

[1] A translation of l. 1 of the Prologue.
[2] He refers to the prophecy about the abbot of Abingdon. Text B. Passus X.
[3] Wright's Piers Plowman, pref. p. ix.
[4] Shipton-under-Wychwood, 4 miles N.N.E. of Burford, Oxon.
[5] See three examples of it quoted in § 5, p. xxv.
[6] See Pass. I. l. 5; cf. VIII 43.

The phrase "oure Wille" is exactly the colloquial way of speaking of a friend or relation which may be heard any day in Shropshire still, as I can well testify, having been called "our Wat" many a time in former days; and it seems to me so utterly unlikely that a man would use a feigned name whilst he was speaking of himself in so familiar a manner. Hence the balance of evidence seems to me in favour of the name William Langland, and we may perhaps further accept the probability that he was born at Cleobury Mortimer, in Shropshire, whilst it is certain that he was familiar enough with Malvern hills, and that he composed the first part of his poem there.[1] He probably afterwards resided a time in London, as he states in the opening lines of Passus VI. (Text C), and was there perhaps "when Chichester was mayor." It is an open question whether he was a monk and unmarried, or whether his wife Kitte and his daughter Calote[2] were real personages. The latter supposition seems to me so very much the more natural that I do not see why it should not be adopted. I can see no reason why we should think that the author is always trying to deceive us about himself; and certainly, Langland is the last man one would suspect of not speaking everything straight out. The opening passage of Passus VI. (Text C)[3] contains many hints which we need not suppose untrue. He has been supposed a monk because of his learning, but his own simple account seems only to mean that he was well educated, probably in a monastery.

"When i yong was, quod I · many ȝer hennes,
Mi fader and my frendes · founden me to scole
Til i wiste withturli · what holi writ bi-menede
And what is best for þe bodi · as þe bok telleþ,"[4] &c.

In the same passage he calls himself a *clerk*, though he has only just mentioned Kitte his wife, so that *clerk* here means no more than a scholar. In another passage he seems to speak of himself as being 45 years old,

"I have folwed thee, in feith !
This fyve and fourty wynter," (ed. Wright, p. 228).

---

[1] Prol. l. 8; Passus VIII. 130.
[2] Kitte is mentioned twice at least; see Wright's ed. p. 395 and p. 514.
[3] Quoted in Wright's ed. vol. ii. p. 514.
[4] Text C; Passus VI. 35.

but the requirements of alliteration are such that no stress can be laid upon this. If true, it would go far to shew that some time probably elapsed before he shaped Text A into Text B. It is in itself quite probable; for, if he wrote the "story of the rattons" in 1376[1] (which seems extremely probable from the very significant quotation " *Ve terre ubi puer rex est* "), and was then forty-five years old, the date of his birth would be 1331, and he would have been 31 years old when first undertaking his poem, a by no means unlikely age. The poem on the " Deposition of Richard II." was written, of course, in 1399, when he would be 68 according to this theory, if still alive. This poem, in the only MS. in which it occurs, follows " Piers Plowman," and is written as a sort of continuation of it. Its author must have been extremely familiar with the " Vision," as he has many half-lines in common with it, and at least one line is quoted from it without alteration, viz.

"Tho ben men of this molde · that most harm worchen."
(Wright, Pol. Poems, i. 408.)[2]

And there are many others where the alteration is very slight, as in
" Trouthe hathe determyned · the tente to the ende " (*id.* p. 385).[3]

To point out all the many points of resemblance between these poems would take up too much space, but we may safely conclude either that the later one was written by some one exceeding familiar with the " Vision " from constant perusal of it, or else by Langland himself at an advanced age. That it was written by an old man seems to be hinted at plainly enough in the lines,

" For it fallith as well · to ffodis [*lads*] of xxiiij ʒeris,
Or *yonge men of ʒistirday* · *to ʒeue good redis,*
As becometh a kow · to hoppe in a cage ! "
(Pol. Poems, i. 405.)

And even were Langland as old as 68 years, this is not equal to the feat performed by Gower, who finished his "Confessio Amantis" in 1393, when he seems to have been upwards of 70, and who had written French ballads in 1350, full 43 years before.[4] Nor does it

---

[1] The Black Prince died in June, 1376, when Richard became heir-apparent.
[2] See Passus III. 1. 71.   [3] See Passus I. 95.
[4] Warton, Hist. Eng. Poetry, ii. 338.

appear that Chaucer even *began* his Canterbury Tales till he was upwards of 60. It is worth noting that the poem now under consideration terminates abruptly, either because (as Mr Wright suggests) the scribe did not partake in the political sentiments of the author, as seems indicated by a marginal note, or because he discovered that it did not form a part of Piers Ploughman. It should be observed, however, that its Passus are numbered from *one* to *four*, so that the latter supposition is hardly tenable, and we are quite as much at liberty to suppose that it was never finished. Lastly, if Langland was really the author of this poem, his death probably took place in the very beginning of the reign of Henry IV.

Scanty indeed are these notes of his life; but the loss of information about him is, after all, of little moment. His poem is a true *autobiography* in the highest sense of the word. It abounds with his opinions, political and religious, from end to end, all expressed in the most decided language and evidently the result of much thought. The allusions to his poverty and the care taken with his education are certainly true; and while he satirizes the friars, he seems not much more friendly to the monks. On two points he is especially clear, viz. on the duty of every man to use his own common sense, and on the simplicity which should characterize a plain Christian man's religion. Better, he says, to do well than to have a whole sackful of pardons, which are but unsafe things to trust to. The law of Love is, with him, the one thing most worthy, the only thing in theology worth knowing. But for the Love which theology enjoins, the study of it would be worthless indeed. He shews himself to us as a man of simple, noble, and pure faith, strong in saving common sense, full of love for his fellows, the friend of the poor, the adviser of the rich, with strong views on the duties of a king towards his subjects, together with a feeling of deep reverence for the kingly character, fearless, unprejudiced, and ever willing to be taught. He does not write to please, but to express earnest and deep convictions, and from a love of contemplating the great problem of life; and there is much that may teach a reader to be earnest, pure, loving, and simple-minded, much that may profit all such as care to be instructed in such things. One point especially deserves attention, the purity of his writings, the great freedom they exhibit from all that is of a prurient tendency. Sometimes, indeed, he speaks out in plain terms, once or twice, but not often, in words that to us are coarse; but it is invariably in a tone of reproof or indignation. In his character of the glutton, he does not scruple to excite our disgust and loathing, but it is in order to shew how debasing and detestable a thing gluttony really is. This passage and one other near the end of the poem are the only ones which Dr Whitaker, who was somewhat scrupulous, thought it at all necessary to omit; and I think that the way in which the poet so frequently insists on the sanctity of the marriage-tie, and on the evil of ill-advised marriages, is greatly against the supposition that he was himself unmarried. To sum up all, his life and thoughts can be easily learnt from his poem, and they seem well worth the learning.

§ 13. ARGUMENT OF THE POEM. (TEXT A.)

The poem is distinctly divisible into two parts, the "Vision of Piers Plowman," and "Vita de Dowel." Of these, the first is again divisible into two distinct visions, which may be called: (1.) The Vision of the field full of folk, of Holy Church, and of Lady Meed, occupying the Prologue and Passus I.—IV.; and (2.) The Vision of the Deadly Sins and of "Pers the Plouhmon,"[1] occupying Passus V.—VIII. The remaining Passus (IX.—XI.) form the Prologue and Passus of the "Vita de Dowel."

I. VISION OF THE FIELD FULL OF FOLK, OF HOLY CHURCH, AND OF LADY MEED. In the PROLOGUE, the author describes how, weary of wandering, he sits down to rest upon the Malvern Hills, and there falls asleep and dreams. In his vision, the world and its people are represented to him by a field full of folk, busily engaged in their avocations. The field was situate between the tower of Truth, who is God the Father, and the dungeon which is the abode of the evil spirits. In it there were ploughmen and spendthrifts, hermits, minstrels, beggars, pilgrims, friars, a pardoner with bulls, law-sergeants, bishops, and all kinds of craftsmen.

Passus I. Presently, he sees a lovely lady, of whom he asks the

[1] So spelt in MS. V.

meaning of the tower. She tells him it is the abode of the Creator, who provides men with the necessaries of life. The dungeon is the castle of Care, where lives the Father of Falseness. He next asks her name, and she says she is Holy Church, and instructs him how great a treasure Truth is, how Lucifer fell through Pride, and that the way to heaven lies through Love.

Passus II. He asks how he may know Falsehood. She bids him turn and see Falsehood and Flattery. Looking aside he sees, not them alone, but a woman in glorious apparel. He is told she is the Lady Meed (i.e. Bribery) who is going to be married to Falsehood on the morrow. Holy Church then leaves him. The wedding is prepared, and Simony and Civil read a deed respecting the property with which Falsehood and Meed are to be endowed. Theology objects to the marriage, and disputes its legality; whereupon it is agreed that all must go to Westminster to have the question decided. Thus all come to the King's court, who vows that he will punish Falsehood if he can catch him. On hearing this, Falsehood flees to the friars, who pity him and house him for their own purposes.

Passus III. Lady Meed is arrested and brought before the king. A justice assures her all will go well. To seem righteous, she confesses and is shriven, offering to glaze a church-window by way of amendment; and, immediately afterwards, advises mayors and judges to take bribes. The king proposes she shall marry Conscience, and she is willing to do so; but Conscience refuses, and exposes her faults. She attempts to retaliate and to justify herself; but Conscience refutes her arguments, quotes the example of Saul to shew the evil of covetousness, and declares that Reason will one day reign upon earth, and punish all wrongdoers.

Pass. IV. Acting upon this hint, the king orders Reason to be sent for; who comes, accompanied by Wit and Wisdom. At this moment, Peace enters, with a complaint against Wrong. Wrong, knowing the complaint is true, gets Wisdom and Wit on his side by Meed's help, and offers to buy Peace off with a present. Reason, however, is firm and will shew no pity, but advises the king to act with strict justice. The king is convinced, and prays Reason to remain with him for ever after.

II. THE VISION OF THE DEADLY SINS, AND OF PERS THE PLOUHMON. *Pass. V.* The king goes to church, and afterwards to meat, and at this point of the vision the dreamer awakes. But it is not for long; he soon falls asleep again, and has a second vision, in which he again sees the field full of folk, and Conscience preaching to the assembled people, reminding them that the late storm and pestilence were judgments of God. Repentance seconds the efforts of Conscience, and many begin to repent. Of these the first is Pride, who makes a vow of humility. The second is Luxury, who vows to drink only water. The third is Envy, who is described with much particularity, and who confesses his evil thoughts and his attempts to harm his neighbours.[1] The fourth, Avarice, who confesses how he lied and cheated, and taught his wife to cheat. The fifth, Gluttony, who (on his way to church) is tempted into a beerhouse, of the interior of which the author gives a life-like and perfect picture. He too repents, though not till he has first become completely drunk and afterwards felt the ill effects of drinking. Lastly, Sloth declares his resolution to amend and to make all due restitution. Robert the robber is also introduced, praying earnestly for forgiveness.

Pass. VI. All the penitents set out in search of Truth, but no one knows the way. Soon they meet with a palmer, who has met with many saints, but never with one named *Truth*. At this juncture Piers the Ploughman "puts forth his head," declaring that he knows Truth well, and will tell them the way, which he then describes.

Pass. VII. The pilgrims think the way long, and want a guide. Piers says he will come himself and shew them, when he has ploughed his half-acre. Meanwhile, he gives good advice to the rich ladies and to the knight. Before starting, Piers makes his will, and then sets all who come to him to hard work. Many shirk their work, but are reduced to subordination by the sharp treatment of Hunger. Next follow most curious and valuable passages respecting the diet of the poor, striking for higher wages, and the discontent caused by prosperity.

Pass. VIII. At this time, Truth (i. e. God the Father) sends

---

[1] The character of Wrath is strangely omitted. Perceiving his mistake, the author, in Text B (his second edition), elaborated this character with much care.

Piers a bull of pardon, especially intended for kings, bishops, honest tradesmen, and the labouring poor, and (in the least degree of all) for even the lawyers. A priest disputes the validity of this pardon, and wants to read it. The dispute becomes so violent between this priest and Piers that the dreamer awakes, and the poem of Piers Ploughman (properly so called) ends with a fine peroration on the small value of popes' pardons, and the superiority of a righteous life over mere trust in indulgences.

III. VITA DE DOWEL, DOBET, AND DOBEST. *Pass. IX.* In introducing a new poem, the Vita de Do-wel, the author begins by describing a dialogue that passed between himself and two Minorite friars upon the doctrine of free-will. After this, he describes himself as again falling asleep, and perceiving a man named Thought. He asks Thought where Do-wel, Do-bet, and Do-best live, and Thought gives him some account of these, but says that the best person to give him further information is Wit. Soon after this, the dreamer (William) and Thought meet with Wit.

Pass. X. Wit tells William that Do-wel dwells in a castle called *Caro*, wherein also is enclosed the lady *Anima*, and they are guarded by constable In-wit and his five sons. Do-wel, he tells him further, consists in fearing God; Do-bet, in suffering patiently; and Do-best, in humility. Then follow very interesting discussions upon the good there is in well-assorted and lawful wedlock, and the evil there is in marriages that are ill-advised or mercenary, and in adulterous connections.

Pass. XI. The dreamer applies to yet one more adviser, viz. Dame Study, the wife of Wit. She inveighs with great justice and force against the way in which shallow would-be theologians cavil about the mysterious things of God, and unworthily amuse themselves with vain quibbles. At last, she commends the dreamer to Clergy and Scripture, from whom he may hope to learn yet more. Accordingly, he seeks these, and is favourably received. Clergy explains that Do-wel is nearly coincident with *Vita Activa* (the Active Life), that Do-bet consists in visiting the sick and those in prison, and that Do-best is—to relieve the poor by means of such vast wealth as was possessed by ecclesiastics for that purpose. But the ecclesiastics were far from doing their duty, and seemed to lie under the ban which declares the impossibility for rich men to enter heaven. Upon this, a dispute arises between Clergy and William, which gives William the opportunity of declaring the insufficiency of mere wisdom to obtain admittance into heaven, and the greater likelihood which honest but ignorant poor men have of attaining to the life eternal;

> "Souteris and seweris · such lewide iottis
> Percen wiþ a *pater noster* · þe paleis of heuene,
> Wiþoute penaunce, at here partyng · into heiȝe blisse!"

THE VISION OF WILLIAM CONCERNING

"PERS THE PLOUHMON."

[*Prologus.*]

IN A somer sesun · whon softe was þe sonne,
I schop me in-to a schroud · A scheep as I were ;
In Habite of an Hermite · vn-holy of werkes,
Wende I wydene in þis world · wondres to here.　4
Bote in a Mayes Morwnynge · on Maluerne hulles
Me bi-fel a ferly · A Feyrie me þouhte ;
I was weori of wandringe · and wente me to reste
Vndur a brod banke · bi a Bourne syde,　8
And as I lay and leonede · and lokede on þe watres,
I slumberde in A slepyng · hit sownede so murie.
¶ þenne gon I Meeten · A Meruelous sweuene,
þat I was in A Wildernesse · wuste I neuer where,　12
And as I beo-heold in-to þe Est · an-heiȝ to þe sonne,
I sauh a Tour on A Toft · [triȝely] I-maket ;
A Deop Dale bi-neoþe · A dungun þer-Inne,
With deop dich and derk · and dredful of siht.　16

[f. 394, b. col. 2.]
One summer season, clothed as a hermit, I went abroad in the world to hear wonders.

On Malvern hills, a strange thing befel me. Being tired of wandering, I rested me by a bourne's side, where I soon fell asleep.

Then dreamt I a wondrous dream, that I was in a strange wilderness, and saw on the east side of it a tower on a toft, and beneath it a deep dale with a dungeon.

Prologus ; *not in any of the* MSS.

1. *whon softe was þe sonne*] as y south wente U.
2. *into*] vndur H ; in U ; to D. *A scheep, &c.*] as I a shep were TH UH₂D.
3. *of*] as TUH₂D.
4. *Wende I wydene*] Wente wyde TH₂D ; I wente wide UH.
6. *A Feyrie*] of fairie THUH₂D.
7. *of wandring and*] of-wandrit & T ; forwandred H₂, forwandryd y U ; for wandryng & D.
9. *leonede*] lened me U.
10. *sownede*] swiȝede T ; swyed H₂ ; schewed D. *hit sownede*] I sweuenyd U.
12. *wuste I*] y wyste UH.
13. *And*] Ac TD ; H omits ; But U. *an heiȝ*] up U.
14. [*triȝely* T ; triely U ; tryelyche H₂] wonderliche VH ; trewliche D. *imaket*] a-tired U.
16. *dich*] dikes T ; diches UH₂. *and dredful, &c.*] þat dredful was of syghte H.

There was also a fair field, full of all manner of folk.	¶ A Feir feld ful of folk · fond I þer bi-twene, Of alle maner of men · þe mene and þe riche, Worchinge and wondringe · as þe world askeþ.
Some of them ploughed, sowed, and worked hard;	Summe putten hem to þe plouȝ · and pleiden hem ful seldene, 20 In Eringe and in Sowynge · swonken ful harde, þat monie of þeos wasturs · In Glotonye distruen.
but some were clad in gay apparel.	¶ And summe putten hem to pruide · apparaylden hem þer-after, In Cuntinaunce of cloþinge · queinteliche de-Gyset ; 24
Others prayed, and led an austere life, like anchorites.	To preyere and to penaunce · putten heom monye, For loue of vr lord · liueden ful harde, In Hope for to haue · Heuene-riche blisse ; As Ancres and Hermytes · þat holdeþ hem in heore Celles, 28 Coueyte not in Cuntre · to carien a-boute, For non likerous lyflode · heore licam to plese.
Some chose merchandise, whilst some were minstrels.	¶ And summe chosen Chaffare · to cheeuen þe bettre, As hit semeþ to vre siht · þat suche men scholden ; 32 And summe Murþhes to maken · as Munstrals cunne, [And gete gold wiþ here gle · giltles, I trowe.]
Some were jesters and slanderers, against whom St Paul preaches.	¶ Bote Iapers and Iangelers · Iudas Children, Founden hem Fantasyes · and fooles hem maaden, 36 And habbeþ wit at heor wille · to worchen ȝif hem luste.

17. *fond I*] I fonde H.
19. H. *omits* this line. *wondringe*] wandringe TUDH₂. *as*] so D.
20. *and pleiden hem*] pleiȝede TUD. *hem ful*] but H.
21. *eringe*] settyng TH₂D; seed tyme U. *harde*] sore HH₂.
22. *þat monie of*] whom that T; And wonnen þat U; whanne þat D. *In*] wiþ TUDH₂.
24. *cuntinaunce*] quoyntyse H. *queinteliche degyset*] comen disgisid TUH₂D ; þei conen hem disgyse H.
25. *To*] In THD. *preyere*] preyers HTUD. *to*] HD *om.*
26. *ful harde*] wel streite TD ; ful strayte HUH₂.

29. *carien*] cairen T; cayren H₂.
30. *non*] no THU. *licam*] lykames U ; lyke hem (!) D.
31. *Chaffare*] to chaffare TUD. *to cheeuen*] þei cheuide TU ; to preue H ; þey cheuen D.
32. *hit semeþ to*] es seen in U. *suche men*] þei so H. *scholden*] þriuen TH₂U; þryueth D.
34. *From* T: *also in* HUH₂D. *giltles*] synles HUD; synfullyche H₂.
35. *Iudas*] Iudases U.
36. *Founden*] þa faynen H ; Gon fynden U ; fynden H₂. *maaden*] maken HUTD.
37. *ȝif hem luste*] ȝif þei wolde H ; what hem liketh U.

þat Poul precheþ of hem · I dar not preouen heere ;
Qui loquitur turpiloquium · Hee is Luciferes hyne.

Bidders and Beggers · faste a-boute eoden,   40
   Til heor Bagges *and* heore Balies · were*n* [bratful]
     I-cromme*t* ;
Feyneden hem for heore foode · fouȝten atte alle ;
In Glotonye, God wot · gon heo to Bedde,
And ryseth vp wiþ ribaudye · þis Roberdes knaues ;   44
Sleep and Sleuȝþe · suweþ hem euere.

¶ Pilgr*i*mes and Palmers · Plihten hem to-gede*r*es
For to seche seint Ieme · and seintes at Roome ;
Wenten forþ in heore wey · wi*th* mony wyse tales,   48
And hedden leue to lyȝen · al heore lyf [aftir].
[Ermytes on an hep · wiþ hokide staues,
Wenten to Walsyngham · & here wenchis aftir ;]

¶ Grete lobres *and* longe · þat loþ weore to swynke 52
Cloþeden hem in Copes · to beo knowen for breþeren ;
And su*m*me schopen [hem] to hermytes · heore ese to
     haue.

I Font þere Freres · all þe Foure Ordres,
   Prechinge þe peple · for p*r*ofyt of heore wombes, 56
Glosynge þe Gospel · as hem good likeþ,

[f. 395 a. col. 1.]
There were beggars, too, dissembling knaves, who lived in gluttony, sleep, and sloth.

Pilgrims and palmers were there, who went to Rome, and had leave to lie ever after.

Hermits, too, went to Walsingham, and their wenches with them; greatlong lubbers were they, and loath to work.

I found friars there, of all four orders, glozing the Gospel,

---

38. *dar*] wol U. *preouen*] proue it TH₂; sey H ; proue yt D.
39. *Qui, &c.*] *Qui turpe loquitur* D. *Hee is*] is HUH₂D; his T.
40. *Bidders and beggers*] beggeris and bydderes U. *eoden*] ȝede TH₂ ; ȝeden H ; ȝedyn U.
41. *bagges—Balies*] bely & here bagge TH₂D ; belyes and here bagges U. [*bratful* T; bretful H₂; bredful UD] faste VH.
42. *Feyneden hem*] Flite þanne T; þei fliten U; Fayteden H; Faytours H₂; Flytteden & D. *atte alle*] at þe ale TD ; at þe nale UH; at nale H₂.
44. *þis*] as TUD ; tho H₂.
46. *Plihten*] pyghten H.
48. *wyse*] vayn H.
49. [*aftir* THUH₂D] tyme V.
50, 51. *From* T ; *also in* UH₂D;

not in VH.
52. *lobres*] lobies TUH₂D ; lobu*rs* H. *þat loþ weore*] loth for U.
53. *for breþeren*] from oþere TU H₂D.
54. *om. the whole line* U. *And summe*] TH₂D *om.* ; summe H. [*hem* THD.] V *omits*.
Obs. After l. 54 *the two following lines occur, in* H₂ *only* ;
Who-so ȝeueth for godes loue · wyl
  nat ȝeue his þankis
But þere his mede may be most · and
  most merytorye.
55. *Font*] fond TUH₂H ; But I fonde D.
56. *heore wombes*] þe wombe TH₂.
57. *Glosynge*] gloside TUH₂ ; gloseth D. *good*] silf H. *likeþ*] likide TUH₂.

covetous cheats, whose traffic had much to do with money.

For Couetyse of Copes · Construeþ hit ille;
For monye of þis Maistres · mowen cloþen hem at lyking,
For Moneye and heore Marchaundie · meeten ofte to-gedere.   60

For since charity has taken to trading, many strange things have happened.

Seþþe charite haþ be chapmon · [and] cheef to schriuen lordes,
Mony ferlyes han bi-falle · in a fewe ʒeres.
But holychirche bi-ginne · holde bet to-gedere,
þe moste Mischeef on molde · mounteþ vp faste.   64

There preached a pardoner, and shewed a bull, saying he could assoil everyone.

¶ þer prechede a pardoner · as he a prest were,
And brouʒt vp a Bulle · with Bisschopes seles,
And seide þat him-self mihte · a-soylen hem alle
Of Falsnesse and Fastinge · and of vouwes I-broken.   68
þe lewede Men likede him wel · and leeueþ his speche,

Men came and kissed it; and he blinded their eyes with it, and got rings and brooches.

And comen vp knelynge · and cusseden his Bulle;
He bonchede hem with his Breuet · and blered heore eiʒen,
And rauhte with his Ragemon · Ringes and Broches.   72
þus ʒe ʒiueþ oure gold · Glotonye to helpen,
And leueþ hit to losels · þat lecherie haunten.

Were the bishop worth his ears, this would not be suffered.

Weore þe Bisschop I-blesset · and worþ boþe his Eres,
Heo scholde not beo so hardi · to deceyue so þe peple.
Saue hit nis not bi þe Bisschop · þat þe Boye precheþ;

---

58. *ille*] ful yuel H; as þei wolde TUH₂; at wille D.
59. *cloþen—lyking*] be clothed the better H.
60. *For moneye*] For here mony TUH₂D. *oft*] THUH₂D omit.
61. *charite—chapmon*] freeris han ben chapmen H. [*and* THUH₂D] V omits.
62. *bifalle*] fallen TUD; falle ryʒt H₂.
63. *biginne*] and þei T; and he U H₂D. *holde—togedere*] þe better to holde togedre H; holde togidre U.
64 *mounteþ, &c.*] is mountyng up faste T; is mowntynge vp wel faste H. H₂D.
65. *as—were*] a prest as he were U; a prest as it were H.
66. *vp*] forth THUH₂.
69. *likede*] leuide T; leued HD; lyueden U. *him*] DH om. *wel*] U om. *leeueþ*] likide TU; lykeden H; liked D; leued H₂.
70. *and cusseden*] to kissen TU H₂D.
71. *bonchede*] bunchiþ T; bunched H₂; blessid UH; bonches D.
72. *And rauhte*] Raughte hym U. *Ringes and broches*] broches and rynges UD.
73. *þus—gold*] þus þei ʒouen here geld TD; þus ʒe ʒyuen ʒoure goodus H. *Glotonye*] glotonis THUH₂D.
76. *Heo—hardi*] His sel shulde not be sent TUH₂D. *to deceyue so*] to bigyle so H; TUH₂D omit so.
77. *Saue—bi*] It is not al be TH;

Bote þe **Parisch** prest and he de-parte þe seluer,   78
þat haue schulde þe pore parisschens · ʒif þat heo ne
   weore.

¶ *Per*sones and parisch p*r*estes · playneþ to heore Bisschops,   80
þat heore Parisch haþ ben pore · seþþe þe Pestilence
   [tyme],
And askeþ leue and lycence · at londun to dwelle,
To singe þer for Simonye · for seluer is swete.

Þ Er houeþ an Hundret · In Houues of selk,   84
   Seriauns hit semeþ · to seruen atte Barre ;
Pleden for pons · and pou*n*des þe lawe,
Not for loue of vr lord · vn-loseþ heore lippes ones.
Þow mihtest beter mete*n* þe Myst · on Maluerne hulles,
   þen geten a Mom of heore Mouþ · til moneye weore
   schewed.   89

¶ I sauh þer Bisschops Bolde · and Bachilers of diuyn
Bi-coome Clerkes of A-Counte · þe kyng for to seruen ;
Erchedekenes and Deknes · þat Dignite hauen,   92
To p*r*eche þe peple · and pore men to feede,
Beon lopen to londun · bi leue of heore Bisschopes,
To ben Clerkes of þe kynges Benche · þe Cuntre to
   schende.

Parish-priests complain that their parishes are poor now since the pestilence, and so they go to London.

There were a hundred sergeants in silk hoods, law-pleaders, who never spoke till they saw their money.

I saw there bishops who became clerks of account, and archdeacons who left the feeding of the poor to be clerks of the king's bench.

---

y trowe it is noght for U ; It is nouʒt be H₂; He is nouʒt al by D. *þe Boye*] þey boþe D.
78. *he*] þe pardoner THUH₂D. *departe*] parte THU ; departid H₂ ; parteth D.
79. *haue—parisschens*] þe pore peple of þe parissh shulde haue TH₂D ; þe poore of þe parysche schuld haue H ; þe pore peple schuld haue U.
80. *parisch prestes*] prouenders H. *playneþ*] playned H ; pleynide hem TD ; playnen hem U. *Bisschops*] bisshop TU.
81. *Parisch*] parischens HU. *haþ ben*] was T ; ben U ; were H₂D. [*tyme* THUH₂D] V *omits.*
82. *And — lycence*] To haue a licence & leue TUH₂. *askeþ*] han H.

D *omits this line.*
84. *houeþ*] houide THUH₂D.
85. *hit semeþ*] it semide THH₂ ; þei semeden U ; it semedyn D. *to seruen atte*] þat seruide at þe T ; pletiden at þe U.
86. *Pleden—poundes*] Pleten for penis & poynteþ T ; For penyes & for powndis pladden H ; þei pletide for pens and poundide U ; plededen for pens & poundes D.
87. *vnloseþ — ones*] openyd his lippes U ; not open her lyppus oouus H.
89. *weore*] be TH₂UD.
90. *Bisschops*] erchebisschopes U.
92. *Erchedekenes*] I saw þere erchedeknes U. *Deknes*] denis THUD ; dekenes H₂.

I saw too barons, burgesses, bondmen,

¶ Barouns and Burgeis · and Bonde-men also   96
I sauȝ in þat Semble · as ȝe schul heren her-aftur.

bakers, butchers, brewsters, and others; and ditchers who lead ill lives, and sing idle songs.

¶ Bakers, Bochers · and Breusters monye,
[Wollene websteris · and weueris of lynen,
Taillours, tanneris · & tokkeris boþe,]   100
Masons, Minours · and mony oþer craftes,
Dykers, and Deluers · þat don heore dedes ille,
And driueþ forþ þe longe day · with " deu vous saue,
    dam Emme ! "   103

Cooks were crying "hot pies," and taverners were praising their wine.

¶ Cookes and heore knaues · Cryen " hote pies, hote !
Goode gees and grys · Gowe dyne, [Gowe] ! "
Tauerners to hem · tolde þe same tale
Wiþ good wyn of Gaskoyne · And wyn of Oseye,
Of Ruyn a[n]d of Rochel · þe Rost to defye.   108
[Al þis I sauȝ slepynge · & seue siþes more.]

96. *and Burgeis*] TU *omit* and. *Bondemen*] bondage TH₂; bondeage D; bondages U.
97. *semble*] semele T. *heren heraftur*] heer aftir TU; seen aftur H; here after D.
98. *Bakers*] Baxteris & T; bakeris and HH₂U; Baksteres & D.
99, 100. *From* T; *also in* UH₂D. [*tanneris & tokkeris*] toucheris and tolleris U; towkers and tollers H₂; & souters and tokkeres D.
102. *heore dedes*] here dede T · here werk U. *ille*] yuol H.

103. *vous*] THU *om. with—saue*] dieu gard D.
105. [*Gowe* THUH₂; V *has* Gouwe]
106. *to hem*] tollid hem U. *Toldetale*] and tolde hem þe same U; tolde þe same TD; tolde hem the same H₂.
107. Wiþ wyn of osay & wyn of gascoyne TH₂D (*but* D *reads* Asay); wiþ white wyn of oseye · and gascoyne U.
108. *Ruyn*] þe ryn THDUH₂. *Rochel*] þe rochel THUH₂.
109. *From* T. *Also in* UD *and* H₂.

PASSUS I.

[*Primus passus de visione.*]

What þis Mountein be-Meneþ · and þis derke Dale,
 And þis feire feld, ful of folk · feire I schal ow schewe.
A louely ladi on leor · In linnene I-cloþed,
Com a-doun from þe [clyf] · and clepte me feire, 4
And seide, "sone! slepest þou? · Sixt þou þis peple
Al hou bisy þei ben · A-boute þe Mase?
Þe moste parti of þe peple · þat passeþ nou on eorþe,
Hauen heo worschupe in þis world · kepe þei no betere;
Of oþer heuene þen heer · [holde] þei no tale." 9
¶ Ich was a-ferd of hire Face · þauh heo feir weore,
And seide, "Merci, Ma dame · What is þis to mene?"
¶ "Þis Tour and þis Toft," quod heo · "treuþe is þer-Inne, 12
And wolde þat ȝe wrouȝten · as his word techeþ;
For he is Fader of Fei · þat formed ow alle
Boþe with Fel and with Face · and ȝaf ow fyue wittes,
Forte worschupen him [þerwith] · while ȝe beoþ heere.

Marginal notes:
I now tell the meaning of the mountain, the dale, and the field.
A lovely lady came down from that cliff, and bade me look at the people;
most of whom seek only worship in this world (here imaged by a field).
I was afraid, and asked what it all meant.
"In the tower," she said, "is Truth, i. e. God the Creator.
[f. 395 a. col. 2.]

Primus, &c.] *found in* TUD.
1. *bemeneþ*] meniþ TD; may mene U. *þis darke*] þis deope H; ek þe derke TD.
2. *feire feld*] THUH₂D *omit* feire; *but see prol.* l. 17.
3. *on leor*] of lire THUD; of lore H₂. *I-cloþed*] was clothid U.
4. [*clyf*] *so in* UDH₂; V *and* H *have* loft; T *reads* fro þat kiþ. *clepte*] clepid H; callide TUH₂D.
5. *slepest þou*] slepistow U. *sixt*] sest T; seest HUD.
7. *nou on*] on þis TH₂; vpon HU;

here on D.
8. *in þis*] of þis HD; of þe U.
9. [*holde*] *so in* TUDH₂; ȝeueþ V; ȝyue H.
11. *is þis to mene*] may þis by-meene HU.
12. *and þis*] of þe T; on þe HDH₂; in þe U.
13. *And*] he H; þat U; D *om.*
14. *Fei*] feiþ THUD. *ow*] ȝow TUH₂D; ȝou H.
16. *Forte*] For to THH₂DU. [*þer-wiþ*] V *omits this word; but it occurs in* THUH₂; D *has* with.

who gives men wool and linen sufficient.	And for he hihte þe eorþe · to seruen ow vchone	17
	Of wollene, Of linnene · To lyflode at neode,	
	In Mesurable Maner · to maken ow at ese ;	
	And Comaundet of his Cortesye · In Comune þreo	
Three things are really needful,— clothes, meat, and drink.	þinges ;	20
	Heore nomes beþ neodful · and nempnen hem I þenke,	
	Bi Rule and bi Resun · Rehersen hem her-aftur.	
	¶ þat on Clothing is · from Chele ow to saue :	
	And þat oþur Mete at Meel · for meseise of þiseluen :	24
But beware of drink, and remember Lot's sin,	And drink whon þou druȝest · but do hit not out of Resun,	
	þat þou weor[þ]e þe worse · whon þou worche scholdest.	
	¶ For Lot in his lyf-dayes · for lyking of drinke,	
	Dude bi his douhtren · þat þe deuel louede,	28
which was caused by drunkenness.	Dilytede him in drinke · as þe deuel wolde,	
	And lecherie him lauhte · and lay bi hem boþe ;	
	And al he witede hit wyn · þat wikkede dede.	
	Dreede dilitable drinke · And þou schalt do þe bettre ;	32
Moderation is wholesome, though the appetite be keen.	Mesure is Medicine · þauh þou muche ȝeor[n]e.	
	Al nis not good to þe gost · þat þe bodi lykeþ,	
	Ne lyflode to þe licam · þat leof is to þe soule.	
Believe not thy	¶ Leef not þi licam · for lyȝere him techeþ,	36

17. *for—eorþe*] þerfore he bad ȝow eche U. *for he hihte*] therefore hooteth H ; þerfore he hiȝte TH₂D. *to—uchone*] to helpe ȝow ichone TDH₂ ; an helpen oþer U.
18. *Of—of*] And wollen & D.
21. *Heore—neodful*] Narn (Are H₂) none nedful but þo TH₂ ; Arn non nedful but þei U ; Ne arn non nedful but þo D.
22. *Bi—bi*] And rekne hem in TD ; And rekene hem be H₂ ; And rekne hem ȝow by U. *Rehersen*] reherse þou TD ; reherse ȝow H₂ ; reherce ȝe U. *heraftur*] aftir UD.
23. *cloþing is*] is vesture TH₂ ; is vesture verrailiche U. *from chele*] fro cold U. *on*] þe TH₂. D *reads*, That on is cloþing for cold · þat it may þee saue.
24. *And—meel*] þe toþer is mete at

ȝour meel U. *meseise*] myschief UH. þiseluen] ȝow selue U.
25. *þow druȝest*] þe driȝeþ TH₂ ; ȝow drieth U.
26. *þou weore*] þou worþe THD ; þe worth H₂ ; ȝe wurche U. *þou—scholdest*] ȝe swynke scholde U.
27. *for lyking*] þorouȝ lykynge H.
28. *louede*] lykide TH₂UH₂D.
29. T *omits this line ; but it occurs in* H₂ *as well as in* HD *and* U. OBS. A whole folio is here lost out of U ; from l. 33 down to l. 99.
33. *ȝeorne*] V ȝeore ; *but* T *has* ȝerne ; *so* H *and* D.
34. *bodi*] gut TD ; gutt H₂ ; *which is perhaps a better reading, as regards the alliteration.* lykeþ] askeþ HH₂D.
36. *lyȝere*] lyar H ; a liþer T ; a lyere H₂ ; a leder D. *techeþ*] ledith H.

THE TREASURES OF THE WORLD.

þat is þe Wikkede word · þe to bi-traye.
For þe Fend and þi Flesch · folewen to-gedere,
And schendeþ þi soule · seo hit in þin herte ;
And for þou scholdest beo war · I wisse þe þe bettre. 40

"A Madame, Merci!" quaþ I · "me likeþ wel þi wordes.
Bote þe Moneye on þis Molde · þat men so faste holden,
Tel me to whom þat Tresour appendeþ ?"

"GO to þe gospel," quaþ heo · "þat god seiþ him-
seluen, 44
Whon þe peple him a-posede · with a peny in þe Temple,
ȝif heo schulden worschupe þer-with · Cesar heore kyng.
¶ And he asked of hem · of whom spac þe lettre,
And whom þe ymage was lyk · þat þer-Inne stod. 48
¶ "Ceesar, þei seiden · We seoþ wel vchone."

[*Reddite ergo que sunt cesaris cesari, et que sunt dei deo.*]

"þenne *Reddite*," quaþ God · "þat to Cesar falleþ,
Et que sunt dei deo · or elles do ȝe ille."
For Rihtfoliche Resoun · schulde rulen ou alle, 52
And kuynde wit be wardeyn · oure weolþe to kepe,
And tour of vr tresour · to take hit [ȝow] at nede ;
For husbondrie and he · holden to-gedere."

þEnne I fraynede hire feire · for him þat hire made, 56
"þat [dungun] in þat deope dale · þat dredful is of siht,
What may hit Mene, Madame · Ich þe bi-seche ?"

body, which is leagued with the fiend; therefore beware."

I thanked her, and asked her to whom the treasures of the world belonged.

She bade me go to the gospel, and read how Christ was tempted by being shown a penny.

"Render unto Cæsar," &c. (Matt. xxii. 21).

Reason and common sense should rule you.

Then I asked her what the deep dale meant.

37. *wikkede*] wrecchide TH₂D. *word*] world THH₂D.
38. *folewen*] foloweþ þee H.
39. *seo*] set T; I see H; & set D; and seith H₂.
40. *bettre*] best HTH₂D.
44. *þat god*] þer god H. *seiþ*] seyde HD.
46. *heo schulden*] þei wile T. *heore*] þe TD.
48. *And—lyk*] And þe imagis like T; And ymage lyk DH₂. *stod*] standis T; stondeth HH₂; standes D.
49. *The Latin quotation following is found in H.*

50. *þenne Reddite*] Reddite cesari TH₂D; ȝeldeþ to cesar H. *falleþ*] befalle TH₂ (*which also om.* to); apendiþ H; he longeþ (be-longeþ ?) D.
51. *Et—deo*] & to god his deel H; Et que sunt dei digno D. *do ȝe*] ȝe don THH₂; also D (*which om.* elles).
54. *tour*] toure H; tutour TH₂D. [ȝow TH₂; ȝou HD] V omits.
55. *he*] witte H.
57. *þat—dale*] þe dungeon in þe dale TDH₂; þe dale & þe dongown H. [*dungun*] V has doun; *but see prol.* l. 15.
58. *hit mene*] þat bymeene H.

"That is the castle of care," she said, "the abode of Satan,

" Þat is þe Castel of care," quod heo · " hose comeþ
    þer-Inne,
Mai Banne þat he born was · to Bodi or to soule.   60
Þer-Inne woneþ a wiht · þat wrong is I-hote,
Fader of Falsness · he foundede [it] him-seluen ;

who deceived Adam and Eve, and Cain, and Judas.

Adam and Eue · he eggede to don ille ;
Counseilede Caym · to cullen his Broþer ;   64
Iudas he Iapede · wiþ þe Iewes seluer,
And on an Ellerne treo · hongede him after.

He hinders love, and deceives all that trust in vain treasure."

He is a lettere of loue · and ly3eþ hem alle
Þat trusteþ in heor tresour · þer no truþe is Inne."   68

Then I wondered who she was, and conjured her to tell me her name.

¶ Þenne hedde I wonder in my wit · what wommon hit
    weore,
Þat suche wyse wordes · of holy writ me schewede ;
And halsede hire in þe hei3e nome · er heo þeonne 3eode,
What heo weore witerly · þat [wisside] me so feire.   72

"I am Holy Church, who received thee in infancy; thou broughtest me then pledges, to work my will."

"Holi churche Icham," quaþ heo · " þou ouhtest me to
    knowe :
Ich þe vndurfong furst · and þi feiþ þe tau3te.
Þow brou3test me Borwes · my biddyng to worche,
And to loue me leelly · While þi lyf durede."   76

Then I prayed her to teach me Christ's will,

¶ Þenne knelede I on my kneos · and cri3ed hire of
    grace,
And preiede hire pitously · to preye for vr sunnes,
And eke to teche me kuyndely · on crist to bi-leeue,

---

59. *quod heo*] TH₂ *and* D *omit.*
hose] who þat THH₂.
61. *wiht*] wy TH₂ ; wey D.
62. *falsnes*] falshed TH₂D.   [*it* T ;
yt D] VHH₂ *omit.*
63. *to don*] hem to TD ; to HH₂.
64. Caym he cownseyled, &c., H.
65. *wiþ*] þorogh H.   *Iewes*] Iewene
T ; Iewyne H₂ ; Iuen D.
66. *on—treo*] siþen on an eldir T ;
sethen on An yllern D ; sithen on an
eldren H₂.
67. *a lettere*] leder D.   *ly3eþ*] by-
ly3eth H.
68. *in heor*] on his TH₂D.   *þer*]
þat H.   *þer—Inne*] betraid arn

sounest TH₂ ; betrayed buþ sounest D.
70. *me*] TDH₂ *omit.*
72. [*wisside* TH₂ ; wysed D] techeþ
V ; tawght H.
74. *Ich—furst*] I undirfange þe
ferst TH₂D ; I þee furst undurfonge
H.þe] D *omits.*
76. *durede*] duriþ TH₂ ; lasted H ;
dureth D.
77. *cri3ed*] prayed H.
78. *And—to*] To haue pytee on þe
pepul & to H.   *vr sunnes*] my sennes
T ; my synnes H₂D.
79. *eke to teche*] to teche H ; ek
kenne TH₂.

þat Ich his willé mihte worche · þat wrouhte me to
Mon.   80

"Tech me to no Tresour · bote tel me þis ilke,
Hou I may saue my soule · þat seint art I-holde."

¶ "Whon alle tresour is I-tryȝed · Treuþe is þe Beste ;
I do hit on *Deus Caritas* · to deeme þe soþe.   84
Hit is as derworþe a drurie · as deore god him-seluen.
For hose is trewe of his tonge · telleþ not elles,
Doþ his werkes þer-with · and doþ no mon ille,
He is a-counted to þe gospel · on grounde and on lofte,
And eke I-liknet to vr lord · bi seint Lucus wordes. 89
Clerkes þat knowen hit · scholde techen hit aboute,
For Cristene and vn-cristene · him cleymeþ vchone.

Kynges and knihtes · scholde kepen hem bi Reson, 92
And Rihtfuliche Raymen · þe Realmes a-bouten,
And take trespassours · and [teiȝen] hem faste,
Til treuþe hedde I-termynet · þe trespas to þe ende.
For Dauid, in his dayes · he Dubbede knihtes, 96
Dude hem swere on heor swerd · to serue treuþe euere.
þat is þe perte profession · þat a-pendeþ to knihtes,
And not to faste a Friday · In Fyue score ȝeres,
But holden with hem and with heore · þat asken þe treuþe,

Side notes: for I wished for no treasure but my soul's salvation. "Truth is the best of treasures whoever is true in word and work is like our Lord. Luke viii. 21. [f. 395 b. col. 1.] Kings and knights should govern rightfully, and bind transgressors. For David dubbed knights to serve Truth: and to do so is far better than to fast on Fridays.

80. *his—worche*] miȝte werchen his wil TH₂D.
81. *to no Tresour*] no tresour, quoþ I H. *tel*] teche H.
82. *I-holde*] yhoten TH₂; D *has, þat senne had y-holden.*
83. *tresour is I-triȝed*] tresours arn triȝed THH₂; *to which* H *also adds* quod heo.
85. Hyt is derworthe & dreury, &c. D. *a*] H *om.*
86. *hose*] whoso THH₂. *not elles*] non oþer THH₂D.
87. *and doþ*] & wilneþ T; & wyllith H₂; willeþ D.
88. *acounted—gospel*] a god be þe gospel TD; good be gospel H₂. *on—lofte*] in heuen & in erþe H.
89. *Iliknet*] lyke THH₂D.
90. *techen hit*] kenne it TH₂D.
91. *him cleymeþ*] cleymeþ it TH₂; claymen it HD.
92. *hem*] it THH₂D.
93. *And—Raymen*] And riden & rappe doun TH₂; And ryden at randoun D. *Raymen*] rule H. *þe Realmes*] in reaumes TH₂; her rewmes H; in reames D.
94. *trespassours*] hem þat trespassen H. [*teiȝen* T; *tyen* H₂; *teyen* D] bynden V; bynde H.
95. *þe trespas*] here trespas THH₂D.
96. *dayes*] lyfdayes D.
97. *Dude*] made TH₂D; & made H. *heor*] his TH₂; a D.
98. *perte profession*] professioun apertly TH₂D; perfyt professyoun H.
99. *a*] oon H. *ȝeres*] wynter TH H₂D.
100. *hem—heore*] hym and wiþ hire TUH₂D; hem and with hers H.

THE FALL OF LUCIFER. [PASS. I.

And leuen for no loue · ne lacching of ʒiftus ; 101
And he þat passeþ þat poynt · is a-postata in þe ordre.
[For crist, kyngene kyng · knyhtide tene,]

And Christ, too, knighted Cherubim and Seraphim, and

¶ Cherubin *and* Seraphin · an al þe foure ordres, 104
And ʒaf hem maystrie *and* miht · in his Maieste,
[And ou*er* his meyne · made hem Archauungelis,]

taught them Truth and Obedience.

And tauʒte [hem] þorw þe Trinite · treuþe for to knowe*n*,
And beo boxum at his biddynge · he bad hem not elles.

Lucifer was most lovely till he brake obedience: and then he and his fellows became fiends.

¶ Lucifer *with* legiou*n*s · lerede hit in heuene ; 109
He was louelokest of siht · aftur vr lord,
Til he brak Boxu*m*nes · þorw bost of him-seluen.
¶ Þene fel he *with* his felawes · *and* fendes bi-comen,
Out of heuene in-to helle · hobleden faste, 113
Su*m*me in þe Eir, *and* su*m*me in þe Eorþe · *and* su*m*me
in helle deope.

Lucifer, for his exceeding pride, lies lowest in hell; with him all wrongdoers shall dwell.

¶ Bote Lucifer louwest · liʒþ of hem alle ;
For pruide þat he put out · his peyne haþ non ende; 116
And alle þat wrong worchen · wende þei schulen
After heore deþ-day · and dwellen *with* þat schrewe.

But they that do after the word may be sure of

¶ Ac heo þat worchen þat word · þat holi writ techeþ,
And endeþ as Ich er seide · in profitable werkes, 120

---

101. *leuen—loue*] neu*ere* leue hym for loue TH₂ ; neither leef hem for loue U ; neu*er* leue hem for loue D. *ne— ʒiftus*] ne for lakkynge of siluer U ; ne lachesse of gyftes D ; ne no lach- ynge of ʒyftus H.
102. *And*] For H. *he þat*] whoso TUH₂D. *þe*] his THUDH₂.
103. This line is a made up one, from H and U. The readings are,
For crist kynge of knyʒt*us* · knytted somtyme H.
And kyng, kyngene kyng · knyhtide tene U.
And crist king of kinges · kniʒtide tene TH₂.
And crist kyng of knyʒtes · knyʒted ten D.
104. *an—ordres*] such seuene & a noþer TH₂ ; and siche mo oþere U ; such seuene & oþer D.
105. *maystrie—miht*] miʒt in his mageste TDH₂U ; honour and myʒte

H. *in—Maieste*] þe meryere hem þouʒte TUH₂ ; þe meryere hym þouʒte D.
106. *From* T. Also in UH₂ *and* D.
107. [*hem* THUH₂D] V *omits*. *treuþe*] þe trouþe THUH₂D.
108. *biddynge*] heste U.
109. *lerede*] lernyd UD ; *also* D *omits* hit.
110. *louelokest*] þe louelyst U. *of siht*] to loke on TH₂.
113. *hobleden*] hobelide þei TH₂ UHD ; hobleden wel H.
115. *liʒþ*] light U.
116. *þat—out*] he was putte out H ; he putte out U ; þat he put out was D. *wende*] wende þedyr H.
117. *wrong worchen*] werchen wiþ wrong TUH₂ ; wurche *with* wronges D.
119. *þat word þat*] in þis world as H (*written over an erasure*).
120. *profitable*] perfite TH₂D.

Mouwen be siker þat heore soules · schullen to heuene,   *heaven; and therefore say I*
þer Treuþe is in Trinite · and Corouneþ hem alle.   *that Truth is the best treasure."*
¶ For I sigge sikerli · bi siht of þe textes,
Whon alle tresor is I-triȝet · Treuþe is þe beste.   124
Lereþ hit þis lewed men · for lettrede hit knoweþ,
þat treuþe is tresour · triedest on eorþe."

"Yit haue I no kuynde knowing," quod I · "þou most   *"But I have no natural*
   teche me betere,   *knowledge of it," said I.*
Bi what Craft in my Corps · hit cumseþ, and where."   128

"Þou dotest daffe," quaþ heo · "Dulle are þi wittes.   *"Thou fool," said she, "It is thy*
   Hit is a kuynde knowynge · þat kenneþ þe in herte   *natural conscience, teaching you*
For to loue þi louerd · leuere þen þi-seluen ;   *to love God, and leave deadly*
No dedly sunne to do · dyȝe þauȝ þou scholdest.   132   *sin.*

Þis I trouwe beo treuþe ! · hose con teche þe betere,   *If any can teach you better, let*
Loke þou suffre him to seye · and seþþe teche hit forþure !   *him !*
For þus techeþ us his word · (worch þou þer-aftur)
þat loue is þe leuest þing · þat vr lord askeþ,   136   *For Love is what God likes best,*
And eke þe playnt of pees ; · prechet [in] þin harpe   *and eke the plant of Peace. Say*
þer þou art Murie at þi mete · whon me biddeþ þe   *this in thy songs, when men ask*
   ȝedde ;   *thee to sing.*

121. *schullen*] shal wende THUH₂D.
122. *Corouneþ hem*] tronen hym T; tryeste of U; trowe him H₂; crownen hem D; crowneþ hem H.
123. *For—sikerli*] For-þi I seye as I seide er TUH₂D; For I saye as I er sayde H. *þe*] þise T; þese U.
124. *tresor—I-triȝet*] tresours arn (ben H) triȝed THUH₂.
125. *þis*] þus TH₂; to H; U omits; *also* D *omits* hit. *lettrede*] lettered men H.
126. *is tresour*] is þe tr. TD; is a tr. H. *triedest*] triȝest here TH₂ ; þe trieste U; tryest D
127. *quod I*] UD *omit*. *þou—betere*] ȝet mote ȝe bet kenne T; ȝe mot me betere kenne UH₂; but ȝe me bet kenne D.
128. *Craft*] kynne craft U. *cumseþ*] compsiþ T; bicomseþ H; comseth UH₂; comsit D.

129. *dotest*] dotide TUH₂; dootest H; doted D.
130. *kenneþ—in*] comseth in þin U. *in*] in þin THDH₂.
131. *leuere*] betere U.
132. *to do*] þat þou do H. *dyȝe—þou*] þoghe þou deye U.
133. *hose con*] who can TUH₂D.
134. *teche—forþure*] lere it aftir TH₂ ; lerne it aftir U; leret after D.
135. *techeþ us*] askiþ wytnesse TH₂; witnesseth UD.
137. *eke þe playnt*] eke þe plante T; eke þe plaunte HH₂ ; also plante U; eke þe plonte D. *prechet—harpe*] preche it in þin harpe THH₂; put it in þin herte U ; preche it in þy herte D; *but* V *has*, prechet þe þin harpe.
138. *whon—ȝedde*] in þi most myrthe (*over an erasure*) H. *me*] men TUH₂. *The line in* D *is corrupt.*

<small>Love began with God the Father, who let His Son die for us;</small>

For bi kuynde knowynge in herte · Cumse[þ] þer a Fitte.
Þat Falleþ to þe Fader · þat formede vs alle.   140
He lokede on vs wit*h* loue · and lette his sone dye
Mekeliche for vre misdede[s] · forte amende vs alle.
And ȝit wolde he hem no wo · þat [wrouȝte] him þat pyne,

<small>even as Christ prayed for His enemies,</small>

But Mekeliche wit*h* mouþe · Merci he by-souȝte,   144
To haue pite on þat peple · þat pynede him to deþe.

<small>granting mercy to them that pierced his heart.</small>

¶ Her þou miht seon ensaumple · in [hymselfe] one,
Hou he was mihtful and Meke · þat merci gon graunte
To hem þat heengen hi*m* heiȝe · and his herte þurleden.

<small>Therefore I advise the rich to have pity on the poor; for "with the same measure," &c. (Matt. vii. 2).</small>

[For-þi I rede þe riche · haue reuþe on þe pore ;   149
þeiȝ ȝe ben miȝty to mote · beþ meke of ȝour werkis ;]
   [*Eadem mensura qua mensi fueritis, remeci*[*e*]*tur uobis ;*]
For þe same Mesure þat ȝe Meten · A-mis oþer elles,
Ȝe schul be weyen þer-wit*h* · whon ȝe wenden hennes.

<small>For though ye be true in word and deed, except ye love the poor, and give alms,</small>

¶ For þauȝ ȝe ben trewe of tonge · *and* treweliche winne,
And eke as chast as a child · þat in Chirche wepeþ,   154
Bote ȝe liuen trewely · and eke loue þe pore,
And such good as God sent · Treweliche parten,   156

---

139. *bi*] in TD ; H *omits. in herte*] U *omits. Cumse—Fitte*] þer comsiþ a miȝt T ; bygynne suche H ; þer comseth it right U ; conseyue þou myȝte D ; þer comeþ a miȝt H₂.
140. *þat*] And þat TUH₂D.
141. *He*] þat U ; TH₂D *omit. and*] he H.
142. *misdede*] misdedis THUH₂D. *forte*] to THUH₂D.
143. [*wrouȝte* THUDH₂] V *has* wolde, *copied from the first part of the line.*
144. *he*] H *and* U *omit.*
145—147 *are omitted in* H.
146. *Her—ensaumple*] Here miȝt þou sen ensaumplis TDH₂ ; Here myght se ensamples U. [*hymselfe* TUDH₂] V *has* þi-self.
147. *Hou*] þat TUH₂D. *þat*] and TUH₂D.
148. *To—heengen*] For hem þat honged H. *heiȝe*] by TH₂DU (*by mistake*).
149, 150. *From* T; *also in* HUD *and* H₂. V *has only* one *line, viz.* For-þi I rede þe Mihtful of Mayn be Meke of þi wordes. *werkis*] hertes D. *The Latin quotation is found in* H *only*.

OBS. MS. H. *is here much tampered with and of little value, for about nine lines.*

151. *þat ȝe meten*] þat þou metest (*over erasure*) H ; ȝe metyn here U. *Amis*] a-riȝt (*over erasure*) H.
152. *ȝe wenden*] þat ȝe gon U.
153. *For —ȝe*] For þi TH₂ ; For þy D. *of*] of ȝoure TUH₂D.
154. *as chast*] U *omits.*
155. *liuen trewely*] loue lelly T ; loue lely UH₂D. *eke loue*] lene (*or* leue) TU ; ȝeue to loue H₂ ; loue D.
156. *And*] Of TUH₂D. *sent*] haþ sent U. *Treweliche parten*] goodliche parteth UTH₂ ; godliche parte D.

CHASTITY USELESS WITHOUT CHARITY.

ȝe naue no more merit · In Masse ne In houres
þen Malkyn of hire Maydenhod · þat no Mon desyreþ.
¶ For Iames þe gentel · bond hit in his Book,
þat [Fey] wiþouten [fait] · Is febelore þen nouȝt, 160
And ded as a dore-nayl · but þe deede folewe.
Chastite wiþouten Charite · (wite þou forsoþe),
Is as lewed as a Laumpe · þat no liht is Inne.   163
¶ Moni Chapeleyns ben chast · but Charite is aweye ;
Beo no men hardore þen þei · whon heo beoþ avaunset ;
Vn-kuynde to heore kun · and to alle cristene ;
Chewen heore charite · and chiden after more !
Such [Chastite] wiþouten [Charite] · worþ claymed in
  helle !   168
¶ Curatours þat schulden kepe hem · clene of heore
  bodies,
þei beoþ cumbred in care · and cunnen not out-crepe ;
So harde heo beoþ wiþ Auarice · I-haspet to-gedere.
þat nis no treuþe of Trinite · but tricherie of helle, 172
And a leornyng for lewed men · þe latere forte dele.
¶ For þeos beþ wordes I-writen · In þe Ewangelye,

ye haue no merit in your prayers.
St James tells us that Faith without works is dead; so chastity without charity is but an unlighted lamp.
Many chaplains are chaste, but have not charity;
they eat up what they should give away, and ask for more.
Curators that should be chaste are encumbered with avarice.
This treachery teaches the laity to put off giving away.
See what is in the

157. *naue*] ne haue TUH₂; haue D. *Masse*] Matynes TUH₂. *houres*] masse TH₂; oures UD.
158. *desyreþ*] desired U.
159. *bond hit*] ioynide TH₂; Iuggid U; hath wryten D.
160. [*Fey*] feiþ THUH₂; fay D. [*fait* TH₁; *feet* D] werk U; warkis H. V *misreads*, þat Treuþe wiþouten Fey.
161. *ded*] as ded TH₂. *but þe*] but ȝif þe THUH₂D.
Obs. *After* folewe H *inserts the weak line*, þat is, to sokoure þe sorowful · & haue charite to alle.
162. *wite—forsoþe*] worth cheynide in helle TH₂; wurþ schryned in helle U; worth shewed in helle D. (*See* l. 168.)
163. *Is*] þat is U; Hit is DT.
164. *Moni*] Now many U.
165. *Beo no men*] Arn none TUH₂; þer beoþ noon H.
166, 167. *Transposed in* H.

166. *and to*] and ek to TUH₂D.
167. *Chewen*] þei chewen H; Chiwen U.
168. [*Chastite, &c.*] chastite withoute charite THUH₂D; V *absurdly transposes* chastite *and* charite; see l. 162. *claymed*] cheynid TH₂; schryned U; shewed D.
169. *Curatours*] ȝe curatours TUH₂D. *schulden—hem*] kepe ȝow TUH₂D; schulden ȝou kepe H. *of heore*] of ȝour TUH₂D. H *has*, in ȝoure soules.
170. *þei—care*] ȝe ben acumbrid wiþ couetise TUH₂D. *& cunnen*] ȝe mowe T; ȝe cunne UH₂; ȝe can D; þei con H.
171. *harde—wiþ*] faste haþ TH₂D; harde haþ U. *I-haspet*] haspide ȝow TUH₂D.
172. þat þe trewe tresoure of trouþe · is almost forȝete H.
173. *latere forte*] lattere to THUH₂; latter for to D.

Gospel (Luke vi. 38).

Date et dabitur vobis · for I dele ow alle.

[ȝoure grace & ȝoure good happe · ȝoure welþe for to wynne,   176

& þerwiþ knoweþ me kyndely · of þat I ȝou sende.]

Love comforts the sad.

[þat is þe lok of loue · þat letiþ out my grace

To counforte þe carful · Acumbrid wiþ synne.

Love is the readiest way to heaven;

Loue is þe leueste þinge · þat our lord askiþ,   180

And eke þe graiþ gate · þat goþ into heuene.

For-þi I seiȝe as I seide er · be siȝte of þise tixtes,

and Truth is the best of all treasures.

Whan alle tresouris arn triȝede · treuþe is þe beste.

Now haue I tolde þe what treuþe is · þat no tresour is betere,   184

I may no lengere lenge · now loke þe oure lord."]

175. After *vobis*, ȝeueþ to myne of ȝoure good*us* for I dele, &c. H. OBS. *The rest is not in* V.

176, 177. *These two lines are in* H *only*.

178—185. *from* T ; *with which* D *and* H₂ *very closely agree ; also found in* H ; *and (partly) in* U.

178. *letiþ—my*] lyth in ȝoure H.

179. U *omits. wiþ*] in H.

181. *graiþ gate*] redyest waye H ; greytheste gate U.

182. *For-þi*] þerfore U. *seide er*] er seyde H ; sayde here D.

184. *þat*] H *omits*.

185. *lenge*] lende H ; duellen U ; lengen D. *now*] but H ; D *om.* *þe*] þou loue H ; by D.

PASSUS II.

[Passus secundus de visione.]

Ȝit kneled I on my knees · and cried hire of grace,   [f. 395 b. col. 2.]
And seide, " Merci, Madame · for Maries loue of   Then I prayed her
heuene
þat Bar þe blisful Barn · þat bouȝt vs on þe Roode,
Teche me þe kuynde craft · forte knowe þe false."   4   to teach me how to know
" Loke on þe lufthond," quod heo · " and seo wher   Falsehood. She bade me turn and see him.
[he] stondeþ!
Boþe Fals and Fauuel · and al his hole Meyne ! "
I lokede on þe luft half · as þe ladi me tauhte ;   I looked, and, first of all, beheld a woman very richly clothed,
þenne was I war of a wommon · wonderliche cloþed, 8
Purfylet with pelure · þe ricchest vppon eorþe,
I-Corouned with a Coroune · þe kyng haþ no bettre ;   decked with a crown and costly rings.
Alle hir Fyue Fyngres · weore frettet with Rynges,
Of þe preciousest perre · þat prince wered euere ;   12

Title; *found in* TH₂UD; H *has* Tercius Passus *by mistake, as it also calls the next Passus by the same name.*
Obs. *The first* 23 *lines occur twice in* U; *readings from the fragment are distinguished by the italic letter* U.
1. *cried*] prayed H.
2. *Merci, Madame*] V *has* Madame Merci, *with marks for transposition.*
3. *blisful*] blisside TU ; blessyd D. *on þe Roode*] wiþ his blood H.
4. *Teche—kuynde*] kenne me be sum TU*U*H₂D; teche me by kynde H. *forte knowe*] to kenne TH₂ ; to knowe U*U*D.
5. *lufthond*] left *U*; left half TU. *quod heo*] TDU *omit* ; quod sche *U*. *seo*] lo TH₂. [*he* TUH₂D] þei H*U*; V *has* heo.
6. *his*] her H. *al—Meyne*] hise feris manye TU*U*H₂D.
8. *cloþed*] atired *U*; clothid U.
Obs. *After* cloþed H *inserts*, In reed scarlet heo rode · rybande wiþ gold (*see* l. 13).
9. *ricchest vppon*] pureste on U*U*D; purest in H₂.
Obs. *Here* H *inserts*, pyȝte ful of perrye · & of preciouse stoones (*see* l. 12).
11. U *omits this line; so also does U.*
12. *preciousest*] pureste TU*U*H₂D. H *reads*,
Of reed gold so ryche · redilyche I-dyȝte
Wiþ preciouse stoones so stoute · stondynge þer-ynne.

	In Red Scarlet heo Rod · I-Rybaunt with gold ;
	þer nis no Qweene qweyntore · þat quik is alyue.
"Who is this?" I asked.	¶ "What is þis wom̃mon," quod I · "þus wonderliche A-tyret?"
"That is Meed (Bribery)," she said, "who has done me much evil.	¶ "Þat is Meede þe Mayden," quod heo · "þat haþ me marred ofte, 16
	A[n]d I-lakked my lore · to lordes aboute.
	In þe pope paleys heo is · as priue as my-seluen ;
Her father was Wrong.	And so schulde heo nouȝt · for wrong was hir syre ;
	[Out of] wrong heo wox · to wroþerhele monye. 20
	Ich ouhte ben herre þen heo · I com of a bettre.
To-morrow shall Meed be married to Falsehood, by help of Flattery and Guile.	¶ To-morwe worþ þe Mariage I-mad · Of Meede and of fals ;
	Fauuel with feir speche · haþ brouȝt hem to-gedere,
	And Gyle haþ bi-gon hire so · heo grauntep al his wille ; 24
	And al is liȝeres ledynge · þat heo leuen to-gedere.
To-morrow you may see the whole crew of them, but beware of them, lest thou fall of bliss.	¶ To-Morwe worth þe Mariage I-mad · soþ as I þe telle,
	þat þou miht [wyte] ȝif þou wolt · whuche þei ben alle
	[þat longith to þat lordschipe · þe lasse and þe more. 28
	Know hem þere ȝif þou canst · and kepe þe fro hem alle,
	Ȝif þou wilnest to wone · with treuthe in his blisse ;]
	[lerne his lawe þat is so lele · & siþþe teche it furþer.]

13. H inserts above ; see obs. on l. 8. heo rod] robid TUUD ; robe H₂. I-Rybaunt] & ribande TH₂D ; rybanyd UU.

14. nis] is HUU.   qweyntore] koynter H. alyue] on lyue HUUDH₂ ; o lyue T.

15. wonderliche] worþily TH₂D.

16. quod heo] TUUDH₂ omit.   me marred] noiȝede me ful TUH₂ ; anoyȝed me H ; noyed me wol U ; noyed me wel D.

19. heo nouȝt] it not be TD.

20. U omits this line.   [Out of TH UH₂D] V has In-to ; U reads, Out of wrong wente sche · wrotherhele manye.

21. herre] hiȝere T ; heyȝer H ; heyere UUD.

23. brouȝt] forgid TUUDH₂.

24, 25. U omits.

25. leuen] liȝen TH₂D ; lyue so H.

26. To-Morwe—I-mad] To-morne schal þei make þe mariage H.   soþ] TUH₂D omit ; D also om. I-mad.

27. þat—wolt] þere miȝte þou wyte ȝif þou wilt (wolt H) THUH₂D ; V has seo instead of wyte.

28, 29, 30. From U ; also in TH₂D ; V has only l. 30, running thus,
Bote ȝif þow wilne to wone · with treuþe in his Blisse, with which H closely agrees.

31. This occurs in H only.

PASS. II.]   TENTS ARE PITCHED FOR THE COMPANY.   19

I may no lengore lette · vr lord Ich þe bi-kenne;   32   I now commend thee to God."
And bi-come a good mon · for eny couetyse, ich rede."
[When heo was me fro · I loked & byhelde]   Afterwards, I beheld the bridal.
Alle þis Riche [Retenaunce] · þat Regneden with Fals
Weoren bede to þe Bruyt-ale · on Bo two þe
sydes.   36
Sir Simonye is of-sent · to asseale þe Chartres,   Sir Simony was sent for to seal the charters.
þat Fals oþur Fauuel · bi eny [fyn] heolden,
And Feffe Meede þer-with · In Mariage for euere.
¶ Bote þer nas halle ne hous · þat miht herborwe þe   But there was not house-room for
peple,   40   all.
þat vche feld nas ful · of Folk al a-boute.
¶ In middes on a Mountayne · at Midmorwe tyde   So a pavilion was pitched, and
Was piht vp a Pauilon · A Proud for þe nones;   10,000 tents, for knights, sellers,
And Ten þousend of Tentes · I-tilled be-sydes,   44   and buyers.
For knihtes of Cuntre · and Comers aboute,
¶ For Sisours, for Sumnors, · for Sullers, for Buggers,
For lewede, for lerede · for laborers of þropes,
[& for the flaterynge freeris · alle þe foure orders],   48
Alle to witnesse wel · What þe writ wolde,   All came to see the marriage.
In what manere þat Meede · In Mariage was [I-feffed],
To beo fastnet with fals · þe fyn was arered.
¶ Þenne Fauuel fet hire forþ · and to fals takeþ,   52   Then Flattery led

32. *lette*] lende H; dwelle D.   *vr*] TD *and* U *omit*. *bi-kenne*] by-take H.
33. *And*] Loke þou H.   *ich rede*] H *omits*.
34. *Occurs in* H *only*.
35. [*Retenaunce* THUH₂D] Retenauntes V. *þat—Fals*] þat with false reigneth U.
36. *Bruyt-ale*] bedale T; bridale UHH₂D.   *Bo two þe*] boþe two THUH₂D.
37. U *omits*. *is of-sent*] is assent T; is a-sent H₂; was aftur sent H; is A-sert D.   *asseale*] a-sele T: seele H; ensele H₂; sele D.
38. [*fyn*] THUH₂D; V *has* peyne.
40. *þat miht*] to THUH₂D.
41. *nas*] was D.   *ful*] filled H.

42. *on*] of HD; T *and* U *omit*.
43. *A proud*] prow U; T *and* U *omit* A; was proud D.
44. *I-tilled*] I-teldyde forþ H; teldit TH₂; tight þer U; teled D.
45. *For*] Of TUD. *and Comers*] of comeres TUH₂D.
46. *Buggers*] biggeres UH; beggeris TH₂D.
47. *lewede—lerede*] lerid for lewid THUH₂D. *þropes*] þrepis U; þorpes D.
48. *Occurs in* H *only*.
50. *manere*] manere and howe H.   *In Mariage*] H *omits*.   [*I-feffed* H] feffid TUH₂D. V *omits, evidently by mistake*.
51. *fastnet*] feffed U.
52. *takeþ*] hir toke H; toket D.

Meed to Falsehood,	In Forwarde þat Falsnesse · schal fynden hire for euere,
	To be Boxum and Boun · his Biddyng to folfulle,
promising that she will obey his will.	In Bedde and at Borde · Boxum and hende,
	And as sir Simonye wol sigge · [to suwen] his wille. 56
	Now Simonye and Siuyle · stondeþ forþ boþe,
Simony and Civil unfold the deed.	Vn-Foldyng þe Feffement · þat Falsnes made,
	[& þus bygonnen þe gomes · & gradden wel hyʒe]:
Carta. "Know all men that I, Flattery, pledge Falsehood to Meed, and grant them the earldom of Envy,	"Hit witen and witnessen · þat woneþ vppon eorþe, 60 þat I, Fauuel, Feffe Fals · to þat Mayden Meede, To be present in pruyde · for Pore or for riche, Wiþ þe Erldam of Envye · euer forto laste,
	Wiþ alle þe lordschupe · of lengþe and of brede, 64
the kingdom of Avarice, and the Isle of Usury,	Wiþ þe kingdom of Couetise · I Croune hem to-gedere; Wiþ þe Yle of vsure · And Auarice þe False,
	Glotonye and grete oþus · Ich ʒiue hem I-feere,
	Wiþ alle delytes and lustes · þe deuel for to serue, 68
	In al þe seruyse of Slouþe · I sese hem to-gedere :
to have and to hold all their lives,	¶ To habben and to holden · and al heore heyres aftur, Wiþ þe purtinaunce of purgatorie · in-to þe pyne of helle :
they yielding their souls to	ʒeldynge for þis þing · at þe ʒeres ende, 72
	Heore soules to sathanas · to senden in-to pyne ;

53. *Falsnesse*] falshed TH₂D ; false U.
54. *To—Boun*] And he (she D) be bounde at his bode TH₂D ; & be buxum at his bode U.
56. *And—sigge*] & at syre symonyes wille UD. *to suwen*] HTH₂ ; to suyen U ; to sewen D ; V *has* schewen.
57. *stondeþ*] stoden H. *forþ boþe*] forþ in-fere H ; vp boþe U.
58. *Vn-Foldyng*] & vn-foldeden H ; And vnfolde TH₂D ; And vnfoldith U. *made*] had made H ; haþ ymakid TUH₂ ; haþ maked D.
59. *From* H ; *also in* TUH₂D.
60. *In the margin of* H *is here written* Carta ; *in the margin of* D, Fauor.
61. *Feffe—Meede*] feffe falsnesse to mede TH D ; haue [feffed ?] falsnesse to mede U.

64. *lordschup—brede*] lordsshipe of leccherie · in lengþe and in brede TH₂ ; worschipe of lecherye in, &c. UD ; H *resembles* T, *but it is written in a later hand.*
65. *hem*] ʒow U.
66. *þe Yle*] al þe Ile TD ; al þe isle H₂ ; alle þe vices U. *False*] faste TU.
67. *hem I-feere*] hem togidere TH₂D ; ʒow togidres U.
68. *delytes—lustes*] delites of lust TH₂D ; þe delytes of deedly synne H ; þe delices of lust U.
69. *seruyse*] seignourie UD. *sese*] ceese H ; set TD.
71. *wiþ*] wiþ al H. *in-to*] & H.
72. *þing*] D omits. *þe*] oon H ; o T ; one UH₂.
73. *senden into*] synken in TH₂D : synke into U.

þer to Wonen with Wrong · whil god is in heuene."   *Satan at a year's end.*
¶ In witnesse of whuche þing · wrong was þe furste,   *The witnesses were Wrong,*
Pers þe pardoner · Paulynes [doctor],   76   *Piers the Pardoner,*
Bette þe Budul · of Bokynghames schire,   *Pauline's doctor, Bette the beadle,*
Rondulf þe Reue · of Rotelondes sokene,   *and many others.*
[Taberes & tomblers · & tapesters fele],
Monde þe Mulnere · and moni mo oþure   80
In þe Date of þe deuel · þe Deede was a-selet,   *The deed was then sealed and signed.*
Be siht of sir Symoni · and Notaries signes.

þEn teonede him Teologye · whon he þis tale herde,   *But Theology was wroth, and said to Civil, "Wo betide thee!"*
    And seide to Siuyle · "serwe on þi lokkes,   84
Such Weddyng to worche · to [wrapþe] with truþe ;
And ar þis weddyng beo wrouȝt · wo þe beo-tyde !
For Meede is a Iuweler · A Mayden of goode,   *[f. 396 a. col. 1.] Meed is rich, and should be wedded where Truth wills.*
God graunte vs to ȝiue hire · þer treuþe wol a-signe.   88
And þou hast ȝiuen hire [to] a Gilour · God ȝiue þe serwe !
þe Tixt telleþ not so · Treuþe wot þe soþe ;   *Remember the text (Luke x. 7).*
    Dignus est operarius mercede sua ;
Worþi is þe Werkmon · his hure to haue ;
And þou hast feffet hire with fals · fy on þi lawe !   92

For lechours and lyȝers · lihtliche þou leeuest,   *Thou believest lechers and liars; but ye shall*
    Simonie and þi-self · Schenden holichirche ;

74. U *omits.*
76. *Pers*] And piers TH H₁. *Paulynes doctor*] poulynes doctor TH₂ ; paulynes dottour (*or* doctour) U ; paulynes doctoure D. V *and* H *have* douhter, douȝter ; *see* l. 152.
78. *of—sokene*] oute of Rotelonde H.
79. *occurs in* H *and* H₂ *only ;* H₂ *reads*, Taylours, tapsters · and tauerners many.
80. *Mulnere*] myllere TH₂ ; mylnere UH ; mellere D. *and—oþure*] of malwiche strete U.
81. *þe—aselet*] þis dede I assele U ; þis dede is seled D.
82. *and—signes*] and signes of notories TUH₂ ; in seals of notoryes D.
83. *teonede*] tenide TH₂ ; tenyd U ; tened D, *which om.* him.
84. *serwe*] now sorewe THH₂D.

lokkes] lockes H ; bokes TUH₂D.
85. [*wrapþe* THUH₂D] teone V.
87. *a Iuweler*] molere T ; muliere U ; a medeler H ; a medlere H₂ ; mulyer D. *A—goode*] of frendis engendrit TUH₂D.
88. *graunte — asigne*] grauntide (graunt H₂, graunteþ UD) to gyue · mede to treuþe TUH₂D. *asigne*] assente H.
89. *And*] For H ; D *omits.* [*to* THUD] V *omits. God*] oure lord H ; now god TUH₂.
90. *telleþ*] telleþ þee H.
91. *hure*] huyre H ; mede TUH₂D.
92. *feffet*] festnyd U ; fastnid TH₂D. *lawe*] lawes TU.
93. *The readings are,* for lesyngis & lecheryes · suche warkes þou louest H ;

abide it at the year's end!	[ʒe schule abygge it boþe · by god þat me made,
	at oo ʒeris ende · whan ʒe reken schul] ; 96
	He and þeose [Notaries] · anuyʒen þe peple.
	For wel ʒe witen, wernardes ! · but ʒif or wit fayle,
Ye well know Falsehood is a traitor, and Beelzebub's bastard son; But Meed (Reward) might kiss the king.	þat fals is a faytur · a faylere of werkes,
	And a Bastard I-boren · of Belsabubbes kunne. 100
	And Meede is a Iuweler · a Mayden ful gent ;
	Heo mihte Cusse þe kyng · for Cosyn ʒif heo schulde.
	Worcheþ bi wisdam · and bi Wit aftur ;
Then take her to London, and see if the law will permit this.	Ledeþ hire to londone · þer lawe is I-hondlet, 104
	ʒif eny leute wol loken · þat þei liggen to-gedere,
	And ʒif þe Iustise wol Iugge hire · to be Ioynet with Fals.
	ʒit be-war of þe weddyng · for witti is treuþe;
	For Concience is of his [counseil] · and knoweþ ou vchone ; 108
If Couscience find this out, it will go hard with you at the last."	And ʒif he fynde such defaute · þat ʒe with Fals holden,
	Hit schal bi-sitten oure soules · sore atte laste."
	[herto assentid syuyle · but symonye ne wolde
	tyle he had syluer · for his sawes & his selynge. 112

For al be (by U) lesinges þou lyuest · & lecherous werkis TUD;
For al ben lesynges þou leuest · and lecherus workes H₂.
95, 96. *From* H; l. 95 *occurs in* TUH₂D *after* l. 97.
95. *it*] TDUH₂ omit.
97. *He and þeose*] for ʒe and þese H; ʒe and þe TH₂D; ʒe and ʒe (*by mistake for* þe) U. [*Notaries*] *See* THUH₂D; V *has the spelling* Nataries, *which looks wrong; for see* l. 115.
98. *or*] ʒoure TH₂; ʒour UD.
99. *a faylere*] feyntles TH₂D; and feythles UH.
100. *Belsabubbes*] belsaboukis T.
101. *a Iuweler*] mulere T; moliere U; a medelar H; mulyer D; mened H₂. *a—ʒent*] of maides engendrit T; amonge men of goode H ; a maiden of gode UH₂D.
102. *heo schulde*] he wolde TH₂D ; sche wolde U.

103. *Worcheþ*] þerfore worcheþ H. *wisdam*] wytte H. *wit aftur*] wysedam boþe H.
105. *leute wol loken*] leaute wile loke TH₂; lewte wil loke U. *þat*] TU *om.* *liggen*] lybbe H; D *reads*, yf ony liaunce wil loke · hem legge to-gidere.
106. *ʒif—hire*] iustise iuggen here U; yf þe Iustice Iugge here DH₂.
108. *of his*] of his counseil TUH₂D; his counseloure H. V *reads*, For Concience is on of his · and, &c.
109. *such—with*] ʒow in defaute · & wiþ þe TUH₂D.
110. *bisitten*] sitt H ; be set on U; be-set DT. *sore atte*] wel (ful H) sore at þe THUD. H₂ *omits the line*.
111—127. *From* H. *Also in* TUD *and* H₂, *except line* 118, *which they omit*.
112. *his—selynge*] his selis & signes TDH₂; selis & signes U.

þen fet fauel forth · floreynes I-nowe,
& bad gyle go to · & ȝyue gold aboute,
& namely to þis notaries · þat hem non lacked ;
& feffe false witnesse · with florens I-nowe, 116
For he may mede a-maysteren · & make hir at his wylle ;
For where falsenes is oft fownden · þere feiþ fayleþ
þoo þe gold was ȝouen · grete were þe thonkes
to false & to fauel · for her feyre ȝyftus. 120
many comen, from care · to counforte þe false,
& sworen on þe hoolydom · þat "cesse schul we neuere
or mede be þi weddud wyf · þorouȝ witte of vs alle.
for we han mede a-maysterd · wiþ oure myri wordis 124
þat heo grаunteþ to goo · wiþ a good wille,
to london to loke · if þe lawe wole
Iugge ȝou Ioyntely · to be Ioyned for euer"].

¶ þenne was Fals fayn · and Fauuel also bliþe, 128
And lette sompne alle men · In Cuntre a-boute,
To Arayen hem redi · Boþe Burgeys and Schirreues,
To weende with hem to westmunster · to Witnesse þe deede.

¶ þenne careden heo for Caples · to carien hem þider ; 132
Bote Fauuel fette forþ · Foles of þe beste,

Then Flattery fetched out florins, and bade Guile give it to the notaries.

Great were the thanks for these bribes.

Meed consents to go to London.

Then were Falsehood and Flattery glad, and bade all be ready to go to Westminster.

Then they all wanted horses.

113. *fett*] fecchide U.
114. *go to &*] go TUH₂D.
115. *lacked*] failede U ; ne failiþ T ; ne fayle H₂ ; fayle D.
117. *hir at his*] at my T ; here at our U ; at his D.
118. *In* H *only.*
119. *were þe thonkes*] was þe þonking TUH₂D.
121. *many—counforte*] And comen to counforte fro care TUH₂D.
122. *sworen—hoolydom*] seide certis TUH₂D.
123. *or*] Til TUH₂D.
124. *myri wordis*] mery speche TH₂D ; faire speche U.
126. *þe lawe*] þat lawe TH₂D ; þat þe lawe U.

127. *Iugge*] Ioyne U. *to—euer*] in ioye for euere TH₂D ; in lawe for euere U.
129. *lette*] bad H. *men*] þe segges TUH₂ ; þe pepul H. *cuntre*] schyres HTUH₂. D reads, And let Symonye seche · al about in shires.
130. The other readings are, þat alle þei myȝten be bowne · beggers & oþer H;
And alle [to H₂] be boun · beggeris & oþere TUH₂D.
132. *careden heo*] cariede hy T ; caareden þei H ; cared þei UD. *caples*] cables D.
133. *Bote—fette*] þanne fette fauel TUH₂D

Meed was set on a sheriff's back, and Falsehood on an assizer's;

And sette Meede on a Schirreues Bak · I-schood al newe,
[& fals on a sysoures backe · þat softly trotted ;
(for falsnes aȝeyn þe feiþ · sisoures he defouleþ,   136
þoruȝ comburance of couetyse · clymben aȝeyn truþe,
þat þe feiþ is defouled · & falsly defamed,
& falsnes is a lord I-woxe · & lyueþ as hym lykeþ) :

Flattery rides upon Fair-speech;

Fauel on a feyre speche · ful feyntly a-tyred ;   140
(For feire speche þat is feiþles · is falsnes broþer ;
& þus sysoures ben sompned · þe false to serue,
& feire-speche fauel · þat moche folke desceyueth)].

¶ þenne Notaries none Hors hedden · anuyed þei
    weore,   144

but Simony and Civil had to go on foot.

þat Symonie and Siuile · schulden go on foote.
¶ þenne seide Siuile · and swor bi þe Roode,

Summoners are to be saddled,

þat Sompnors schulde ben sadelet · and seruen hem
    vchone;
" And lette apparayle prouisours · on Palfreis wyse, 148
[Sire symonye hym-selfe · shal sitte on here bakkis],

and provisors and deans to be used as horses.

And alle Denes and Sodenes · as Destreres dihten,
For þei schullen beren Bisschops · and bringen hem to
    reste.

"Pauline's people shall serue myself," said Civil.

¶ Paulines peple · for playntes in Constorie   152
Schal seruen my-self · þat Siuile hette ;

---

134. *Schirreues bak*] shirreue TUH₂D.
135—143. *These lines are quoted from* H; *and those in parentheses occur in* H *only.* V *has only the one line,*
And Fauuel on a Feir speche · Feyntliche atyret.
T *and* D *have only the two lines,*
And fals sat on a sisour · þat softeliche trottide,
And fauel vpon fair speche · fetisliche atirid.
U *has the same, omitting* sat ; H₂ *has also two similar lines.*
144. *Notaries — hedden*] hadde notories none TUD ; Notaries had noo horses H ; þer hadde notories non hors H₂.

145. *Symonie—siuile*] siuile and symonie H. *go on foote*] on here fet gange TUD ; on fote gange H₂.
146. *seide*] swor TH₂D. *swor*] seide TH₂D.
OBS. H² *has been closely collated only thus far* ; *see the Preface.*
147. *seruen*] beren U.
148. *prouisours*]. þise prouisours THD ; þe prouisours U. *on*] in THD.
149. *From* T; *also in* HUD *and* H₂. *here backes*] hym oone H.
150. *Denes—Sodenes*] þe denis & southdenis TH₂ ; þe denes and sudenes U ; þise officyales & deenys H ; the denys sodenys D. *Destreres*] palfreyes H (*in later hand*). *dihten*] hem diȝte THUH₂D.
152. *Constorie*] þe constrye H.

Let Cart-sadele vr Commissarie · vr Cart he schal drawe, *Yoke our commissary.*
And fetten vr vitayles · of þe Fornicatours ;
And make liȝere a long cart · to leden alle þis oþure 156 *and make of Liar a long cart."*
Fabulers and Faytours · þat on Fote rennen."

NOw Fals and Fauuel · fareþ forþ to-gedere, *Thus all fare forth together.*
 And Meede in þe Middel · and al þe Meyne aftur.
I haue no [tome] to telle · þe Tayl þat hem folweþ, 160
Of so mony Maner Men · þat on Molde liuen.
¶ Bote gyle was for-goere · and [gyede] hem alle. *Guile led the way; but soon*
Soþnesse sauh hem wel · and seide bote luyte, *Soothness spurred on, and went and*
Bote prikede on his palfrey · and passede hem alle, 164 *told conscience.*
And com to þe kynges Court · and Concience tolde,
And Concience to þe kyng · Carpede hit aftur.

"NOw be crist," quod þe kyng · "ȝif I mihte Chacche
 Fals oþur Fauwel · or eny of his Feeres, 168 *"If I could but catch Falsehood,*
I wolde be wreken on þis wrecches · þat worchen so ille, *or Flattery," said the king,*
And don hem hongen bi þe hals · and al þat hem *"I would hang them both.*
 Meyntenen ;
Schal neuer [mon] vppon Molde · Meyntene þe leste,
But riht as þe lawe lokeþ · let fallen of hem alle. 172
¶ And Comaunde þe Cunstable · þat Com at þe furste, *Command the constable to*
To a-Tache þe Traytours · for eny Tresour, *attach them,*

154. *Cart-sadele*] sadele U; cartesadil T. *commissarie*] comysaries H. *vr—drawe*] oure long carte þei schul drawe H.
155. *of þe*] at H ; fro T; of UD.
156. *make*] makiþ of TUD.
157. *Fabulers*] flaterers H ; As folis TUD. *rennen*] iotten T.
158. *Now*] TUD omit. *fareþ*] goþ U.
159. *middel*] myddes U ; myddis TD.
160. [*tome* T] tyme for H ; tunge UD ; V *has* while.
161. *Of—men*] Of many maner of men TD ; of alle manere of men U. *Molde*] þis molde TUD.
162. [*gyede* TUD] bygyed H (*with by partly erased*). V *has* gilede, *a mistake evidently due to the word* gyle *preceding.*

163. *wel*] D omits. *luyte*] a lytel HU; litel TD.
164. *prikede*] prikede forþ TU.
167. *ȝif*] And THD. *mihte*] mowe U.
168. *his*] her H.
169. *on þis*] on þoo H ; of þise T; on þo UD. *wrecches*] U *omits*. *worchen*] wroughten U.
170. H *omits this line*. *al*] þey D.
171. *neuer—vppon*] neuer man of þis T; no man on H; neuer [man] on þis UD ; *where* man *is* (*in* U) *omitted ; for* mon V *has* non. *meyntene þe leste*] meynprise þe lest H ; meynprise þe beste TUD.
172. *lokeþ*] wola loke H ; wele D. *of*] on TUD.
173. *Comaunde*] comaunded HTUD. *þe*] a THUD. *þat com*] he com U.
174. *a-Tache*] take U. *þe Tray-*

FALSEHOOD FLEES TO THE FRIARS. [PASS. II.

fetter Falsehood, and cut off Guile's head.

Ich hote, ȝe Fetere Fals faste · for eny kunnes ȝiftus,
And gurdeþ of gyles hed · let him go no forþer ; 176
And bringeþ Meede to me · Maugre hem alle.

Simony and Civil I warn; and let not Liar escape.

¶ Symonye and Siuile · I seende hem to warne,
þat holichirche for hem · worþ harmet for euere.
And ȝif ȝe chacche lyȝere · let him not a-skape, 180
To ben set on þe pillori · for eny preyere ;
[I bydde þee awayte hem wele · let non of hem ascape]."

Dread was at the door, and heard the doom, and bade Falsehood flee.

Dreede at þe dore stood · and þe [dume] herde,
And wihtliche wente · to Warne þe False, 184
And bad him faste to fle · and his feeres eke.

Then fled Falsehood and Guile;

Þenne Fals for fere · fleih to þe Freeres,
And gyle doþ him to go · a-gast for to dyȝe ;

but tradesmen prayed Guile to keep their shops for them.

Bote Marchaundes Metten with him · and maaden him
 to abyden, 188
Bi-souȝten him in heore schoppes · to sullen heore ware,
Apparayleden him as a prentis · þe Peple for to serue.

Liar leapt away through by-lanes, being nowhere welcome.

Liȝtliche Lyȝere · leop a-wey þennes,
Lurkede þorw lones · to-logged of Monye ; 192
He nas nouȝwher wel-come · for his mony tales,
Bote ouur al I-hunted · and hote to trusse.

[f. 396 a. col. 2.] Pardoners hedden pite · and putten him to house,

---

tours] þis tiraunt T; þese tirauntes U; þese tyrans D. *Tresour*] tresour, I hote TUD.

175. *Ich hote ȝe*] THUD omit. *eny kunnes*] ony kynne U; any skynes T; eny kynnes D; ony kynnes H.

176. *gurdeþ*] gederith T; gadereth U; gurde D.

177. *to me*] forth U.

OBS. *In the margin of D is here written*, Falsitas Deceptura Merces Simonia Mendax.

178. *seende*] sente TD. *warne*] seye H.

180. *chacche*] take H; lacche TUD.

181. *To ben set*] Er he be put TD; Sette him H ; Til he be set U. *preyere*] preyour, I hote TD ; tresour, y hote U.

182. *Occurs in* H *only*.

183. *stood*] stant U. [*dume*] V has dune, *clearly by mistake for* dume; þis dome H ; þat doom TD; þe dome U.

184. *wente*] wente he þo H

185. *faste to fle*] fleo fast H; fle for fere UTD. *eke*] alle TUD.

186. *fals*] falsnesse TUD.

187. *doþ*] dide H. *to go*] awey U. *a-gast for*] and gast D.

189. *Bi-souȝten*] & busscheden H; besshette TD; By-schytten U. *sullen*] shewen TD.

192. *Lurkede*] lurkynge TUD; H *om. lones*] hyrnes & lanus H; lanes TUD. *to-logged*] to-luggid THUD.

194. *Bote*] TUD *omit. ouur al I-hunted*] honsched as an hounde H. *hote to*] y-hote T; yhote go U.

195. *pite*] pytee of him H. *putten*] pulden TD ; pullid UH.

Wosschen him and wrongen him · *and* wounde*n* him in cloutes, 196
And senden hi*m* on sonendayes · w*ith* seales to churches,
And ȝaf pardun for pons · poundmele a-boute.

¶ þis leornden þis leches · and lettres hi*m* senden
For to [wone] with [hem] · watres to loke. 200
Spicers speeken w*ith* him · to a-spien heore ware,
For he ke*n*nede hi*m* in heore craft · *and* kneuȝ mony gummes.

¶ Mu*n*strals and Messagers · metten w*ith* him ones,
And wit*h*-heo[l]de hi*m* half a ȝer · and elleuene wykes.

¶ Freres w*ith* feir speches · fetten him þennes ; 205
For knowynge of Comers · kepten him as a Frere ;
Bote he haþ leue to lepen out · as ofte as him lykeþ, 207
And is wel-come whon he wole · *and* woneþ w*ith* hem ofte.

And alle fledden for fere · and flowen in-to huirnes ;
Saue Meede þe Mayden · no mon dorste abyde ;
But trewely to telle · heo tremblede for fere,
And eke wepte and wrong hire hondes · who*n* heo was a-tachet. 212

But pardoners took him in, washed him, clothed him, and sent him to church with pardons.

Then leeches begged him to dwell with them;

and spicers asked him to be shopkeeper.

Minstrels entertained him half a year;

but Friars fetched him thence, and clothed him as a Friar.

Thus all fled into corners for fear, and only Meed durst stay; and even she wept when taken prisoner.

196. *Wosschen*] wysshen TD; waschid · U. *wrongen*] wypide TUD. *wounden*] leyden H. *cloutes*] cloþis TUD.
197. *senden*] senten T; sent U. *churches*] þe churche H; chirche TUD.
198. *pons*] pans H; panis T; pens UD.
199. *þis—leches*] þanne louride lechis TUD; þerof herden leches H. *him senden*] besente T; he sente U; ben sent D.
200. [*wone* THUD] ben V. *For— wone*] þat he schuld wone H. [*hem* THD] hym U. V *has* him, *but the* i *is over an erasure.*
201. *In* H *this line follows* l. 208; *and the lines answering to* ll. 201, 202 *run differently, viz. as follows :—*
Spicers aspieden him · & speken wiþ him feyre,
& preyeden him pr*i*uely · to putte forþ her ware,
& he asured hem forsoþe · to serue hem for euer.
202. *kennede—craft*] knewe her craft H; coude on here craft TUD. *kneuȝ—gummes*] couþe many Iapes H ; knowith many gommes D.
203. *Munstrals, &c.*] Messangers and mynstrels, &c. H.
204. *with-heo*(l)*de*] wiþ-helden H ; of-heeld U; withheld T; helden D. *half a ȝer*] an half ȝer H ; half ȝer TU. *wykes*] dayes TUD.
205. *Freres, &c.*] wiþ faire speche freres, &c. U
206. *kepten*] copide TUD; copeden H.
207. *lykeþ*] luste H.
208. *wole*] cometh HU.
209. *And—fere*] Alle oþur fledde for ferd H. *huirnes*] hernis T; hyrnes HU; hernes D.
210. *no mon*] no mo TUD; none H.
211. *fere*] drede HU.
212. *wepte*] wep T; wepe HD; weep U. *hire hondes*] TUD *omit*.

PASSUS III.

[Passus Tercius de Visione.]

<small>Now is Meed, all alone, brought to the king.</small>

NOw is Meede þe Mayden I-nomen · and no mo of hem alle,
Wiþ Beodeles *and* Baylyfs · I-brouht to þe kyng.
þe kyng clepet a Cler[ke] · (I knowe not his nome),
To take Meede þe Mayden · *and* Maken hire at ese.   4

<small>"I shall ask her," said the king, "whom she wishes to wed; and perhaps I may forgive her."</small>

" Ichulle assayen hire my-self · *and* soþliche aposen
What Mon in þis world · þat hire weore leouest.
And ȝif heo worche be my wit · and my wil folewe,
I schal for-ȝiue hire þe gult · so me god helpe ! "   8

<small>So a clerk brought her to the chamber.</small>

¶ Corteisliche þe Clerk þo · as þe kyng hihte,
Tok þe Mayden bi þe Middel · *and* brouhte hire to chaumbre.
¶ þer was Murþe and Munstralsye · Meede wi*th* to plese;
Heo þat woneþ at westmu*n*stre · worschipeþ hire alle.   12

<small>Gladly the Justice went to see her, and said, "Mourn</small>

Gentiliche with Ioye · þe Iustise soone
Busked him in-to þe Bour · þer þe Buyrde was Inne,

Passus, &c. ; *found in* THUD.
1. *I-nomen and no mo*] I-nomen H; and no mo TD; name U.
2. *wiþ*] And with U.   *Baylyfs*] with bayles H; baillys U.   *I-brouht*] & brouȝt H.
3. *clepet*] calliþ TD; called HU. *cler(ke)*] clerke THUD.   *knowe*] con H; can TUD.
4. *To take*] & bade him take H.
5. *Ichulle*] I wolde U; I wile TD; I wole H. *After* my-self H *inserts* seyd þe kyng.   *soþliche*] softly hir H.
6. *in þis world*] of þis moolde U.
7. *ȝif*] H *omits.*   *my wit*] wyt TD.

8. *I schal*] I wile TD; I wole HU.
þe *gult*] þis gulte H; þis mysgilt D.
9. *þo*] þanne TU; þen H; þan D.
as þe king hihte] as his kynde wolde H.
10. *þe mayden*] mede TUD.
11. *with*] TUD *omit.*
12. *Heo*] þei H; TUD *omit.*   *alle*] ychoone H.
13. *Iustise*] Iustices THD.   *soone*] wel soone H; to sowpen U.
14. *him*] hem THD.   *in-to*] to TUD. *Bour*] chaumbur H.   *buyrde was Inne*] burde dwelliþ TUD.

THE JUSTICE COMFORTS HER.

Cumfortede hire kuyndely · and made hire good chere,   *not, Meed, we will get thee clear off.*
And seide, "Mourne þou not, Meede, · ne make þou no
  serwe,   16
For we wolen wysen þe kyng · and þi wey schapen,
For alle Concience Craft · and Casten, as I trouwe,
[þat þou schalt haue boþe myȝt & maystrye · & make
  what þe likeþ
wiþ þe kynge & þe comyns · & þe courte boþe]."   20
¶ Mildeliche þenne Meede · Merciede hem alle   *Then Meed thanked them all,*
Of heore grete goodnesse · and ȝaf hem vchone   *aud gave them gold cups and*
Coupes of clene Gold · and peces of seluer,   *ruby rings.*
Rynges with Rubyes · and Richesses I-nouwe,   24
[þe leste man of here mayne · a mutoun of gold].
¶ Þenne [lauȝten] þei leue · þis lordynges, at Meede.
Wiþ þat þer come Clerkes · to Cumforte þe same :   *Then came clerks, and said, "Be*
"We biddeþ þe be bliþe · for we beoþ þin owne,   28   *blithe, Meed, we will work thy*
Forte worche þi wil · while vr lyf dureþ."   *will."*
¶ Hendeliche þenne heo · be-hihte hem þe same,   *She promised to love them, and*
To louen hem lelly · and lordes to maken,   *make them lords.*
And in Constorie at Court · to tellen heore names.   32
"Schal no lewednesse hem lette · þe lewedeste þat I loue   *"Naught shall prevent one*
þat he ne worþ avaunset ; · for Icham I-knowe   *whom I love*

---

15. *good cheere*] at eese H. *and—chere*] be clergie leue TD. U *reads,* Curteisly confortide mede · by clergies leue.
16. *Mourne þou*] ne mowrne þou H; mourne TUD.
17. *schapen*] make TUD.
18. *The readings are,*
For al consiences cast · a cruft as I trowe T.
For al concience caste · a crafte can we schewe H.
For al consciences cast · or craft as y trowe U.
For Al concience cast · a craft as I trowe D.
19, 20. *In H only.*
21. *Mildeliche*] Mekely H. *þenne Meede*] mede þanne TD; mede U.
22. *grete*] U *omits.*

24. *I-nouwe*] manye THUD.
25. *From* T; *occurs also in* HUD.
26. [*lauȝten* HD] lauȝte TU; tok V. *leue*] her leue H. *lordynges*] lordis TUD.
27. *þer*] THUD *omit.* *Cumforte*] conforten hire TUD.
28. *We biddeþ þe*] And bidden hire TD; & bade here U.
29. *vr*] þi TD. *dureþ*] lastiþ THD.
31. *hem*] ȝow U. *lelly*] truly H. *to maken*] hem make TH; ȝow make UD.
32. *at*] at þe U. H *reads,* In courte & in constrye, &c. *to tellen heore*] callen here T; calle ȝour U; telleþ D.
33. *Schal*] þer schal HU. *lewedeste*] lede TU; ladde D.
34. *he*] þei H. *worþ*] worþ ferst TUD. *I-knowe*] beknowe TUD.

from being advanced." Then came a confessor, and said,	þer Cunnynge Clerkes · schul Couche be-hynde." þEnne com þer a Confessour · I-Copet as a Frere ; 36 To Meede þe Mayden · ful Mekeliche he loutede, And seide ful softely · in schrift as hit weore,
"Though learned and lay had all lain by thee, I would assoil thee for a load of wheat."	" þauh leredo and lewede · hedden leyen bi þe alle, And þauȝ Fals hedde folewed þe · þis Fiftene winter, 40 I schal asoyle þe my-self · for a summe of whete, And eke be þi Baude · and Bere wel þin ernde Among Clerkes and knihtes · Concience to falle." 43

Then Meed knelt to him, and shrove her, and gave him a noble.	þEnne Meede For hire misdede · to þat Mon knelede,
	    And schrof hire of hir sunnes · schomeliche, I
	        trouwe.
	Heo tolde him a tale · and tok him a noble,
	For to ben hire beode-mon · and hire Baude after. 47

Then he assoiled her, and said that If she would glaze a window, she should be saved.	¶ þene he asoylede hire soone · and [siþ] to hire seide, " We han a wyndow in worching · wol stonden vs ful heiȝe : Woldustow Glase þe Gable · *and graue þerinne þi nome*, Siker schulde þi soule ben · for to dwellen in heuene."
She said that, were that only sure, she would glaze all she could.	¶ " Wust I þat," quod þe wommon · " þer nis nouþur Wyndou ne Auter, 52 þat I ne schulde maken oþur mende · and my nome write, þat vche mon schulde seye · Ich were suster of house."

35. *þer*] þere as H. *Couche*] clokke TUD.
37. *ful*] THUD *omit*.
38. *ful*] wol U ; wil D.
39. *alle*] ichone T ; boþe H ; echone D.
40. *Fals*] falsnesse UH ; falshed TD. *Fiftene*] four score U.
41. *summe of*] sem of T ; seem U ; seme of D.
42. *Baude*] baudekyn TU ; bawd-strot H. *ernde*] arnede T ; erande HD ; arende U.
43. *falle*] felle THUD.
44. *knelede*] lowtide U.
45. *sunnes*] shrewidnesse THD. *schomeliche*] shameles THUD.
46. *Heo*] TUD *omit*. *tale*] tokne U.
47. *beodeman—after*] bawde · and bere wel hir erand H.
48. V *omits* siþ ; *but* H *has* siþ, TU siþen, D sethen.
49. *in*] of T. *ful*] wel T ; wol U.
50. *Woldustow*] woldist þou THUD. *þerinne*] þere TUD.
51. *for—heuene*] heuen to haue TUD ; heuen for to haue H.
52. *nouþur*] THUD *omit*.
53. *þat—mende*] þat I schulde mende or make H ; þat I ne schulde graue and mende U. D *omits* ne.
54. *þat—seye*] þat iche segge shal se T ; þat men schulden sey H ; þat eche segge schulde wite U ; That eche man shal se D. *Ich were*] þat I were H ; þat I am D ; I am T. *of*] of ȝour TUD ; of þe H.

PASS. III.] ALMS-DEEDS SHOULD BE DONE IN SECRET. 31

¶ Bote god to alle good folk · such grauynge defendet, *But remember ye the text, Matt vi. 3.*
And seiþ, *Nesciat sinistra quid faciat dextera.*
Lete not þi luft hond · late ne raþe, 56
Beo war what þi riht hond · worcheþ or deleþ ;
Bote parte hit so priueli · þat pruide beo not seʒen *Give alms without pride, for God knoweth the heart.*
Nouþer in siht, ne in soule · for god him-self knoweþ
Ho is Corteis, or kuynde · Couetous, or elles. 60
¶ For-þi I lere ʒou, lordynges · such writynge ʒe leue, *Cease, lords, to write on windows, and to shout when ye give alms.*
To writen in Wyndouwes · of ʒoure wel dedes,
Or to greden aftur Godus folk · whon ʒe ʒiuen or doles ;
Parauenture ʒe han · oure hure þerfore here. 64 [f. 396 b. col. 1.]
¶ For vr saueour hit seiþ · and him-seluen precheþ, *For what saith Christ? see Matt. vi. 2.*
Amen dico vobis, receperunt mercedem suam ;
[Here forsoþe þei fongen · her mede forþ-wiþ].
¶ Meires and Maistres · and ʒe þat beoþ mene *Hear this, mayors and masters, and punish butchers and bakers on the pillory.*
Bitwene þe kyng and þe Comuns · to kepe þe lawes, 68
As to punisschen on pillories · or on pynnyng stoles
Brewesters, Bakers · Bochers and Cookes ;
For þeose be Men vppon Molde · þat most harm worchen, *For they defraud the poor that buy by retail.*
To þe pore people · þat [percel-mel] buggen. 72

55. *to*] and UD; T *omits. defendet*] defendiþ THUD. *sinistra*] sinister TD. *dextera*] dexter TD.
56. *hond*] halfe U.
57. *Beo war*] wite U. *hond*] half U. *or*] ne U.
58. *Bote—priueli*] And (Ac D) so preuyliche parte it TUD ; so priuely be it parted H.
61. *lere*] rede HU. *lordynges*] lordis TUD. *such—leue*] leuiþ such wrytyng TD ; such lernyngus to leue H ; to leue swiche writynge U.
63. *folk*] men TUD. *or*] THUD *omit*.
64. *Parauenture*] An aunter TU ; In auntur lest H ; On Awnter D. *oure*] ʒoure THUD. *þerfore*] þerof TD. *oure—here*] ʒour mede for ʒour gode U.
65. *seiþ*] seide TUD. *precheþ*] prechid TUD. H *reads*, For of suche men oure sauyoure · seiþ in þe gospel. *Amen*] Amen, amen U.
TD *read*, Amen, amen, recipiebant, &c.
66. *Occurs in* H *only*.
OBS.: ll. 67—77 *comprise the passage of which readings from* 29 MSS. *are given in a pamphlet entitled* "Parallel extracts from 29 MSS. of Piers Plowman," &c.; *by the Rev.* W. W. Skeat (published for the E. E. T. S.).
67. *Meires*] ʒe meyres H. *Maistres*] macerys U. *and—mene*] hij þat ben mene T; þat beoþ ordeyned meenes H; þei þat ben mene UD; hij þat ben menene dwellyn H₂.
68. *þe*] his U. *to kepe þe lawes*] þe lawe for to kepe H.
70. *Brewesters*] Breweris TUH₂D.
71, 72. H *omits these lines*.
72. [*percel-mel*] TUD (*and* 14 *other MSS.*); V *reads*, þat al schal a-buggen.

¶ þei punisschen þe peple · priueliche and ofte,
And recheþ þorw Reg[r]atorie · *and* Rentes hem buggeþ,
With þat þe pore people · schulde puten in heore wombe.
¶ For toke þei on trewely · þei timbrede not so hye, 76
Ne bouȝte none Borgages · beo ȝe certeyne.

BOte Meede þe Mayden · þe Meir heo bi-souȝte,
Of alle suche sullers · seluer to taken,
Or presentes withouten pons · as peces of seluer, 80
Rynges with Rubyes · þe Regratour to fauere.
"For my loue," quod þe ladi · "loue hem wel vchone
And soffre hem to sulle · sumdel aȝeyn Resoun."

¶ Bote Salamon þe Sage · a Sarmoun he made, 84
To a-Mende Meires · and men þat kepeþ þe lawe ;
And tolde hem þis teeme · þat I wol telle nouþe :
*Ignis deuorabit tabernacula eorum qui libenter
accipiunt munera.*

Among þis lewede men · þis latin Amounteþ,
þat Fuir schal falle · and brenne atte laste 88
þe houses and þe homes · of hem þat desyreþ
For to haue ȝiftes · in ȝouþe or in elde.

[Now beoþ ȝe war, if ȝe wole · ȝe maysturs of þe lawe ;

---

73. *punisschen*] poisone TUH₂D; pylen H. *peple*] pore pepul H. *and ofte*] wel ofte TUH₂D.
74. *recheþ*] risen vp TH₂; richen UD. H reads, & waxen ryche regratoures, &c.
75. *With þat*] Of þat TUH₂D. *wombe*] wombes HU.
76. *toke—trewly*] if þei token with trouthe H; ne toke þei so wrongwisly U; took he but trewly H₂.
77. *bouȝte none*] schulde oye noo H. *borgages*] bargaynes U; bargages H₂. ȝe] ȝe wel TH₂; þou wol UD.
79. *suche sullers*] selleris U. *seluer to taken*] for to take syluer H.
80—127. *Transposed in* D; *see preface.*
80. *withouten pons*] oþer pens U; withoute panis T. *as*] os H; or U.
81. *with Rubyes*] or oþer richesse T; or richesses U; or other richesses D. *þe—fauere*] þat regratour to meynteyne T; þese regratoures to fauoure H; þese regratours to meyntene U; Regratours to mayntene D.
82. U *omits this line. wel*] THD *omit.*
84. *Bote*] TUD *omit.*
85. *To—moires*] For to amende men TD; to amende wiþ þise meyres H. *and men*] TD *omit.*
86. *And—teeme*] And tok hym þis teeme TUD; lo, þis was his teme H. *wol—nouþe*] telle þenke THUD.
87. *lewede men*] lettride lordis TD lettride men U.
88. *brenne*] forbrenne TD; forbrenne right U.
90. *For—ȝiftes*] To haue ȝeftis for here seruice TD; to take ȝyftes amysse H; to haue mede for here seruyse U.
91—94. *Occur in* H *only.*

MEED CONSENTS TO MARRY CONSCIENCE.

for þe soþe schale be souȝte of ȝoure soules · so me god helpe, 92 *Ye who permit wrong must answer for it.*
þe suffraunce þat ȝe suffre · such wrong*us* to be wrouȝt ;
While þe chaunce is in ȝoure choyse · cheose ȝe þe best].
Þ̶E king com from Counseyl · and cleped aftur Meede,
    And of-sente hire a-swiþe · Seriauns hire to fette, 96 *Then the king sent for Meed, who was brought with mirth and song.*
And brouȝte hire to boure · w*ith* Blisse and w*ith* Ioye ;
[wiþ myrþe & wiþ mynstrasye · þei pleseden hir ychoone].
Corteisliche þe kyng · Cumseþ to telle, *Then the king courteously spake thus:*
To Meede þe Mayden · [meleþ þeose] Wordes : 100
"[Unwittily, ywys,] · wrouht hastou ofte ;
Bote worse wrouhtest þou neue*re* · þen whon þou fals toke. *"Never hast thou done worse than now; but do so no more.*
Ac I forȝiue þe þis gult · and graunte þe my grace ;
Hennes to þi deþ day · do so no more. 104
¶ Ichaue a kniht hette Concience · com late from bi-ȝonde, *I have a knight named Conscience; wilt thou marry him?"*
Ȝif he wilne þe to wyf · wolt þou him haue ? "
¶ " Ȝe, lord," quaþ þat ladi · "[Lord] for-beode hit elles ! *"Yes," said she, "I will do your will."*
Bote Ich holde me to oure heste · honge me sone!" 108

---

95. þe—*counseyl*] þe king*e* fro counseil com T; þan þe kyng fro Counceil come D ; Then ca*m* þe kyng from þe counseyle H ; þe king & his conseil com U. *cleped*] callide THUD.
96. *The readings are,*
  And ofsente hire as swiþe *seriauntis* hire fecche (fette D) TD ;
  And sent aftur hir asswiþe · seriawntis hir fette H ;
  & of-sente here swithe · wiþ seriauntes here fette U.
In the latter, fette *is transferred by mistake to the beginning of the line following.*
97. *boure*] borugh T; þe boure H. *with*—*Ioye*] þere þe king was ynne H.
98. *Occurs in* H *only.*
99. *Corteisliche*] Certis TD. *cumseþ to telle*] þoo seyde to mede H.
100. H *omits this line.* [*meleþ þeose*] *There is no doubt that such should be the reading; but in* V *the scribe has mis-written it* melodyes, *which is nonsense; in* T *and* H$_2$ *we find* melis þise ; *in* U *it is* moueþ þese ; D *corruptly has* mekely þese.
101. *From* T. V *has the inferior reading,* Qweynteliche, quaþ þe kyng ; *which makes the king begin to talk a third time. The other readings are,* Certis unwysely H ; Vnwittily wrought · hast þou wol ofte UD.
103. H *omits by mistake the last half of this line, and the first half of l.* 104. *my*] TU *omit.*
104. *do so*] do þou so TUD ; so þou do H.
105. *hette*] U *omits ;* D *is here again corrupt.*
106. *him haue*] assente H.
107. ȝe] ȝa TU ; ȝea H. [*Lord* TUD] V *and* H *have* God, *which spoils the alliteration. hit*] TH *omit ;* U *reads,* lord it forbede elles.
108. TDH$_2$ *omit this line. The*

Then was Conscience called, who knelt and asked the king's will.	¶ Þenne was Concience I-clepet · to comen and apeeren To-fore þe kyng and his Counsel · Clerkes and oþure. Kneolynge Concience · to þe kyng loutede, [to wyte what his wille were · & what he do schulde].
"Wilt thou wed this woman?" said the king.	¶ "Woltou wedde þis wommon," quod þe kyng · "ȝif I wol assente? 113 Heo is fayn of þi felawschupe · for to beo þi make."
"Nay, Christ forbid!" quoth Conscience.	¶ "Nay," quaþ Concience to þe kyng · "Crist hit me forbeode!
	Er Ich wedde such a wyf · wo me bi-tyde! 116
"She is frail and fickle, and makes men sin.	¶ Heo is frele of hire Flesch · Fikel of hire tonge ; Heo makeþ men misdo · moni score tymes ; In trust of hire tresour · teoneþ ful monye.
She teaches women wantonness.	¶ Wyues and widewes · wantounesse heo techeþ, 120 Lereþ hem lecherie · þat loueþ hire ȝiftes ;
She caused Adam's fall; and harms Holy Church.	Vr Fader Adam heo falde · wiþ Feire biheste ; Apoysende Popes · and peyreþ holy chirche. Þer nis no beter Baude · (bi him þat me made !) 124 Bitwene heuene and helle · In eorþe þauȝ men souhte.
She is frail, and a tale-bearer; common as a	¶ Heo is Tikel of hire Tayl · Talewys of hire tonge, As Comuyn as þe Cart-wei · to knaues and to alle ;

others give,
Bote ich hoolly be at ȝoure heest ·
 gurd off my nek H.
But y be holy at ȝour heste · hange me
 elles U.
109. *I-clepet*] callid THD ; ycalled
U. D *omits* coucience.
110. *Tofore*] Before THUD.
111. *to*] þen to H.
112. *From* H. What þat his wille
were, &c. TD; What his wille were, &c.
U. *Omitted in* V *by mistake, for it
leaves the sentence incomplete*.
113. *quod þe kyng*] THUD *omit*.
I] he D.
114. *Heo*] for sche UD ; for heo TH.
115. *Nay*] TUD *omit*. *me*] T *omits*.
117. *Flesch*] feiþ TUD. *tonge*]
speche TUD ; feiþ H.
119. *teoneþ*] sche teniþ T ; heo
teoneþ H ; sche troyteþ U ; sche tenes
D.

120. *heo*] TUD *omit*.
121. *Lereþ hem*] leride hem TUD ;
lereþ hem to H. *loueþ*] louiden TD ;
louedyn U. *þat—ȝiftes*] & lecching
of ȝeftis H.
122. ȝoure fadir he fellide · þoruȝ
 false behest T ;
fele men heo falliþ · wiþ faire
 behestis H ;
ȝour fadir sche fellide · þurw
 false byhestes U ;
ȝoure fader sche felde · with
 fals be-hestes D.
123. *Apoysende*] Apoisonide TD ;
Apo[i]sowned U. H *reads*, & popes
heo poiseneþ. *and peyreþ*] apeiride al
TU ; Apeyred D.
124. *þer nis no*] I not a TD ; Is
noght a U.
125. *In*] & TU.
127. *knaues—alle*] knaue & to
monke TU ; knaues & to monkes D.

To Preostes, to Minstrals · to Mesels in hegges.   128   cartway to every knave. Assizers and summoners and sheriffs praise her.
Sisours and Sumpnours · suche men hire preisen ;
Schirreues of schires · weore schent ȝif heo nere.

¶ Heo doþ men leosen heore lond · and heore lyues after,   She makes men lose both land and life, and releases prisoners by bribes.
And leteþ passe prisons · and payeþ for hem ofte.   132
Heo ȝeueþ þe Iayler Gold · and grotes to-gedere,
To vn-Fetere þe False · and fleo where hem lykeþ.
Heo takeþ þe trewe bi þe top · and tiȝeþ him faste,   She ties true men fast, and hangs the innocent.
And hongeþ him for hate · þat harmede neuere.   136
Heo þat ben Curset in Constorie · counteþ hit not at a Russche ;
For heo Copeþ þe Comissarie · and Coteþ þe Clerkes ;
Heo is asoyled as sone · as hire-self lykeþ.   She is assoiled when she pleases.

Heo may as muche do · In a Mooneþ ones,   140
As [ȝoure] secre seal · In Seuen score dayes.
Heo is priue with þe Pope · Prouisours hit knowen ;   She is intimate with the pope, and seals bulls.
Sir Simonie and hire-self · asselen þe Bulles ;
Heo Blessede þe Bisschopes · þouȝ þat þei ben lewed.   144

¶ Prouendreres, persuns · Preostes heo meyntenep,   She maintains priests in concubinage.
To holde Lemmons and Lotebyes · al heor lyf-dayes,

128—142. *Omitted in* D.
128. *To—minstrals*] To mynstrelis, to messangeris TUH₂ ; To monkis, to minstrals H. *to mesels*] many tyme U.
129. *sumpnours*] schereues U.
130. U *omits this line. nere*] ne were T.
131. *lond*] lyf U. *lyues*] lond U ; life T. *after*] eke H ; boþe T.
132. *passe prisons*] prisouns passe H ; passe prisoners T ; passe þe prisoneres U.
133. *Heo*] And THU. *Iayler*] gaileris TU. *to-gedere*] among H.
134. *And—lykeþ*] fle where hym likeþ TU.
135. *þe trewe*] treuþe HU. *tiȝeþ him*] teieþ hym vp U.
136. *hate*] hattrede THU. *harmede*] harm dide H.
137. *Heo þat ben*] þeiȝ heo be H ; To be TU. *counteþ*] heo countiþ TH ;

sche ȝyueþ U. *at*] THU *omit. Russche*] cresse H.
138. *coteþ þe*] cloþiþ hise TU.
140. *Heo may*] She may neiȝ T ; Sche may ny U. *as muche do*] do as myche H.
141. [ȝoure TH] vre V ; þe U. *seuen—dayes*] foure score wintris H.
143. *asselen*] selen HU ; seliþ TD.
144. *Heo—þe*] She blissiþ þise TUD ; Heo examyneþ þe H. *þouȝ—ben*] ȝif þei be T ; if þei beþ H ; þo þat ben D.
145. Prouendrours, prestis & persones · she mayntenip to holde T ; (D *same, omitting* prestis &) ;
Prouendrours, persones · prestes sche meyntenep to holde U.
146. TUD *omit* to holde *here ; see l.* 145.

And bringeþ forþ Barnes · aȝeyn forbodene lawes.
Þer heo is wel with þe kyng · wo is þe Reame !   148
For heo is Fauerable to Fals · and fouleþ Treuþe ofte.
¶ Barouns and Burgeis · heo bringeþ to serwe,
Heo Buggeþ with heore Iuweles ; · vr Iustises heo schendeþ.
Heo lihþ aȝeyn þe lawe · and letteþ so faste,   152
Þat Feiþ may not han his forþ · hir Florins gon so þikke.
Heo ledeþ þe lawe as hire luste · *and* loue-dayes makeþ,
Þe Mase for a Mene mon · þauȝ he mote euere.
Lawe is so lordlich · and loþ to maken eende,   156
With-outen *p*resentes or pons · heo pleseþ ful fewe.
Clergye an Couetise · heo Coupleþ to-gedere.
Þis is þe lyf of þe ladi · vr lord ȝif hire serwe !   159
And alle þat Meynteneþ hire · [myschau*n*ce hem bytide] !
For [þe] pore may haue no pouwer · to playne, þauȝ he*m* smerte,
Such a Mayster is Meede · A-Mong Men of goode."

Þ Enne Mornede Meede · and Menede hire to þe kyng
    To haue space to speken · spede ȝif heo mihte.   164
Þenne þe kyng graunted hire *g*race · with a good wille :
" Excuse þe, ȝif þou const · I con no more seye ;
For Concience haþ a-cuiset þe · to Congeye for eu*er*e."

[f. 306 b. col. 2.]
She brings barons and burgesses to sorrow.

She lies against the laws,

and appoints love-days.

Law will not make an end without bribes.

Such is her evil life.

The poor cannot make their complaints known."

Then Meed was sorry, and asked leave to speak.

The king bids her excuse herself.

147. *bringeþ*] bringen TUD. *forbodene*] forbode HU.
148. *wel*] U *omits*.
149. *fouleþ*] falliþ H ; foloweþ D.
150. *Burgeis*] bachelers H. *to*] in TD.
151. Be Ihesu, wiþ hire Iuelx · ȝoure Iustice she shendiþ TUD; *where for* Iuelx U *has* Ieweles, D Iuels. *heo*] & hem H.
152. *Heo lihþ*] And leiþ TD; Sche leyth U ; Makiþ hem liȝe H. *letteþ so faste*] lettiþ þe treuþe T; letteþ treuthe ofte U; letteþ it so fast H. D *corrupt, here and in next line*.
153. *not—forþ*] haue no forþ H.
154. *Heo—þe*] She let T. *hire luste*] heo wol H.
155. *Mene*] pore U. þauȝ—euere] þei he plede euere H.

156. *so lordlich*] now lordschipe D.
157. *pons*] panis T ; penyes H ; pens UD. *ful*] wel H.
158. *an*] & THD ; and U.
159. *þe*] þat TUD ; þy H.
160. *Meynteneþ hire*] hire meynteneþ H ; meintene here men UT. [*myschaunce hem bytide*] *From* H ; TUD *have the same*. V *merely repeats*, vr lord ȝif hem care.
161. V *omits* þe, *but it is found in* H. TUD *have*, For pouere men, &c. *to—smerte*] to pleyne hem þeiȝe þei smerte U.
163. *menede*] pleyned HU.
165. *þenne*] THUD *omit*.
166. *no more seye*] sey no more H.
167. *haþ a-cuiset*] acusiþ TUD. *congeye*] cunge T ; conieye þe H ; conge þe D ; cunge þe U.

"Nay, lord," quaþ þat ladi · "leef him þe worse 168 *"Disbelieve Conscience," said she;*
Whon ȝe witen witerliche · Wher þe wrong lihþ.

¶ Þer Mischef is gret lord · Meede may helpe,
And þou knowest, Concience · I com not to chyde,
Ne to depraue þi persone · *with* a proud herte. 172

¶ Wel þou wost, Concience · (But ȝif þou wolt lyȝe), *"for well knowest thou, Conscience, thou hast hung on my neck eleven times, and taken money from me,*
Þow hast honged on my Nekke · Enleue tymes;
And eke I-gripen of my gold · and ȝiuen þer þe lykede.
Whi þou wraþþest þe now · wonder me þinkeþ! 176
For ȝit I may as I mihte · menske þe wiþ ȝiftes,
And Meyntene þi Monhede · more þen þou knowest,
And þou hast famed me foule · bifore the kyng heere. *and hast defamed me. And yet I never killed a king, as thou didst.*
¶ For Culde I neuere no kyng · ne counseilede þer-after;
Ne dude i neuere as þou dust · I do hit on þe kyng! 181

¶ In Normandie nas he not · a-nuyȝed for my sake;
Ac þou þi-self soþliche · schomedest him þere, *'Twas thou who madest him return from Normandy,*
Creptest in-to a Caban · for Colde of þi nayles, 184
Wendest þat wynter · wolde haue last euere,
And dreddest to haue ben ded · for a dim Cloude,
And hastedest hamward · for hunger of þi wombe! *hastening home for hunger*

¶ Wi*th*outen pite, pilour! · pore Men þou robbedest,

169. *lihþ*] liggeþ TD; liþ H; duellith U.
170. *grete lord*] gret TUD; most H. *mede—helpe*] mede it may amende H; mede mayde may helpe D.
171. *And þou knowest*] þou knowist wel H. *com not*] can nouȝt for T.
172. *depraue*] dispise U.
174. *Nekke*] half TUD (*one would expect to find* half (= hals, *a neck*) *but it is plainly* half). *Enleue*] enleuene TU; elleuen DH.
175. *I-gripen of*] grepe TD; gripen U. *ȝyuen þer*] gyue it where TD. *lykede*] list H; likiþ TD.
177. *For*] THUD *omit*. *menske*] mylde U; auaunce TD.
179. *And*] But H. *heere*] nowþe H.
180. *Culde*] kilde TU; kelled D. H *reads*,
& I agult hym neuer · ne his counsel neþer.
181. *Ne—dust*] Ne dide as þou demist TUD; for I dede neuer as þou didest H. *þe kyng*] þy-silue H.
182. *anuyȝed—sake*] noied for me U.
183. *schomedest*] asshamidest T; aschamyd H; schamed D. *þere*] ofte TD. U *reads*, Ac þou self sikerly · conseiledest hym þennes: *see* l. 199.
184. *Creptest*] þou creptest H; Crope TD; creep U.
185. *Wendest*] þou wendest H. *haue*] UD *omit*. *last*] y-last H.
186. *to—ded*] þe to be deed U; to be ded T; for to be ded D.
187. *And hastedest*] And hastide þe TD; þou hastedest þee H; & hastidest þe U.
188. *pite*] riȝt H. *pilour*] þou pilour HU.

And beere heor bras on þi Bac · to Caleys to sulle. 189
But I laughed, and made my lord merry, and made his men hopeful.
Þer I lafte with my lord · his lyf forto saue,
Maade him murþe ful muche · Mournynge to lete,
Battede hem on þe Bakkes · to bolden heore hertes,
Dude hem hoppe for hope · to haue me at wille. 193

Had I been marshal then, he should have been lord of all the laud!
Hedde I be Marchal of his Men · (bi Marie of heuene)!
I durste haue I-leid my lyf · and no lasse wed,
He hedde beo lord of þat lond · in lenkþe and in brede;
And eke kyng of þat cuþþe · his cun for to helpe; 197
Þe leeste barn of his blod · a Barouns pere.

But thou, Conscience, didst counsel him to leave that richest realm.
¶ Soþliche, þou Concience · þou counseildest him þennes,
To leue þat lordschupe · for a luitel seluer, 200
Þat is þe Riccheste reame · þat Reyn ouer houeþ!

A king should reward them that serve him.
Hit bicomeþ For a kyng · þat kepeþ a Reame
To ȝiue meede to men · þat mekeliche him seruen;
To Aliens, to alle Men · to honoure hem with ȝiftes. 204
Meede makeþ him beo bilouet · and for a Mon I-holden.

Thus emperors and earls get their young servants.
Emperours and Eorles · and alle maner lordes
Þorw ȝiftes han ȝonge men · to renne and to ride.

Thus, too, the pope gives rewards to men.
¶ Þe pope and his prelates · presentes vnderfongen, 208
And Meedeþ men hem-seluen · to meyntene heore lawes.

---

190. *lafte*] lefte TU.
191. & made him merie · mornynge to lete H;
And made hym murþe · mournyng to leue TD;
And made hym mirthes · fro morwe til eue U.
192. *Battede—Bakkes*] And baterride hym on þe bak T; & batrid men on here backis H; I batride on þe bak UD. *to—hertes*] boldite his herte TUD.
193. *Dude hem*] Dede hym TD; & dide hym U; I made hem H. *hoppe*] D omits. *hope*] ioiȝe H. *wille*] here wille H; his wille U.
194. *Marchal*] marchaunt (!) TD. *Men*] oost H. *Marie*] maries loue H; mary loue U.
195. *lyf*] heed U. *lasse*] wors D.
196. *hedde be*] schuld haue be THUD.
197. *cuþþe*] kiþ TH₂; kytthe U; countrey H; kyth D. *cun*] kyn THUD.
198. *barn*] brol TUD.
199. *Soþliche*] but soþely H; Cowardliche UD. T *omits this very necessary line*.
200. *þat*] his TUD. *seluer*] disese H.
201. *þat—houeþ*] þat regniþ ouer on T; þat regneþ ouer one D.
202. *for*] to H; TUD *omit*.
203. *mede—men*] hise men mede TUD. *mekeliche*] menskly H.
204. *To*] And U. *hem*] U *omits*.
205. *him*] U *omits*. *beo*] H *omits*.
206. *Emperours*] dukis H.
208. *and*] wiþ TUD.
209. *men hemseluen*] men hymselfe T; gretly men H; hem hym-selue U; men here-self D. *heore*] here THD; his U.

¶ Seruauns for heore seruise · (ȝe seon wel þe soþe), *Servants receive wages.*
Takeþ Meede of heore Maystres · as þei mowen a-corde.
Beggers for heore biddyng · Biddeþ Men [meede] ; 212 *Beggars ask for gifts, and so do minstrels.*
Munstrals for heor Murþe · Meede þei asken.
¶ Þe kyng Meedeþ his Men · to maken pees in londe ; *The king pays his men to keep the peace.*
Men þat knoweþ Clerkes · Meede hem craueþ.
¶ Prestes þat precheþ · þe peple to goode   216 *Priests expect mass-pence.*
Askeþ Meede and Masse-pons · and heore Mete eke.
Alle kunne craftes men · craueþ Meede for heore prentys ; *Trade and payment go together; none can live without reward."*
Meede and Marchaundie · mot [nede] go to-gedere. 219
Þer may no wiht, as I wene · with-outen Meede libbe."
" NOw," quod þe kyng to Concience · " be crist, as me þinkeþ, *"Then Meed is worthy to rule," said the king.*
Meede is Worþi · Muche Maystrie to haue ! "
'Nay," quod Concience to þe kyng · and knelede to grounde ; *"Nay," said Conscience, "there are two kinds of Meed:*
" Þer beoþ twey maner of Meedes · my lord, bi þi leue.
Þat on, good God of his grace · ȝiueþ, in his blisse, 225 *the one, such as God gives men on earth*
To hem þat wel worchen · whil þat þei ben here.
¶ Þe Prophete hit prechede · and put hit in þe psauter,
Qui peccuniam suam non dedit ad vsuram, &c. (Ps. xv. 5) ;

210. *Seruauns*] seruauntis THUD. ȝe—soþe] we se wel þe soþe TUD; wite ȝe for soþe H.
212. U *omits this line.* biddyng] bedis H. [mede THH₂D] V *has* mete, *which is out of place entirely.*
214. *Meedeþ*] haþ mede of U; haþ nede (*sic*) of TD.
215. Men þat ben clerkis · crauen of hym mede TUD ; & þese kunnynge clerkis · crauen vpon mede H.
217. *Masse-pons*] messe-penis TUD; maspenyes H. *eke*] also TUD.
218. *Alle—craftes*] Of alle kyn crafty T; Alle kynne crafty U; & alle manere craftis H; alle kende crafty D. *for*] to H.
219. [*nede*] V *has* not, *which is contrary to the sense ; the others have these half-lines :* mote nede go to-gidere TH₂D ; most nede holde to-gedris H ; mot nede mete to-gidres U.
220. No wiȝt as I wene · wiþoute mede miȝte libbe TU. *mede*] mete D. *libbe*] lyue H.
221. *Now*] þo H ; TUD *omit.* as me þinkeþ] þat me made H.
222. *muche*] þe TUD.
223. *grounde*] þe grounde H ; þe erþe TUD.
224. *my*] U *omits.* þi] ȝour THUD.
225. *þat on*] þe ton U. *good*] THU *omit.* ȝiueþ] haþ grauntid H. D *is corrupt.*
226. *wel worchen*] werchen wel TUD. *þat*] THUD *omit.*
227. *hit prechede*] prechiþ it T ; prechide it UD. *and—psauter*] and preued it in þe sauter H. *non dedit*] dat H ; dedit TH₂D. *ad*] in H.

40 LABOURERS RECEIVE NOT MEED, BUT HIRE. [PASS. III.

[f. 397 a. col. 1.] and such as God will give you if you love good men;

Tak no Meede, mi lord · of Men þat beoþ trewe ; 228
Loue hem, and leeue hem · for vr lordes loue of heuene;
Godes Meede and his Merci · þer-*with* þou maiht winne.

the other, such as maintains misdoers, and of which the psalter speaks (Ps. xxvi. 10).

¶ Bote þer is a Meede Mesureles · þat Maystrie desyret,
To Meyntene Misdoers · Meede þei taken ; 232
And þerof seiþ þe psauter · in þe psalmes eende,

In quorum manibus iniquitates sunt ; dextera eorum repleta est muneribus ;

[þat here riȝthond is hepid · ful of ȝeftis],

Such as take bribes will have to answer for it.

And heo þat *gripeþ* heore ȝiftus · (so me God helpe!)
þei schullen a-Bugge bitterly · or þe Bok lyȝeþ ! 236

Priests that take money shall have the reward St Matthew speaks of (Matt. vi. 5).

¶ Preostes *and* Persones · þat plesyng desyreþ,
And takeþ Meede *and* moneye · for Massen þat þei syngen,
Schullen han Meede in þis Molde · þat Matheu haþ I-grauntet ;

Amen dico vobis, receperunt mercedem suam.

But that which labourers receive is not Meed (Bribery), but wages.

þat laborers and louh folk · taken of heore Maystres, 240
Nis no Maner Meede · bote Mesurable huyre.

In trading is no

¶ In Marchaundise nis no Meede · I may hit wel avoue ;
Hit is a permutacion · a peni for anoþer.

228. *men*] hem T.
230. *þou maiht*] miȝte þou THD; myghtow U.
231. *Bote*] TUD *omit. Maystrie desyret*] maystrie desireþ H ; maistris desiriþ TD ; maistres desyren U.
233. And þerof seide þe sauter · in a salmis ende T;
And þat witnessiþ wel þe sauter · of wicked men H ;
UD *like* T, *but with* seith *for* seide. *In quorum*] *Inimicorum* (!) H.
234. *In* H *only.*
235. *And—ȝiftus*] But he þat gripeþ siche ȝeftis H. *ȝiftus*] gold U.
236. *þei*] he H; TUD *omit. þei—bitterly*] he schal abigge it bitterly H ; Schal abye ful bitere U.
237. *Preostes—Persones*] Persouns & prestis H. *þat — desyreþ*] þat penyes desiren H ; þat plesynges de-

siren U.
238. *And takeþ*] to take H ; Schal take U; þat take TD. D *omits* & moneye.
239. *Schullen*] þei H. *Meede*] þe mede U; here mede H. *in*] on THD; of U. *þat—I-grauntet*] withouten eny more H. H *omits the Latin quotation. Amen — vobis*] Amen, amen TD. *receperunt*] recipiebant TUD.
240. *louh folk*] lewid men H ; loud (*or* lond) folk U.
241. *Nis*] hit nis H ; It is UD ; Is T. *Meede*] of mede T. *bote*] but a TUD.
242. *nis*] is TUD.
243. It is a permutacion apertly, &c. TD; but a-*pert* permytacion · as n, &c. H ; It is apertly a permutacion, &c. U. *peni*] peny-worth UD.

PASS. III.] HOW SAUL WAS RUINED BY COVETOUSNESS. 41

But Raddest þou neuer *Regum* · [þou] recreiȝede Meede, *Meed, but only barter.*
Whi þat veniaunce fel · on Saul and his chi[l]dren? 245 *Hast thou not read, in Kings,*
God sende to seie · Bi Samuels mouþe, *how God told Saul to slay Agag for Amalek's sin against Israel?*
  þat Agag and Amalec · and al his peple aftur,
Schulden dye for a dede · þat don hedde his eldren
Aȝeynes Israel and Aaron · and Moyses his broþer. 249 *(1 Sam. xv.; Exod. xviii. 8).*
¶ Samuel seide to Saul · God seendeþ þe and hoteþ *Samuel said to Saul,*
To beo boxum and boun · his biddyng to worche;
"Weend þider with þin host · wymmen to Culle, 252 *"Go and kill women and children, and king Agag; but covet not his goods.*
Children and Cheorles · Chop hem to deþe,
Loke þow culle þe kyng · Coueyte not his goodes
For Milions of Moneye; · Morþer hem vchone.
Bernes and Beestes · Brenne hem al to askes." 256 *Burn both barns and beasts."*
¶ And for he culde not þe kyng · as crist him-self hihte, *But because he did not so,*
Coueytede feir catel · and [culde] not his Beestes,
Bote brouhte wiþ him þe Beestes · as þe Bible telleþ,
¶ God sende to seye · þat [Saul] schulde dye, 260 *God sent to say that he should die.*
And al his seed for þat Sunne · schendfulliche ende.
Such a Mischef Meede · made þe kyng to haue, *Thus did Meed make God hate him.*
þat God hatede him euere · and his heires after.

244. [þou TUH₂D] þat VH.
245. *whi*] how H. *and*] and on TU; and eke on D.
246. *sende—seie*] soute hym to segge TU; sende him to say H; sent hym to sayne D.
247. *Agag*] achar U. *and Amalec*] of amaleg TH; for Amalec D. *al*] TD omit.
248. *his*] here T.
249. TUD *omit this line*.
250. *and hoteþ*] to say H.
251. *boun*] bold U. *worche*] fulfille TUD.
252. Wend þou to amalek wiþ þine ost · þe cuntre to quelle H.
253. *chop*] dryue H; schap D.
254. U *omits this line, and also ll*. 255, 256.
255. *Milions*] any mylionis THD. *morþer*] murdre T; molde H; morder H₂; muldre D.
256. burwes & bernes · & bestis þou

brenne H. *al to askes*] to deþe TD.
257. *him-self hihte*] hymself sende H; hym selue bad U; bode sente T; hym boþe sente D.
258. *Coueytede*] but coueyted UH. *feir*] here TU; þe H; his D. *his*] here H. *and—Beestes*] kilde not hire bestis TH₂UD; *hence* culde *is the reading;* V *and* H *read* slouh, slow.
259. *him—Beestes*] hem here goodis H. *telleþ*] techiþ H; hym tolde (!) T; tolde D.
260. God seide to samuel · þat saul shulde deiȝe TUD. [*Saul*] So in THUH₂D; V *has* Samuel, *which is obviously wrong*.
261. *schendfulliche*] senfully schulde T; schendfully schuld D.
262. *Mischef*] mysdede U.
263. *hatede—euere*] hatiþ þat kinge T; hateth þe kyng D; hatid hym for euer H; hatide þe kyng for euere U. *his*] alle hise THUD.

REASON SHALL ONE DAY BANISH MEED. [PASS. III.

    þe Culor*um* of þis [clause] · kepe I not to schewe, 204
    In Auenture hit [nuyȝed] me · an ende wol I make :
    ¶ And riht as Agag hedde · hapne schulle su*m*me ;

Saul shall be blamed, and David diademed.
    Samuel schal slen him · and Saul schal be blamet,
    Dauid schal ben Dyademed · and daunten hem alle, 268
    And on cristene kyng · kepen vs vchone.

I, Conscience, well know that Reason shall reign ;
    Concience knoweþ þis ; · for kuynde wit me tauȝte
    þat Resun schal regne · and Reames goue*r*ne ;
    Schal no more Meede · be Mayster vppon eorþe, 272

and there shall be Love, Humility, and Loyalty ; Loyalty shall punish trespassers.
    Bote loue and louhnesse · and leute to-gedere.
    ¶ And heo þat trespasseþ to trouþe · or doþ aȝeyn his wille,
    Leute schal don him lawe · or leosen his lyf elles.
    Schal no seriau*n*t for þat seruise · were a selk houue,
    Ne no Ray Robe · wiþ Riche pelure. 277

Meed makes Law rich, and Loyalty poor.
    ¶ Meede of misdoers · makeþ men so riche,
    þat lawe is lord I-waxen · and leute is pore.
    Vnkuynde[n]esse is Comau*n*dour · *and* kuyndenesse is
        Banescht. 280

But Common Sense shall yet return, and make Law a labourer.
    [Ac]-kuynde wit schal come ȝit · *and* Concience to-gedere,
    And make of lawe a laborer · such loue schal aryse !"

264. *culorum*] coloure H. [*clause*] *Inserted on the authority of* T *and* H₂ ; *not in* VHU ; D *has the paraphrase*, The ende of þis terme · y oute to schewe.

265, 266. *Omitted in* H.

265. *In—me*] An Aunter it me noiȝide T ; An aunt*er* ȝif it noiede me U ; On Aunter it noyed me now D. [*nuyȝed*] *Such should be the reading ; cf.* l. 182. *In* V *it is miswritten* munged.

266—269. *In* TUD *these four lines follow* l. 271, ll. 270, 271 *being made to follow* l. 265.

266. *hapne—summe*] happe shal som*m*e T ; hap men schul se som tyme U ; happed ende schul som*m*e D.

267. þen samuel slowe agag · and saul was y-blamyd H.

268. & dauid was diademyd · and daunted hem alle H. *daunten*] damnen D.

269. *on*] o T ; one U. *kepen vs*] kept hem H ; to kepen vs U.

270. *Concience knoweþ*] In consience knowe I TU ; I consciens knew H. *kuynde wit*] kynde it TD ; resoun it U.

273. *leute*] leaute T ; lyaunce D.

274. And who-so trespassiþ trewely · & takiþ to þe wronge T ; And who tr*e*spaseth treuliche · and taketh aȝens right U ; And ho-so trespaced treuþe · & takeþ ony þyng D.

275. His wykkide leaute shal do hym lawe · or lese his lif ellis TU ; D *similar, with* liaunce *for* leaute, *and* and *for* or.

276. *a—houue*] no selk gowne U.

277. *wiþ*] of HT ; with no D.

278. *Meede—misdoers*] meede wiþ her mysdedis H. *men*] hem THUD.

279. *leute*] lyaunce D.

280. *Vnkuynde(n)esse*] wickednes HU ; vnkyndenesse TD.

281. [*Ac*] V *has* And ; *but* Ac (TUD) *gives far better sense, and* H *has* but.

PASSUS IV.

[*Passus Quartus de Visione.*]

"SEseþ," seide þe kyng · "I suffre ȝou no more.
Ȝe schulle sauȝtene forsoþe · and serue me boþe.
Cusse hire," quaþ þe kyng · "Concience, Ich hote."
"Nay, be Crist," quod Concience · "Congeye me raþer !
Bote Reson Rede me þer-to · Arst wol I dye !" 5
¶ "And I comaunde þe," quod þe kyng · to Concience þenne,
"Þat þou Rape þe to ride · And Reson þou fette ;
Comaunde him þat he come · my Counseil to here. 8
For he schal reule my Reame · and Rede me þe beste
Of Meede, and of oþer mo · and what mon schal hir wedde ;
And A-Counte with Concience · (so me [Crist] helpe !)
How þou ledest my peple · Lered and Lewed." 12
¶ "I am Fayn of þat foreward" · seide þe Freike þenne,
And Rod riht to [Reson] · and Rouned in his Ere,

Side notes:
"Be reconciled," said the king. "and kiss her, Conscience."
"Not unless Reason advises me so to do."
"Then ride and fetch Reason here," said the king.
"He shall give us good advice."
Conscience gladly rode off, and gave

[Passus, &c.] THUD.
1. *suffre ȝou*] ne mote ȝe H. *more*] lengere TUD.
2. *Sauȝtene*] sauȝte T; saghtlyn U; *in* H *acoorde is written, as a gloss, above* saȝtene; saghten D.
3. *Cusse*] Kisse TH; kys D.
4. *Crist*] god TUD. *congeye*] cunge TU; counge D.
5. *Rede*] radde H; rewle D. *arst*] erst T; first U. *arst—dye*] leuer hadde I deyȝe H.
6. *þenne*] as swiþe H.
7. *þat þou*] TUD omit. *and*] H omits. *þou*] þat þou TD; þou me U; to H.
9. *me*] me for H.
10. *oþer mo*] mo oþere TU. *and what*] what TUD. *wedde*] haue H.
11. *a-counte*] counte TUD. *with*] wiþ þee H. [*Crist* T] god VHUD.
12. *ledest my*] lerist þe TD; lernest my H; rewliste þe U.
13. *seide*] quod H. *Freike*] frek TH; freek U; frayk D.
14. *Rod riht*] rideþ riȝt H; riȝt renneþ TUD. [*Reson*] *So in* THUD; V *has* Concience, *which is clearly wrong. Rouned*] rouniþ TH; rownes UD.

Reason the king's message.

Seyde as þe kyng sende · and seþþe tok his leue.

¶ "I schal araye me to Ride," qu*o*d Reson · "Reste þe
 a while"—   16

Reason bids his knave Oato saddle his horse called Suffer-till-I-see-my-time.

And clepte Caton his knaue · Curteis of speche—
"Sette my Sadel vppon Soffre- · til-I-seo-my-tyme,
And loke þou warroke hi*m* wel · wiþ swiþe feole gurþhes;
Hong on him an heui Bridel · to bere his hed lowe, 20
Ʒit wol he make moni a whi · er he come þere."

Then Conscience and Reason rode to the king, and

Þenne Concience on his Capul · Carieþ forþ Faste,
 And Resun wi*th* him Rideþ · Rappynge Swiþe;

[f. 397 a. col. 2.]

Wisdom and Wit followed them in a wain, for they wanted Reason's advice.

Bote on a wayn [witti] · and wisdame I-feere   24
Folweden hem faste · for þei hedden to done
In Esscheker and Chauncelrie · to ben descharget of
 þinges;
And Riden faste, for Reson · schulde Rede*n* hem þe
 beste
For to sauen hem-self · from schome and from harme.
¶ Bote Concience com arst · to Court bi A Myle, 29
And Romede forþ bi Reson · Riht to þe kyng.

The king receives them courteously.

COrteisliche þe kyng · þenne com to Resou*n*,
 Bitwene himself and his sone · sette hi*m* on Benche,

---

15. *Seyde*] Seide hym TD; & seide
H. *sende*] him sente U; bade H.
seþþe] siþþe TH; sitthe U; sethen D.
17. *And*] he H. *clepte*] calde TUD.
Caton] conscience U.
18. *soffre*] soffre, quoþ he H.
19. *loke þou warroke*] let warroke
TUD. *swiþe—gurþhes*] riʒtful gerþis
TU; wytful gartys D.
20. *an*] þe THD. *to bere*] to holde
TD; & hoold U.
21. *he*] we TD (*wrongly*). *moni a
whi*] many wehe TU; many a wehe
H; many wey D. *er he*] er we TU;
or he H; or we D.
22. *carieþ*] cairiþ T; caried HD.
23. *Rideþ*] rit T; right U. *Rappynge swiþe*] & rapiþ hym ʒerne TH;
& rapide hym faste U; & hastid hem
swiþe H. D *omits this line*.
24. Ac vnwary wisdom · & witty
 his (wyt his ovne D) fere
 TD;

Ac on-were wysdom · & wytty
 his fere U;
& in a wayn wysdome · and
 witty his fere H.
V *has* Bote on a wayn wyd, &c. *which
gives no sense; see* Folweden *in next
line*. N.B. V *has* witti *in* l. 141 *below*.
25. *hem faste*] faste forþ U.
26. *Esscheker*] cheker TUH₂D; court
HU. *chauncelrie*] in chauncelrie H; in
chaunceric TD; in þe chancerye U.
ben descharget] deschargen hem H.
27. & for reson shulde reule hem ·
& rede hem for þe best H.
28. & saue hem fram harme · &
fram shame also H.
29. *Myle*] myle wey TUD.
30. *Romede*] rombide T; rowned
U. *bi*] wiþ THU; D *omits*. *Riht*] &
rauʒt H.
31. *þenne—Resoun*] þanne com in
to resoun TU; welcomed resoun H.
32. *Bitwene*] And betwyn TD. *him-*

PEACE BRINGS A COMPLAINT AGAINST WRONG.

And wordeden a gret while · wysliche to-gedere.   33
þene Pees com to parlement · and put vp a Bille,   *Enter Peace, with a plea against Wrong.*
Hou þat Wrong aȝeyn his wille · his wyf hedde I-take,
And [hou] he Rauischede Rose · Reynaldes lemmon,   36
And Mergrete of hire Maydenhod · maugre hire chekes.
" Boþe my Gees and my Grys · [his] gadelynges fetten;   *"Wrong (said he) has stolen my geese and pigs, and my horse Bayard,*
I dar not for dreede of hem · fihte ne chide.
He Borwede of me Ayȝard · and brouhte him neuer
    aȝeyn,   40
Ne no Ferþing him fore · for nouȝt þat I con plede.
He meynteneþ his Men · to Morþere myn owne,
Forstalleþ my Feire · Fihteþ in my chepynges,
Brekeþ vp my Berne-dore · and bereþ awei my whete,   *murdered my men, stolen my wheat, and beaten myself."*
And takeþ me bote a tayle · of Ten quarter oten;   45
And ȝit he bat me þerto · and liȝþ be my Mayden.
I nam not so hardi for him · vp for to loke."
þe kyng kneuh he seide sooþ · for Concience him tolde.
¶ Wrong was a-Fert þo · and Wisdam souhte   49   *Then was Wrong afraid, and tried to bribe Wisdom to plead for him,*
To Make his pees with pons · and proferde forþ
    Moneye,

self] hym U. *on*] a T. H *omits this line.*
33. *wordeden*] speken H. *wysliche*] wel wisly TU.
34. *Pees com*] com pes THD. *vp*] forth U. *Bille*] bulle H.
35. *his—I-take*] hadde his wyf take THU; D *omits* hadde.
36. V *omits* hou, *but it is in* THUD. *lemmon*] loue TUD; douȝter H.
37. *Mergrete*] molde H.
38. [*his*] V *has* þe, *but this is inferior to* his, *which is in* THUD. *fetten*] fecchen THU. *gadelynges fetten*] gadlyng fecches D.
39. *dar*] durst H; þer D. *dreede of*] U *omits*; for of TD.
41. *Ferþing—fore*] ferþing þerfore TD; ferthyngworth þerfore U; ferþing for hym H. *nouȝt—plede*] nouȝt I couþe plete T; ouȝt þat I cowde pleden H; ought I coude plete U; nouȝt y couþe plede D.

42. *to morþere*] forto sle H. *owne*] hynen TD; hyne U.
43. *Feire*] feires HTD. *chepynges*] chepynge THUD.
44. *dore*] dores HTUD.
45. *bote*] þen H. *of ten*] for ten TUD. *oten*] of otis T; otes U; ootis H; otys D.
46. *bat*] betiþ THUD.
47. *vp for*] vneþis H.
And I am not hardy vnneþe · on hym for to loke TD ;
And I am noght so hardy · ones on hym to loke U.
48. *þe—kneuh*] þo kneuȝ þe kinge TU; That knewe þe kyng D. H *has*, þe king seide, þis is soþ · for conscience hit me tolde.
49. *a-fert*] aferd THD; aferid U. *souhte*] he souȝte THD; bysoughte U.
50. *pons*] his panis T; penyes H; his pens U; his pans D. *forþ Moneye*] hym manye TD; manye U.

And seide, "Hedde I loue of þe kyng · luite wolde I recche
Þauh pees and his pouwer · playneden on me euere!"

Wisdom and Wit told him

¶ Wisdam wente þo · and so dude Wit, 53
And for wrong hedde I-do · so wikked a dede
And warnede wrong þo · with such a wys tale;
"Whose worcheþ bi wil · wrappe makeþ ofte; 56

that, unless he could get Meed to help, he was ruined.

I sigge hit bi þi-seluen · þou schalt hit sone fynde.
Bote ʒif Meede make hit · þi Mischef is vppe,
For boþe þi lyf and þi lond · liʒþ in þe kynges grace."

Then Wrong wept, and got Wisdom and Wit to take Meed with them.

Wro[n]g þenne vppon Wisdom · wepte to helpe, 60
Him for his handidandi · Rediliche he payede.
Þene wisdam and wit · wente to-gedere,
And nomen Meede with hem · Merci to wynne.

Peace shows the king his bloody head.

¶ Pees putte forþ his hed · and his ponne blodi: 64
"Withouten gult, god wot · gat I þis scaþe."
¶ Concience and þe kyng · knewen þe soþe;
Wusten wel þat wrong · was a schrewe euere.

But Wisdom and

¶ But wisdam and wit · weoren ʒeorne aboute faste 68

---

51. H *omits*. TUD *read*,
And seide, hadde I loue of my lord þe kinge · litil wolde I recche;
but in UD *the last half-verse is at the beginning of the next line; in* V *we should perhaps read*, of my lord.
52. but pes wiþ his powere · playned on hym euere H. þauh] if U. on me] hem T; hym UD. D *omits* and his pouwer.
53. wente] wan to T; wan U; ran D. dude wit] dede wyt also TUD; dide hym witt H.
54. And for] For þat THUD. I-do] ywrouʒt H; wrouʒt TD; don U.
55. þo] U *omits*. a wys tale] wyse talys D.
56. wrappe makeþ] makiþ wrappe H.
57. I sigge] we say H. þi-seluen] my-self TUD.
58. Bote—hit] But mede þi pees make U. þi] TD *omit*.

59. lond] lyme H. liʒþ—kynges] liþ in his TD; liþ in here H; ben in his U.
60. Wrong] THUD. vppon] on TU. wepte] wepiþ TD. to helpe] to helpe hym at nede U; to hym helpe ; hym to helpe T.
61. For of hise penys he proffride handy dandy to paye T; For right þer of is handy dandy payd U; For of his handy-dandy payd (*sic*) D.
63. nomen] toke THD; token U.
64. ponne] panne TUDH₂; hode H. ponne blodi] blody panne U. (*In* D Blody *begins the next line.*)
65. gat] hent H.
66. U *omits*. Concience—kyng] þe king & conscience H. knewen] kneuʒ wel TD.
67. Wusten] And wisten THUD.
68. weoren ʒeorne] were THUD.

To ouercome þe kyng · with [catel] ȝif heo mihten.
¶ þe kyng swor þo bi crist · and bi his Coroune boþe,
þat wrong for his werkes · schulde wo þole,
And Comaundede A Constable · to casten him in Irens.
"He ne schal þis seuen ȝer · seon his feet ones." 73
¶ "God wot," quaþ wisdam · "þat weore not þe beste ;
And he amendes make · let Meynprise him haue ;
And beo borw of his bale · and buggen him bote, 76
And a-Menden his misdede · and euer-more þe bettre."
¶ Wit a-Cordede herwith · and seide him þe same :
"Hit is betere þat boote · Bale a-doun bringe
þen Bale be beten · and boote neuer þe better." 80
þEnne Meede Meokede hire · And Merci bi-souhte,
And profrede pees a present · al of pure Red gold:
"Haue þis of me," quod heo · "to Amende with þi scaþe,
For Ichul wage for wrong · he wol do so no more." 84
Pees þenne pitously · preyede þe kyng
To haue merci on þat Mon · þat mis-dude him ofte :
"For he haþ waget me a-mendes · as wisdam him tauhte,
I Forȝiue him þat gult · with a good wille ; 88
So þat ȝe assented beo · I con no more sigge :

Wit tried to overcome the king.
The king swears Wrong shall suffer, and shall be cast into irons.

Wisdom offers bail, and says Wrong will pay damages.

Wit seconds this

Then Meed proffers Peace a present of gold, and engages that Wrong shall keep the peace.

Peace begs Wrong off, and forgives him, since Meed has made amends.

---

69. [*catel* TUD] Meede VH.
70. þo] THUD *omit*.
71. TUD *omit this line*.
72. T *omits this line*; UD *omit down to* Constable.
73. *ne schal*] shal not H; shulde not T. to 'casten hym in yrens he schal þis vij ȝer sen his fet onys (!) U; D *similar, but has* he schal not.
75. *And*] ȝef H. *make*] mowe make TU; wol make H.
76. *borw of*] borugh for T; brouȝt of H; borw for U; borow for D. *buggen*] bringen T; bigge HU; beggyn D.
77. *And*] TUD *omit*. *his*] þat UD ; þat he T. þe] do þe U.
78. *him*] TUD *omit*. D *is corrupt*.

79. *Hit is betere*] Betere is THUD.
80. *beten*] bote U.
81. *Meede Meokede*] gan mede to meke TUD.
82. *pure Red*] purid TH; pure U ; pured D.
83. *me*] me, mau TUD. *with*] TUD *omit*.
84. *Ichul*] y wile T ; y wol HU; I wyl D. *wol*] shal TUD.
87. *For—a-mendes*] For he haþ wagid me wel TUD; For he hadde wagid hym wel H.
88. *him—gult*] þee þis gult quod pees H.
89. *þat—beo*] ȝe assente perto TU ; ȝe Assente D ; þat ȝe assent, my lord H. *no—sigge*] sey no more TUD.

For Meede haþ maad me amendes · I may no more aske."

But the king swears that Wrong shall not get off so lightly.

¶ "Nay," quod þe kyng þo · "(so god ȝiue me blisse !)
Wrong went not so awei · til ich wite more ;   92
Lope he so lihtliche awei · lauȝwhen he wolde,
And eft be þe baldore · forte beten myne [hynen ;]
Bote Reson haue reuþe of him · he resteþ in þe stokkes
Also longe as I lyue · bote more loue hit make."   96

Then some advised Reason to take pity on Wrong.

¶ þenne summe Radde Reson · to haue reuþe of þat schrewe,
And to Counseile þe kyng · and Concience boþe,
þat Meede moste be Meynpernour · Reson heo bi-souȝte.

"Nay," says Reason, "not till all lords and ladies love truth,

"Rede me not," quod Reson · "Reuþe to haue,   100
Til lordes, and ladies · louen alle treuþe,
And perneles porfyl · be put in heore whucche ;
Til children Chereschinge · be chastet wiþ ȝerdes,
Til harlotes holynesse · be holden for an hyne ;   104

[fol. 397 b. col. 1.]
rioters are holy, clerks and knights courteous, and

Til Clerkes and knihtes · ben Corteis of heore Mouþes,
And haten to don heor harlotrie · and vsun hit no more ;

---

90. H *omits this line.* *Meede*] he U. *me amendes*] my mendis TD. *aske*] axen TU ; axe D.
91. *god*] crist U.
92. *went*] wendiþ THU ; wendes D. *til*] er TU ; or D.
93. for yf he lept so liȝtly · he wolde vs alle scorn H. *awei*] U *omits.* *lauȝwhen*] lauȝen T; laghen U ; lawhen D.
94. *eft*] ofte THUD. *baldore*] boldere HTD ; baldere U. *forte, &c.*] to bete my hynen TUD ; to mysdo my puple H. V *omits* hynen.
95. *of*] on TDHU. *resteþ in þe*] shal reste hym in þe TD ; schal resten in U ; shal into þe H.
96. *Also longe*] As long TUD ; be as longe H.
97. *þenne*] TD *omit.* *summe*] summe men TD ; U *omits.* *of*] on THUD.

98. *to counseile*] þo conseilede U.
99. *heo bisouȝte*] þei besouȝte TUD ; þei preied H.
100. *Rede*] Rediþ H. *Reuþe*] no reuþe TUD ; reuþe for H.
102. *porfyl*] purfile TH ; purfil U ; purfyl D. *whucche*] hucche TU ; whicche H ; huche D.
103. *children*] childris T ; childrens H ; childrenes U. *chereschinge*] chiding H. *chastet*] chastid U ; chasted D ; chastisid TH.
104. *Til*] And THUD. *holynesse*] harlotrie U. *be—hyne*] be preised ful hiȝe H (TUH₂D *like* V). *an*] any D.
105. *Clerkes— knihtes*] kniȝtes & clerkis H.
106. *to don*] TD *omit.* *don*] U *omits.* *heor*] H *omits.* *and—more*] oþer mouþe it with tungis T ; & no more it vsen H ; or mouthe it hemselue U ; oþer hit mouþen D.

PASS. IV.] WRONG MUST BE PUNISHED. 49

Til prestes heore prechyng · preuen hit in hem-seluen, <small>priests practise what they preach·</small>
And don hit in dede · to drawen vs to gode ; 108
Til seint Iame beo I-souht · þer I schal a-signe,
And no mon go to Galys · bote he go for euere ; <small>till men go no more to Galicia, and Rome-seekers no more bear the king's coin over the sea,</small>
And alle Rome Renners · for Robbeours of bi-ʒonde
Bere no seluer ouer see · þat bereþ signe of þe kyng,
Nouþer Grotes ne gold I-graue · with þe kynges Coroune,
Vppon Forfet of þat Fe · hose hit fynde at douere,
Bote hit beo Marchaund oþur his men · or Messager <small>unless they be merchants, messengers, provisors, or priests.</small>
  with lettres,
Or Prouisours or Preestes · þat Popes a-vaunset. 116
¶ And ʒit (quod Reson) bi þe Roode · I schal no reuþe <small>I will have no pity while Meed is here.</small>
  haue,
While Meede haþ eny Maystrie · to Mooten in þis halle ;
[Ac y mai schewe ʒow ensamples · y seie be myselue].
¶ For I sigge hit for my soule · And hit so weore 120
þat Ich weore kyng with Croune · to kepen a Reame, <small>Were I king, no Wrong should go unpunished, or get grace by bribes.</small>
Scholde neuer wrong in þis world · þat Ich I-wite
  mihte,
Ben vn-punissched beo my pouwer · for peril of my
  soule !
Ne gete grace þorw ʒift · (so me [god] helpe !) 124

107. U *omits the line.* in] TH *omit.* preuen hit in] preued D.
108. vs—gode] men to goode H.
109, 110. H *omits these lines.*
110. And] þat TUD. bote] but ʒif T ; but yf D.
111. And] til H. alle] alle þe T. Robbeours] Robberis THUD.
112. bereþ—kyng] signe of kinge shewide T ; coyn of kyng schewith U ; syne of kyng schewith D.
113. Neiþer grotis ne gold · ygraue wiþ kinges coyn TUD.
114. Vppon Forfet] For faytour D. þat] þe H. hose—douere] who fynt hym do euere TD ; whoso fynt hit at douere H ; who fynt hym diuerse U.
115. Marchaund] messingere H. men] man TUD. Messager] messangeris T. or—lettres] þat wiþ hym beriþ lettris H.

116. Or—Preestes] oþer prestis oþer prouisours H ; oþer prouisour or prest TUD. Popes avaunset] þe pope auaunciþ TUD ; popis doþ auaunce H.
117. ʒit] D *omits.* schal] wol U.
118. eny] þe TUD. Mooten] moten U ; mo T ; moo D.
119. From U. *Also in* T, *which has* Ac I may shewe ensaumplis · as I se forsoþe ; D *like* T, *but omits* forsoþe. *The line is not in* V *or* H.
120. U *omits down to* soule. *for*—soule] be myself T ; myself H.
121. kyng—croune] a king crowned H. kepen] gouern H. UD *mis-written, including part of l.* 120.
122. neuer] no D. wrong] U *omits.* Iwite mihte] myʒte wete D.
123. beo] be U ; by D ; at THH₂.
124. grace þorw] my grace by H ; my grace þoruʒ T ; my grace with

4

GOOD SHOULD BE REWARDED. [PASS. IV.

No evil ought to go unpunished, nor good unrewarded.

Ne for Meede haue Merci · but Mekenesse hit make.
For *nullum malum* þe Mon mette · [with] *inpunitum*,
And bad *nullum bonum* · be *irremuneratum*.
Let þi Clerk, sire kyng · Construe þis in Englisch ;

Were this rule kept, Law might go and cart manure, and Love should rule over all."

And ȝif þou worchest hit *in* wit · Ich wedde boþe myn
    Eres, 129
þat lawe schal ben a laborer · and leden a-feld dounge,
And loue schal leden þi lond · as þe leof lykeþ."

Clerkes þat were *con*fessours · Coupled hem to-gedere,
  Forte Construe þis Clause · *and* distinkte hit after.

When Reason said this, all thought he was right, and that Meed was a wretch.

Whon Resun to þis Reynkes · Rehersede þeose wordes,
Nas non in þat Moot-halle · more ne lasse,
þat ne held Reson a Mayster þo · And Meede a muche
    wrecche; 136

As for Love, he laughed her to scorn, and said,

Loue lette of Meede luite · and louh hire to scorn,
And seide hit so loude · þat soþnesse hit herde,

"Whoever marries her will surely prove a cuckold."

" Hose wilneþ hire to wyue · for weolþe of hire godes,
Bote he beo A Cokewold I-kore · cut of boþe myn Eres !"

¶ Was nouþer wisdam þo · ne witti his feere, 141

UD. *ȝift*] giftes TD ; ȝeftis H ; ȝiftes U. [*god*] So in THUD ; V *has* gold.
125. H *varies, reading,*
for loke what þese wordis seyn · þat writen beþ in latyn.
Meede] no mede TUD. *make*] made TUD.
126, 127. *In these lines H has only the Latin words.*
126. For *nullum malum* · he may mete with *Inpunitum* TD ; For *nullum malum* · *inpunitum* þe may mete with U.
[*with* TUD] *with*-outen U.
127. *bad*] bad quod (!) D. *be*] TUD omit.
128. *Clerk*] clerkis H ; confessour TUD. *þis in*] it þe on TD ; it þe in U.
129. *worchest—wit*] worche þis werk T ; worche it *in* werk UD ; werchest þer-after H. *Ich wedde*] y lay H. *boþe*] TD omit.
130. *a-feld*] to feld U ; on felde D.
131. *þe leof*] þe lefe T ; þe best U ;

þy self H ; þe lef D.
132. *Clerkes—confessours*] þo alle þe grete clerkis H.
133. *and—after*] declynede fast TH₂ ; & declyne aftir U ; & wite what it moned H ; declyned it faste D.
134. *Whon—reynkes*] Ac resoun amonge þise renkis T ; Ac whan resoun among þe renges U ; but when resoun among hem H ; Ac resou*n* among þe reules had D.
135. *Nas non*] þer nas no manTD ; þer nas man HU. *þat Moot-halle*] þe court H.
136. *þo*] TUD *omit*. *wrecche*] shrewe H.
137. *Meede luite*] hire liȝt TUD ; hire liȝtly H.
138. *seide*] gredde U. *so*] to D.
139. *wyue*] wyf H.
140. *I-kore*] ycald TU ; ykyd H ; I-callid H₂ ; called D. *boþe myn eres*] myne eeris H ; my nose TUD.
141. *Was — þo*] Warne wisdom þo

THE KING ELECTS TO LIVE WITH REASON.

þat couþe warpen a word · to wit*h*-siggen Reson;
Bote stareden for studiing · and stooden as Bestes.
¶ þe kyng acordede, bi crist · to Resons Connynge,
And rehersede þat Reson hedde · Rihtfoliche I-schewet:
"Bote hit is hard, be myn hed · herto hit bringe, 146
Al my lige leodes · to lede þus euene."
¶ "Bi him þat rauhte on þe Roode," · quod Reson to þe kyng, 148
"Bote I Rule þus þi Reame · Rend out my Ribbes!
ȝif hit beo so þat Boxumnesse · beo at myn assent."
¶ "Ich assente," quod þe kyng · "bi seinte Marie mi ladi,
Beo my counseil I-come · of Clerkes and of Erles. 152
¶ Bote Rediliche Reson · þou Rydest not heonnes.
For as longe as I liue · lette þe I nulle."
¶ "Icham Redi," quod Reson · "to Reste with þe euere;
So þat Concience beo vr counseiler · kepe I no betere."
¶ "I graunte gladly," quod þe kyng · "God forbeode he fayle 157
And also longe as I lyue · leue we to-gedere."

Neither Wisdom nor Wit could gainsay Reason's speech.
The king decreed that Reason was right, but said it was hard to govern so.
Reason declares it is easy.
The king says he assents to Reason's counsel;
and hopes he will stay with him.
"I will stay if Conscience be your counsellor."
"Yes," said the king, "let us live together till I die.

TD; I warne þat wysdom H; Vnwar was wisdom U. *witti*] no wyt T; ynwit U. *ne—feere*] & wyt his owne fere D.
142. U *omits this line*. *þat—warpen*] ne couþe seie H; couþe nouȝt warpen TD. *with-siggen*] aȝenscie H.
143. *stareden—studiing*] stareden & studeden H; staringe & stodyenge TD; starende & studiande U. *and stooden*] stoden TD; stode forþ U.
144. *acordede*] a-cord H. *connynge*] kunnyng H; sawis TUD.
145. *hedde*] TD *omit*.
146. *hard*] wel hard T; wol hard U; ful hard D. *herto—bringe*] herto to bringe it T; it þer to to brynge U · herto to brynge D.
147. *þat eny lyuyng men · shulde lede hem þus euen* H. *Al*] And alle T. *leodes*] ledes TUD. *þus*] hem þus TUD.
148. *rauhte*] deiȝede T; rest hym H; deyde D.
149. *Bote*] But ȝif TD. *þi*] ȝoure D. *out*] of U.
150. *so*] TD *omit*. *beo at*] be of HUD.
151. *quod þe kyng*] H *omits*.
152. *of erles*] erlis T; of kniȝtis H.
153. *Rydest, &c.*] shalt not wende henne T; schalt not riden henne U; shalt wende henne D (*sic*).
154. H *varies, reading*
For into my deþday · we nele not depart.
lette—nulle] loue þe I wile TUD.
156. *þat*] TUD *omit*. *vr counseiler*] of oure counseil HU; of ȝour counseil TD.
157. *gladly*] wel H; TUD *omit*. *God—fayle*] godis forbode he faille (failed U) TU; god forbode I fayle D.
158. *And also*] As TUD; for as H. *I*] we H. *leue*] libbe TUH₂D; loue H.

PASSUS V.

[Passus quintus de visione.]

<small>The king goes to matins.</small>

Þ E kyng and his knihtes · to þe Churche wenten
  To heere Matyns and Masse · and to þe Mete aftur.

<small>The FIRST VISION ends.</small>

Þenne Wakede I of my wink · me was wo with alle
þat I nedde sadloker I-slept · and I-seʒe more.   4

<small>Here begins the SECOND VISION, viz. of the Deadly Sins, and of PERS THE PLOUHMON.</small>

Er I a Furlong hedde I-fare · A Feyntise me hente,
þat Forþer mihti not a-fote · for defaute of Sleep.
I sat Softeliche a-doun · and seide my beo-leeue,
And so I blaberde on my Beodes · þat brouhte me
  a-Slepe.   8
Þen sauh I muche more · þen I beofore tolde,
For I sauh þe Feld ful of Folk · þat ich of bi-fore
  schewede,
And Concience with a Crois · com for to preche.

<small>The sermon of Conscience upon the pestilence and the violent wind of Jan. 15, 1362.</small>

¶ He preide þe peple · haue pite of hem-selue,   12
And preuede þat þis pestilences · weore for puire synne,
And þis souþ-Westerne wynt · on a Seterday at euen

Passus, &c. *In* THUD.
1. *his*] T *omits.*
2. *to þe*] sithe to U.
3. *wink*] wynkyng TUH. *me—wo*] & wo was TU; wo was me H. *with alle*] þerfore H.
4. *nedde*] ne hadde TU. *sadloker I-slept*] yslepe saddere TU. *I-seʒe*] yseyn TH; yseie U.
5. *a—I-fare*] hadde faren a furlonge THU. *A*] swiche U; TH *omit. Feyntise*] fantesie U. *hente*] hadde T.
6. *Forþer—a*] I ne miʒte ferþere a TU; ferþer ne miʒte y one H. *sleep*] slepynge TU.
7. *a-doun*] in my bedis T (*wrongly; see l.* 8).
8. *blaberde*] babelide T; bablide U; blaberid H. *þat*] þei TU.
9. *sauh I*] y sawe H. *muche*] meke T. *tolde*] shewid H.
10. TH *omit. For*] U *omits. of—schewede*] byfore nempnyd U.
11. *And*] & how H. *com*] bygan H.
12. *He*] And TH. *preide*] prechide U. *haue*] to haue U. *of*] on THU.
13. *þis pestilences*] þe pestilence H; þis pestilence U. *weore*] wern T; was HU.
14. *þis*] þe THU. *wynt*] wynd TU. *a*] TU *omit.*

CONSCIENCE PREACHES A SERMON.

Was a-perteliche for pruide · and for no poynt elles.
¶ Piries and Plomtres · weore passchet to þe grou*n*de, 16
In ensau*m*ple to Men · þat we scholde do þe bettre.
Beches and brode okes · weore blowen to þe eorþe,
And t*ur*ned vpward þe tayl · In toknyng of drede
þat dedly Synne or domesday · schulde fordon hem alle. 20
¶ Of þis Matere I mihte · Momele ful longe,
Bote I sigge as I sauh · (so me god helpe) !
How Concience w*ith* a Cros · Comsede to preche.
¶ He bad wastors go worche · what þei best couþe, 24
And wy*n*ne þat þei wasteden · w*ith* su*m* mane*r* craft.
¶ He preiȝede Pernel · hire Porfil to leue,
And kepen hit in hire Cofre · for Catel at neode.
Thomas he tauȝte · to take twey [staues], 28
And fette hom Felice · From wyuene pyne.
¶ He warnede watte · his wyf was to blame,
þat hire hed was worþ a Mark · *and* his hod worþ A Grote.
¶ He chargede Chapmen · to Chasten heore children ; 32
Let hem wonte non eiȝe · while þat þei ben ȝonge.

marginalia:
Pear-trees, plum-trees, beeches, and oaks were blown down.

The dreamer gives an outline of Conscience's sermon.

Conscience bids wasters work,
[fol. 307 *b*. col. 2.]
and tells Pernel to put her finery away.

Thomas is to fetch home his wife Felice ; and Wat's wife is to blame.

Chapmen are to chastise their children, and

---

15. *pruide*] synne U. *no poynt*] nothyng U.
16. *Piries*] peretrees H. *Plomtres*] plantes T. *passchet*] possid H ; put TU. *grou*n*de*] erþe TU.
17. *to men*] sent god T ; seith god U. *þat we*] þat ȝe T ; þat þei H ; ȝe U.
18. *þe eorþe*] grounde T ; þe grounde U.
19. *vpward*] vp U. *þe tayl*] here tail T ; here tailes H.
20. *dedly synne*] deth U. *schulde*] shal TU. *hem alle*] þe world H.
21. *of—mihte*] vpon þis ilke matere y H ; Of þis matere myght y U. *momele*] mamele T ; mamle U ; momelid H. *ful*] wel TU.
22. *Bote-sigge*] Ac I shal seiȝe TU ; but y say H. *sauh*] saiȝ T ; sauȝ H ; seide U.
23. *comsede*] cumside T ; bygan for H ; com for U.
24. *He*] & H. *wastors*] wastour TU. *þei*] he TU.
25. *þei wasteden*] þei wasted H ; he wastide TU ; V *has* þei ne wasteden, but *I propose to omit* ne. *maner*] maner of T ; kynne U.
26. *He*] And TH. *preiȝede*] prechid U.
27. *kepen*] kepte T. *cofre*] whicche H. *for—neode*] lest rattis hit eten H.
28. [*staues* THUH₂] V *has* stauenes ; *prob. from* wyuene *in l. below.*
29. *hom Felice*] felis his wyf T ; home his wyf H. *wyuene*] heuene wyuene U, *with stroke through* heuene. *See* Critical Notes.
30. *watte*] also watte H.
31. *worþ* (2)] not worþ TH ; not a U.
32. *chasten*] chastice TU.
33. *Let*] & lete H. *Let—eiȝe*] let no wynnyng for-wanye hem T ; let no

priests to practise what they preach.
¶ He preyede Preestes · and Prelates to-gedere,
þat þei prechen þe peple · to preuen hit in hem-seluen—
"And libben as ȝe lereþ vs · we wolen loue ow þe
    betere."   36

Religion should rule strictly.
¶ And Seþþe he Radde Religioun · þe Rule for to holde—
"Leste þe kyng *and* his Counseil · ȝor Comunes apeire,
And beo stiward in oure stude · til ȝe be stouwet betere.

Pilgrims should seek St Truth.
¶ And ȝe þat secheþ seynt Iame · *and* seintes at Roome,
Secheþ Seint Treuþe · for he may sauen ow alle ;   41
Qui cum patre et filio · feire mote you falle."

Þenne Ron Repentaunce · and Rehersed þis teeme,
    And made William to weope · wat*ur* wit*h* his eȝen.

I. PRIDE. Pernel repents her pride,
Pernel proud-herte · platte hire to grounde,   45
And lay longe ar heo lokede · and to vr ladi criede,
And beo-hiȝte to him · þat vs alle maade,

and vows to wear a hair shirt, and to be ever humble.
Heo wolde vn-souwen hire smok · *and* setten þer an here
Forte fayten hire Flesch · þat Frele was to synne :   49
"Schal neuer liht herte me hente · bote holde me lowe,
And suffre to beo mis-seid— · *and* so dude I neu*er*e.
And nou I con wel meke me · and Merci be-seche   52
Of al þat Ichaue I-had · envye in myn herte."

---

welthe for-wany hem U. *while þat*]
whiles þat U ; whiles T.
34. *preyede*] prechiþ T; preohide
U. *Preestes—prelates*] prelatis &
prestis THU.
35. *prechen*] shulde preche H. *to*]
& THU. *in*] THU *omit.*
36. *ȝe—vs*] þei tauȝte hem H; ȝe
lerne vs U. *we wolen*] þei wolde H;
for we wol U. *loue ow*] leue ȝow T;
loue hem H ; loue ȝou U.
37. *þe—for*] here reweles T; here
rule HU. *holde*] kepe U.
38. *kyng and his*] kyngis H. *ȝor*]
here H. *apeire*] apeiriþ T; apeired H.
39. *beo*] were H ; be TU. *in—
stude*] of ȝoure stede T ; in ȝore stede
U; in here stude H. *til—betere*]
til ȝe be stewid bet*er*e T ; til þei were
amendid H ; so þat ȝe cheue þe betere
U.

40. *at*] in U.
41. *Secheþ*] Sekiþ at hom T.
42. *feire*] þat faire UH. *falle*] befalle TU.
43. *Ron*] ran H ; TU *omit. and*]
TU *omit.* þis] his TU.
44. *William*] wil T ; wille U. *his*]
V *has* boþe his ; *but* boþe *is best
omitted, as in* THU.
45. *grounde*] þe erþe TU.
46. *to vr ladi*] lord mercy THU.
48. *wolde*] shulde TU. *smok*]
serke TU ; shert H.
49. *Forte fayten*] For to affaiten
TH; To affayten U. *frele*] fers T;
fresch HU.
50. *liht*] heiȝ T; hye U. *hente*]
hente, quoþ heo H.
52. *And—wel*] But now wile I TU;
Now wol y H. *me*] myself H.

¶ Lechour seide " Allas ! " · and to vr ladi criede
To maken him han Merci · for his misdede,
Bitwene god almihti · and his pore soule, 56
Wiþ-þat he schulde þe seterday · seuen ȝer after
Drinken bote with þe Doke · and [dynen] but ones.
¶ Envye wiþ heui herte · asket aftur schrift,
And gretliche his gultus · bi-ginneþ to schewe. 60
As pale as a pelet · In a palesye he seemede,
I-cloþed in A Caurimauri · I couþe him not discreue ;
[A kertil & a courtepy · a knyf be his side ;
Of a Freris frokke · were þe fore sleuys]. 64
As a leek þat hedde I-leiȝen · longe In þe sonne,
So loked he with lene chekes ; · lourede he foule.
His Bodi was Bolled · for wrappe he bot his lippes,
Wroþliche he wrong his fust · he þouȝte him a-wreke 68
Wiþ werkes or with Wordes · whon he seiȝ his tyme.
" Venim or vernisch · or vinegre, I trouwe,
Walleþ in my wombe · or waxeþ, ich wene.
I ne mihte mony day don · as a mon ouhte, 72

II. LECHERY.
Lechour repents,
and vows henceforth to drink only with the ducks.

III. ENVY. Envy confesses his misdeeds.

He is pale, paralytic, and like a dried leek for leanness.

He bites his lips, and wrings his fist.

"There is venom," he says, " in my belly, filling me with wind.

---

54. *Lechour*] þe lechours H. *to—criede*] lord mercy had H; on our lady cride U.
55, 56. *As one line in* H ; *so also we find* To make mercy for his mysdede · betwyn god & hym T; To make amendes for his mysdede · bytwene god & hym U.
57. *schulde*] T *omits*. *þe seterday*] saterdayes U.
58. *Drinken*] Schulde drinke T. *doke*] goos U. [*dynen*] dyne TU; eten VH.
59. *heui*] hiȝe H.
60. *gretliche*] carfulliche THU. *gultus*] cope T; coupe U. *biginneþ*] begynneþ he T; he gynneþ U.
61. *As*] He was us TU. *pelet*] palet T; pelat U. *As—pelet*] þe pelour was pelled H. *In a*] & on þe T; in þe H. *In a palesye*] & peralatik U.
62. *I-cloþed*] He was cloþid TU; cloþid H. *caurimauri*] caury maury T; cawrymawry H (*which omits* a);

caurymawry U; caurimauri H₂. *coupe hym*] can it T.
63, 64. *From* T; *also in* HUH₂.
64. *frokke*] frogge U. *þe fore*] his two H; þe forme U.
65. *As—þat*] like as he H.
66. *lene*] his lene H. *lourede he*] lourande T; lourynge U; lowring ful H. *foule*] lowe H.
67. *bolled*] bolnid TU. *he bot*] þat he bot TU ; he bote boþe H.
68. *wrong*] wroþ TU. *he—awreke*] to wreke hym he þouȝte TU; he þouȝte hym to wreke H
69. *werkes—wordes*] werkis & wordis T; werk or wiþ word U. *seiȝ*] saiȝ T; sey U ; sawe H.
70. *vernisch*] verious T ; vergeous U; verdegrese H.
71. *Walleþ*] walewiþ T; walweþ U. *wombe*] wombe, quoþ he H. *or waxeþ*] & waxiþ as TU.
72. *I—mony*] I miȝte not many TU; I miȝt not many a H. *ouhte*] miȝte TU.

56 ENVY CONFESSES HIS SIN. [PASS. V.

Such wynt in my wombe · waxeþ, er I dy[n]e.

I annoy my neighbour, blame him behind his back,
¶ Ichaue a neihȝebor me neih · I haue anuyȝed him ofte,

Ablamed him be-hynde his bak · to bringe him in disclaundre,

Injure and revile him.
And peired him bi my pouwer · I-punissched him ful ofte,   76

Bi-lowen him to lordes · to make him leose Seluer,
I-don his Frendes ben his fon · with my false tonge;
His grase and his good hap · greueþ me ful sore.   79

I stir up strife between him and his household,
¶ Bitwene him and his Meyne · Ichaue I-Mad wrappe,
Boþe his lyf and his leome · was lost þorw my tonge.
Whon I mette him in þe Market · þat I most hate,

yet I pretend to be his friend.
Ich heilede him as hendely · [as I his frend] weore.

He is douȝtiore þen I · i dar non harm don him.   84
Bote hedde I maystrie and miht · I Morþerde him for euere!

When I kneel in church, I pray Christ to curse them that have borne away my bowl.
¶ Whon I come to þe churche · and knele bi-fore þe Roode,

And scholde preiȝe for þe peple · as þe prest vs techeþ,
þenne I crie vppon my knes · þat crist ȝiue hem serwe   88

---

73. *wynt*] wynd TU. *dy(n)e*] dyne THUH₂; *V has* dye, *by mistake.*
74. *a neihȝebor*] neȝeboris H. *me neih*] neiȝ me TU; many H. *him*] hem H.
75. *After* l. 74, H *inserts* l. 77, *slightly varied.* *Ablamed*] And blamide THU. *him*] hem H. *his*] here H. *him*] hem H. *disclaundre*] fame TU; defaut H.
76. *And—him*] To apeire hym TU; to apeiren hem H. *I-punissched, &c.*] I pursuide wel ofte T; y pursuyed ofte U; y preued ful oft H.
77. *Bilowen*] And belowen T; And yley on U. *make*] don TU. H *reads,* & eke y-bulled hem to þe lord to make hem lese siluer (*see note to* l. 75).
78. *I-don*] And don TU. *with my*] þoruȝ my T; þurw his U. H *reads,* I made here frendis be here foon, &c.

80, 81. H *omits.*
80. *I-mad*] mad T; mad ofte U.
81. *lyf—leome*] lyme & his life TU.
82. *whon*] but when H. *in þe*] in a T; in U. *hate*] hatide THU.
83. *heilede*] hailside THUH₂. [*as —frend*] *So in* THU; *V has* his frend *as* I.
84. *He is*] but he was H. *i—him*] y durst bede hym none harm H.
85. *Bote—I*] Ac hadde I TU; ȝif y had H. *I morþerde*] I wold murdre T; I wolde murthre U; y hadde maymed H.
86. *and*] to H. *knele*] knelide T. *bifore*] afore U; to TH.
87. *And scholde*] To THU. *vs techiþ*] techiþ T; me techith U; precheþ H.
88. Aftir þanne I criȝe on my knes þat crist gyue hym sorewe T; Aftir

ENVY LAMENTS HIS BITTER FEELINGS.

þat haþ I-bore a-wei my Bolle · and my brode schete.
¶ From the Auter I turne · myn eiȝe, and bi-holde   *I envy Heyne his new clothes.*
Hou heyne haþ a newe Cote · and his wyf anoþer ;
¶ þenne I wussche hit weore myn · and al þe web
    aftur.   92
Of his leosinge I lauhwe · hit likeþ me in myn herte ;   *laugh when he loses, weep when he wins,*
Ac for his wynnynge I wepe · and weile þe tyme.
¶ I deme men þat don ille · and ȝit I do wel worse, 95 *judge ill-doers, and do worse*
For I wolde þat vch a wiht · in þis world were mi knaue, *myself.*
[And who-so haþ more þanne I · þat angriþ myn herte].
¶ þus I liue loueles · lyk A luþer dogge,   *So live I loveless, and my breast*
þat al my breste Bolleþ · for bitter of my galle ;   *swells with bitterness, which*
May no Suger so swete · a-swagen hit vnneþe,   100   *nothing can assuage."*
Ne no Diopendion · dryue hit from myn herte ;
ȝif schri[f]t schulde hit þenne swopen out · a gret wonder
    hit were."
¶ "ȝus, rediliche," quod Repentaunce · and Radde him   *Repentance bids him be sorry*
    to goode,
"Serw for heore sunnes · saueþ men ful Monye."   104

þat I pray on my knees our lady ȝyue hym sorwe U ; þenne bidde I wiþ my mouþ þat crist, &c. H.
89. *haþ Ibore*] bar THU. *brodo*] broken TH.
90. Fro þe auter myn eiȝe I turne & beholde T; *Fram þe auter I turne me, & byholde heyne* H.
91, 92. T *one line*, How heyne haþ a newe cote, I wysshe it were myn howne (howue?); U *has two lines*, How hayne haþ a newe cote, And al þe wele þat he haþ greueth me wol sore, *with which cf. l.* 94. *heyne*] he H. *þe web*] his wele H.
93. *lauhwe*] smyle U. *hit—in*] þerof in T; and þerof lawheþ U ; it likeþ H.
94. *Ac for*] Ac of TU ; & for H.
95. *þat—ille*] þere þei don ille T ; þer y do ille U ; þei don yuel H. *wel*] THU *omit*.
96. *voh—wiht*] iche wiȝt TU ; alle wiȝtes H. *in—world*] in world H ;

TU *omit*. *knaue*] knaues H.
97. *From* T; *also in* HUH₂.
98. *lyk*] as T. *luþer*] lyþer T; lither UH₂ ; leþer H.
99. *þat*] And T. *my—bolleþ*] my brest bolniþ T; bolnyth my breste U.
100, 101. *This arrangement suits the alliteration, and occurs in* TUH₂ ; V *has* May no suger so swete · dryue, &c. ; Ne no Diopendion · aswagen, &c. ; *which* H *resembles.*
100. *so swete*] ne swet þinge THU. *vnneþe*] An vnche TU ; vneþ H.
101. *Diopendion*] dyapendyon TH ; diapenydion UH₂.
102. *schrift*] THU ; V *has* schrit. *hit—out*] it shop T ; U (*wrongly*) *omits ;* aswage it (*cf. l.* 100) H. *a—were*] a gret wondir T; it were a gret wondir U; wonder me þinkeþ H.
103. *ȝus*] ȝis TH ; ȝys U. *goode*] þe best H.
104. *heore sunnes*] synne TU. *men ful*] wel TU ; ful H.

DESCRIPTION OF AVARICE. [PASS. V.

"I am never otherwise," said he.

¶ "Icham sori," quod Envye · "I ne am but seldene oþer,
And þat Makeþ me so mad · for I ne may me venge."

[IV. WRATH; caret.]
V. AVARICE. Then came Avarice, [f. 308 a, col. 1.]

¶ Þenne com Couetyse · I couþe him not discreue,
So hungri and so holewe · sire herui him loked. 108
He was bitel-brouwed · with twei blered eiȝen,
And lyk a leþerne pors · lullede his chekes ;

with a threadbare and torn coat.

¶ In A toren Tabart · of twelue Wynter Age ;
But ȝif a lous couþe lepe · I con hit not I-leue 112
Heo scholde wandre on þat walk · hit was so þred-bare.

"I acknowledge I am covetous, for I once served Sim at the Oak,

¶ "Ichaue ben Couetous," quod þis Caityf · "I be-knowe hit heere ;
For sum tyme I Seruede · Simme atte noke,

where I learnt lying and false weights.

And was his pliht prentys · his profyt to loke. 116
¶ Furst I leornede to Lyȝe · A lessun or tweyne,
And wikkedliche for to weie · was myn oþer lessun.

I went to Winchester and Weyhill fair, and

¶ To Winchestre and to Wych · Ich wente to þe Feire
With mony maner marchaundise · as my mayster hihte ;

sold my wares by cheating.

Bote nedde þe grace of gyle · I-gon a-mong my ware, 121
Hit hedde ben vn-sold þis seuen ȝer · so me god helpe!

---

105. *ne am*] nam H; am TU. *seldene*] selde TH; seldom U.
106. *And*] U omits.
107. *couþe*] can THU. *him*] U omits.
108. *hungri*] hungrily T. *so*] TH omit. *herui*] heruy THU.
109, 110. He was bittirbrowid & babirlippid boþe Wiþ two bleride eiȝen as a liþene purs lollide his chekis T; He was bitelbrowid & babirlippid wiþ two brode iȝen And as a leþerne pors lollide his chekes H; He was babirlippid and eek biterbrowed Wiþ two blerid eyȝen as a lethern purse U; (TU faulty)
111. *toren*] broun H; tore U. *age*] old H.
112. *ȝif*] U om. *con*] may THU. *I-leue*] yleue H; leue T; trowe U.
113. *Heo*] he T; how heo H; þat he ne U. *nandre—walk*] wandre on þat walsshe scarlet T; walke on þat wede H; slideren þeron U. *hit—so*] so was it T; so was U.
114. *Two lines in* U, *viz.* I haue louyd couetise al my lif tyme, I knowe it here byforen crist & his cleue modir; T *has*, I haue ylouid coueitise, quaþ he, al my lif tyme, *and also* I knowe hire *at begin. of l.* 115; H *and* V *shew the true old form.*
115. *simme*] symoun H. *atte*] at þe THU.
116. H omits. *pliht prentys*] prentis ypliȝt T; prentis aplight U.
117. *lessun or*] lef oþer T; leef oþer U.
118. *weie*] wynne U. *was—lessun*] was my ferste lesson TU; certis was þe þridde H.
119. *Wych*] wy TU; wellis H.
120. *hihte*] me hiȝte T; me bad H; me tauȝte U.
121. *Bote nedde*] Ne hadde TU.
122. *ben—ȝer*] ofte be vnsold H.

PASS. V.]   HOW AVARICE LEARNT TO CHEAT.   59

¶ þenne I drouȝ me a-mong þis drapers · my Donet to   Then I went to
   leorne,   the drapers, and
                                                          learnt from them
                                                          false measure
To drawe þe lyste wel along · þe lengore hit semede ;
Among þis Riche Rayes · lernde I a Lessun,   125   There I learnt to
                                                          fasten pieces of
Brochede hem with a pak-neelde · and pletede hem to-   stuff together,
   gedere,
Putte hem in a pressour · and pinnede hem þer-Inne   and press them
                                                          out till they
Til ten ȝerdes oþer twelue · tolden out þrettene. 128   seemed longer
¶ And my Wyf at Westmunstre · þat Wollene cloþ made,   My wife made
                                                          woollen cloth,
Spak to þe spinsters · for to spinne hit softe.   and sold it by false
                                                          weight.
þe pound þat heo peysede [by] · peisede a quartrun more
þen myn Auncel dude · whon I weyede treuþe.   132
¶ I Bouhte hire Barly · heo breuh hit to sulle ;   She brewed
                                                          barley, and
Peni Ale and piriwhit · heo pourede to-gedere   made mixed
                                                          drinks for poor
For laborers and louh folk · þat liuen be hem-seluen.   people,
¶ þe Beste in þe Bed-chaumbre · lay bi þe wowe, 136   and sold ale
Hose Bummede þerof · Bouȝte hit þer-after,   at a groat a
                                                          gallon.
A Galoun for a Grote · God wot, no lasse,
Whon hit com in Cuppemel ; · such craftes me vsede.
¶ Rose þe Regratour · Is hire rihte name ;   140   Her name is
                                                          Rose the regrater.
Heo haþ holden hoxterye · þis Elleuene wynter.
¶ Bote I swere nou [soþely] · þat sunne wol I lete,

123. *among þis*] among T ; among þese H ; to U.   *leorne*] lere TU.
124. *lyste wel*] list TH ; lysour U.   *semede*] semyth U.
125. *þis*] þe THU.   *lernde I*] I rendrit TU.
126. *Brochede*] Prochid U.   *pak-neelde*] paoneld H ; pakke nedle TU.   *pletede*] pleit T.
127. *pressour*] presse H.   *pinnede*] peyned H.
128. U omits.   *out*] H om.
129. *And — þat*] my wyf was a wynstere & T ; my wif was a breustere & U.
130. *Spak*] And spake TU.   *spinsters*] spynstere TU.
131. *þe*] two H.   *peysede*] weid by TU ; VH omit by.   *peisede*] was U ; weied H.
132. *myn—dude*] any aunsel dede T ; ony almesdede (!) U.   *whon I*] & I T ; whan sche U.
133. *hire*] lire also H.
134. *piriwhit*] pile-whey T ; pilewhew U ; pilwhay H₂.
135. *and louh*] & louȝ T ; & lewid H ; for loþ U.   *liuen*] lay T
136. *þe*] my TU.   *Bed*] H om.   *lay—wowe*] lith by þe wowes U.
137. *Bummede*] dronke H.   *Bouȝte*] he bouȝt U ; shulde bye H.
139. *com*] comeþ HU.   *cuppemel*] cop-mele H ; cuppemale U.   *such—vsede*] þat craft my wyf vside TU ; such crafte heo vsiþ H.
140. *Is*] was TH.
141. *Hoxterye*] osterye U.   *þis elleuene*] elleuene T ; all þis xxxti H.
142. *I—soþely*] now I swere soþely

GLUTTON THINKS OF REPENTING. [PASS. V.

But now I repent and will make restitution"
And neuere wikkedliche weye · ne fals chaffare vsen,
Bote weende to Walsyngham · and my wyf alse, 144
And bidde þe Rode of Bromholm · bringe me out of dette."

VI. GLUTTONY. Glutton goes to church to confess,
NOu ginneþ þe Gloton · for to go to schrifte,
And carieþ him to chircheward · his schrift forte telle.

but on the way Betun the brewster hails him.
Þenne Betun þe Breustere · bad him gode morwe, 148
And seþþen heo asked of him · "Whoder þat he wolde?"
¶ "To holi chirche," quod he · " for to here Masse
And seþþen I-chule ben I-schriuen · *and* sunge no more."

She offers him ale; he asks if it is spiced; she says, yes.
¶ "Ichaue good ale, gossib," quod heo · "gloten, woltou asaye?" 152
"Hastou ouȝt I þi pors," quod he · " eny hote spices?"
"Ȝe, glotun, gossip," quod heo · "god wot, ful goode;
I haue peper and piane · and a pound of garlek, 155
A Ferþing-worþ of Fenel-seed · for þis Fastyng dayes."

Glutton goes in.
¶ Þene geþ Gloton in · and grete oþus after;

There were Cis the shoemaker's wife, Wat the warrener, Tomkyn the
Sesse þe souters wyf · sat on þe Benche,
Watte þe warinar · and his wyf boþe,
Tomkyn þe Tinkere · and tweyne of his knaues, 160

H. [*soþely* HTU] V (*wrongly*) omits. *wol—lete*] wole I leue H; shal I lete TU.
143. *And*] Ne TU. *wikkedliche weye*] wickedly forto weye H; wynne wykkidly U. *fals*] wykkide T; no U. *vsen*] make TU.
145. *bringe me*] to brynge vs U.
146. *þe*] TU *om. go to*] T *om*.
147. *carieþ*] cariede TU; wendiþ H. *schrift*] synnes T; synne U. *telle*] shewe THU.
148. *þenne Betun*] And Betoun TU; bele H. *bad him*] þer bad he T; þere bad him U; þen bade hym H.
149. *seþþen*] THU *om. whoder þat*] wheþer þat H; whidirward TU.
151. *Ichule*] I wile THU. *sunge*] synne THU.
152. *gossib*] U *om. gloten*] H *om*.

153. *I þi pors*] in þy pors H; U omits. *ouȝt—pors*] T omits.
154. *ȝe*] ȝhe H; ȝa TU. *quod heo*] U *om. ful goode*] wel hote TU. H reads, ȝhe, god wot, quod heo, ful hote I haue.
155. *I haue*] H *om. piane*] peynye T; pianye HU. *pound—garlek*] pomgarnade (!) H.
156. *Ferþingworþ*] pound T. *Fenel seed*] felkene sedis T; fenkil seed U. *þis*] þese H; TU *om*.
157. *geþ*] goþ TH; gooþ (*sic*) U.
158. *Sesse*] Cisse T; Cesse U; Symme H. *Souters wyf*] soutere TH; soustere U.
159. *warinar*] waffrer TU. *boþe*] after H.
160. *Tomkyn*] Symme T; Thomme U. *tweyne*] two HU.

PASS. V.]   SCENE IN A PUBLIC-HOUSE.   61

Hikke þe hakeney mon · and hogge þe neldere,
Clarisse of Cokkes lone · and þe Clerk of þe churche,
Sire Pers of pridye · and pernel of Flaundres,
Dauwe þe disschere · and a doseyn oþere.   164
[A] Ribibor, [a] Ratoner · a Rakere of chepe,
A Ropere, a Redyng-kyng · and Rose þe disschere,
Godfrei of Garlesschire · and Griffin þe walsche,
And of vp-holders an hep · erly bi þe morwe   168
ȝiue þe gloton with good wille · good ale to honsel.
Þ Enne Clement þe Cobelere · caste of his cloke,
  And atte newe Feire · he leyde hire to sulle ;
And Hikke þe Ostiler · hutte his hod aftur,   172
And bad bette þe Bocher · ben on his bi-syde.
Þer weore chapmen I-chose · þe chaffare to preise ;
Hose hedde þe hod · schulde haue Amendes.
Þei Risen vp Raply · and Rouneden to-gedere,   176
And preiseden be peniworþus · and parteden bi hem-
    seluen ;
Þer weoren oþes an hep · hose þat hit herde.
Þei couþe not bi heore concience · a-corde to-gedere,
Til Robyn þe Ropere · weore Rad forte a-ryse,   180

tinker, Hick the ostler, Hogge the needle-seller, Clarice of Cook's lane, the clerk of the church, Sir Pers of Pridye, Pernel of Flanders, Daw the ditcher, a ribibe-player, a ratcatcher, and many others, who all welcomed Glutton.

Clement the cobbler offers to barter his cloak,

and Hick the ostler his hood.

Then all rose together, and chaffered, and swore.

Robyn the roper is made

161. *hakeney mon*] hakeneman U. *hogge—neldere*] hobbe þe neldere H ; hogge þe myllere T ; hobbe þe mylner U.
162. *Clarisse*] Claris T ; Clares U ; Clarice H. *lone*] lane TU. *churche*] werkis H.
163. TU *omit*. H *reads*, Sire peris of pryde, pernel of flaundris.
164. *disschere*] dykere TU.
165. [A] *so in* TU. [a] *so in* TU ; V *reads*, And Ribibor þe R. ; H *reads*, Robyn þe r. *a Rakere*] & a rakiere T ; a rakiere H.
166. *a*] & a H. *disschere*] ribbere H.
167. TU *omit*. *Garlesschire*] garle-kiþe H. *Griffin*] gruffiþ H.
168. *And of*] And HU. *Of* T. *an hep*] U *om*.
169. *ȝiue þe*] ȝeue T ; Gaf U. *good wille*] glad chiere TU. *honsel*] hansele T ; drinke HU.

170. *þenne*] TU *omit*.
171. *atte*] at þe THU. *he—hire*] nempnide it TU. *sulle*] selle TU.
172. *And*] THU *omit*. *hutte*] hitte TU ; cast H.
173. *bad*] U *omits*. *bi-syde*] side THU.
175. *Hose*] þat who so U. *A-mendes*] amendis of þe cloke TU.
176. *þei—vp*] þo risen þei vp T. *Raply*] in a rape T ; in rape U. *rouneden*] rombeden T.
177. H *omits*. *and parteden*] apertly TU.
178. *an*] on an U. *hose—herde*] þanne þei ne couþe T ; þei couthe not ȝit iugge U ; ouer þe ware H.
179. *þei—heore*] Be here T ; þei couþe not by H ; Ne by here clene U.
180. *weore*] was THU. *forte aryse*] to arisen TH ; vp to rise U.

umpire, who

And nempned for a nou*m*pere · þat no de-bat neore,
[for he schulde p*reise* þe penyworþes · as hym good
þouȝt,].

decided that Hick should have the cloak, and Clement have the hood and fill the cup.

¶ Þenne Hikke þe Ostiler · hedde þe cloke,
In Couenaunt þ*at* Clement · schulde þe Cuppe fulle,
And habbe hikkes hod þe ostiler. *and* hold hi*m* wel I-
seruet ;   185
And he þ*at* repenteþ Raþest · schulde arysen aftur,
And grete*n* Sir gloten · wi*th* a galun of ale.

Then came much laughing and drinking, till Glutton had swallowed more [f. 398 a. col. 2.] than he could well hold.

¶ Þer was lauȝwhing *and* lotering · and "let go þe
cuppe ;"   188
Bargeyns *and* Beuerages · bi-gonne to aryse,
And seeten so til Euensong · And songen su*m* while,
Til Gloten hedde I-gloupet · A Galoun and a gille.
He pissede a potel · In a *pater-noster* while,   192
And Bleuh þe Ronde Ruwet · atte Rugge-bones ende,
Þat alle þat herde þe horn · heolden heore neose after,
And weschte þat hit weore I-wipet · wi*th* a wesp of
Firsen.

He could scarce stand, and walked all ways, like a gleeman's bitch,

¶ He hedde no strengþe to stonde · til he his staf
hedde ;   196
Þenne gon he for to go · lyk A gleo-monnes bicche,

---

181. *nempned*] nempnide hym T. *And—for*] þei named hym H. *neore*] nere T; were HU.
182. *In* H only.
184. *clement*] clement þe coupe*re* T. *schulde—fulle*] shulde felle þe cuppe T; þe cuppe schulde fille U.
185. *wel*] TU *omit*. H *reads*,
And klement hadde hickis hood ·
& held hym wel apaied.
186. *And he þat*] And whoso TU; whoso H. *repenteþ Raþest*] repentid hym raþest H; repentist raþere U. *aftur*] afore U.
187. *of*] TH *omit*.
188. *lauȝwhing—lotering*] myche lauȝhing H; lawhynge & lurkynge U; lauȝinge and lourynge TH₂.
189. *Beuerages*] beuerechis TU. *to aryse*] for to arise T; þo to rise H ; .

to rise U.
190. *Euensong*] mydnyȝt H.
191. *Igloupet*] ygloppid H ; y-gulpid T; y-golped U.
193. *Ruwet*] rewet H ; ryuet TU.
194. *herde þe*] herden þat THU.
195. *The readings are*,
And wisshide it hadde be wexid ·
 · wiþ a wysp of firsen T ;
And wyȝschid it hadde be waxed ·
wiþ a wips of ferse H ;
And wysschide it hadde waxid ·
wiþ a wyspe of fyre (!) U.
196. *til*] er T.
197. *þenne—go*] þen bygan he to go H ; & þan gan he go U. *lyk*] as H.
OBS. *In* T ll. 197, 198 *are mixed up, thus :—*
And þanne gan he to go sum tyme asid & sum tyme arere.

Sum tyme asyde · and sum tyme arere, or a man setting bird-catching lines.
As hose leiþ lynes · to [lacche] wiþ Foules.
¶ Whon he drouh to þe dore · þen dimmede his eiȝen,
He þrompelde atte þrexwolde · and þreuh to þe grounde. He stumbled at the threshold,
[Clement þe coblere · cauȝte glotoun by þe mydle, 202 when Clement caught him and carried him,
And for to lyfte hym aloft · leide hym on his knees ;
And glotoun was a gret cherl · and grym in þe lyftynge,
And cowhede vp a cawdel · in clementis lappe, 205 for which service he was ill repaid.
þat þe hungriest hound · of hertforde schire
Ne durst lape of þat laueyne · so vnloveli it smakith].
þat with al þe wo of þis world · his wyf and his wenche 208
Beeren him hom to his bed · and brouhten him þer-Inne. His wife put him to bed, and he slept all Saturday and Sunday.
And after al þis surfet · an Accesse he hedde,
þat he slepte Seturday and Sonenday · til sonne wente to reste.
¶ þenne he wakede of his wynk · and wypede his eiȝen ; 212 Then he woke up, rubbed his eyes, and asked where the cup was,
þe furste word þat he spac [was] · " wher is þe Cuppe ? "
His wyf warnede him þo · of wikkednesse and of sinne.
þenne was he a-schomed, þat schrewe · and schraped his eren, but soon feels ashamed.
And gon to grede grimliche · and gret deol to make
For his wikkede lyf · þat he I-liued hedde. 217

198. *asyde*] auaunt H.
199. *leiþ*] leide TU. [*lacche*] *So in* TU ; VH *have the mis-reading* cacche. *wiþ Foules*] wiþ larkes T ; wiþ briddis H ; wilde foules U.
201. *He—atte*] He stumblide on þe TU ; he stumblid to þe H. *þrexwolde*] þresshewold T ; þreschfold H ; throschfold U. *þreuh*] fel TH ; stey U. *grounde*] erþe TU.
202—207. *In* U *only*.
208. *þat*] U *omits*. *þis*] þe TH.
209. *hom*] TU *omit*.
210. *accesse*] axesse TH ; accidie U.
211. *wente*] ȝede TU.

212. *he—wynk*] wakide he of his wynkynge THU.
213. *word*] word was H. *spac*] spak was T ; spak, what U. [*was* TH] V *omits*. *cuppe*] bolle TU.
214. *warnede—þo*] blamide hym þanne THU. *& of*] of H ; & TU.
215. *he—schrewe*] þat schrewe asshamide THU. *schraped*] robbed H.
216. *gon—grimliche*] gan grete grymly T ; gan to grete grymly U ; bygan to be sory H. *to make*] made TU.
217. *his*] þe HU. *wikkede*] liþer TU.

"I vow," said he, "henceforth to observe abstinence."

"For hungur oþer for Furst · I make myn A-vou,
  Schal neuer [fysch] on Frydai · defyen in my mawe,
Er Abstinence myn Aunte · haue I-ʒiue me leue ; 220
And ʒit Ichaue I-hated hire · al my lyf tyme."

VII. SLOTH. Sloth falls dowr. swooning, but *Vigilate* wakes him,

¶ Sleuþe for serwe · fel doun I-swowene
Til *vigilate* þe veil · fette water at his eiʒen,
And flatte on his face · and faste on him criʒede, 224
And seide, "war þe for wonhope · þat Wol þe bi-traye.

and bids him repent.

¶ 'Icham sori for my sunnes' · sei to þi-seluen,
And bet þi-self on þe Breste · and bidde god of grace,
For nis no gult her so gret · his Merci nis wel more."

Then Sloth sat up and sighed,

¶ Þenne sat sleuþe vp · and sikede sore, 229
And made a-vou bi-fore god · for his foule sleuþe ;

and vowed he would always go to church early and regularly,

"Schal no sonenday þis seuen ʒer · (bote seknesse hit make),
þat I ne schal do me ar day · to þe d[e]ore churche, 232
And here Matins and Masse · as I a Monk were.
¶ Schal non ale after mete · holde me þennes,
Til ichaue Euensong herd · I beo-hote to þe Rode.

218. *The readings are,*
  And auowide to faste · for any hungir or þrist T ;
  þo to fast he made a uow · for hunger or for þurst H ;
  And avowed to faste · for hungir or for þriste U.
219. V *omits* fysch; *but it is in* HTU. *After* Frydai H *inserts* quod he. *mawe*] wombe T.
220. Er—*aunte*] er into tyme þat abstinence H.
221. *I-hated hire*] hire hatid H.
222. *Sleuþe*] þo sleuþe H. *Iswowene*] a swowe TH ; aswoune U.
223. *þe veil*] þer while T ; U *omits. fette*] wol fecche U. *at*] to TU.
OBS. H *makes two lines of this, thus :—*
  til he woke & wept · water wiþ his iʒen,
  & *vigilate* þe wakere · warned him þo.

224. *And flatte*] heo flat H ; And flattide it T.
225. *war þe for*] þat H. *þat—þe*] wile þe T ; wolde hym H ; he wil þe U.
226. U *omits this line.*
227. *þe*] þy H. *god*] hym TU.
228. U *omits. For*] þer H. *her*] H *omits. his*] þat H. *his—more*] þat his goodnesse nis more T.
229. *sikede sore*] seide to hymsiluen H ; seynide hym faste TU.
230. *bifore*] tofore T ; to H ; to verrey U. *foule*] wicked H.
231. *þis*] be þis TU. *ʒer*] U *omits.*
232. *do me ar*] euery H. *to—deore*] to the dere T ; rise erly to H ; to þe parische U.
233. *Matins—Masse*] masse & matynes TH. *as—Monk*] a monk as I H.
234. *non ale*] no riot H.
235. *beohote to*] behote TU ; swere by H.

And ȝit I-chulle ȝelden aȝeyn · ȝif I so muche haue,
Al þat I wikkedliche won · seþþe I wit hade.   237
¶ And þauh my lyflode lakke · letten I nulle
þat vche mon schal habben his · er ich henne wende :
And with þe Residue and þe remenaunt · (bi þe Rode
  of Chester !)   240
I schal seche seynt Treuþe · er I seo Rome !"
¶ Robert ȝe Robbour · on *Reddite* he lokede,
And for þer nas not Wher-with · he wepte ful sore.
But ȝit þe sunfol schrewe · seide to him-seluen :   244
"Crist, þat vppon Caluarie · on þe Cros diȝedest,
þo Dismas my broþer · bi-souȝte þe of grace,
And heddest Merci of þat mon · for *Memento* sake,
þi wille worþ vppon me · as Ich haue wel deseruet
To haue helle for euere · ȝif þat hope neore.   249
So rewe on me, Robert · þat no Red haue,
Ne neuere weene to wynne · for Craft þat I knowe.
Bote for þi muchel Merci · mitigacion I be-seche ;   252
Dampne me not on domes day · for I dude so ille."
¶ Ak what fel of þis Feloun · I con not feire schewe,
But wel Ich wot he wepte faste · watur with his eiȝen,
And knouhlechede his gult · to Crist ȝit eft-sones,   256

attend evensong, and make amends.

Robert the robber thought to make restitution, and prayed to Christ, saying,

"Christ, that saved Dismas on the cross,

thy will be done upon me; have mercy upon me!"

What became of him I know not; yet he wept sore,

236. *Ichulle ȝelden*] wile I ȝelde T; y wold ȝelde H ; y wol ȝelde U.
237. *Al*] U omits.
238. *And þauh*] þeiȝ T. *my—lakke*] lyflode me faile U. *nulle*] ne wolle U.
239. *vche*] euery HU; iche A T.
241. *seynt*] TU omit. *seo*] seke T; se H ; see U.
242. *on—he*] rufulliche H. *he*] TU omit.
243. *And—wherwith*] for þat he was wicked H. *ful*] swiþe THU.
244. *But ȝit*] And ȝet TU ; But H.
245. *vppon*] on THU. *on*] vpon TH. *cros*] rode T. *diȝedest*] deide HU.
246. *þe*] hym U.
247. *And*] And þou TU ; as þou

H. *of*] on THU. *memento*] memento-is TH.
248. *worþ*] werche TU. *as*] for H. *wel*] U omits.
250. *me*] þis TU. *no Red haue*] red non ne hauiþ T; no reed ne haue H ; reed non haueþ U.
251. *weene*] weniþ TU. *for—knowe*] wiþ craft þat he knowiþ TU.
252. *muchel*] grete U. H *reads,* bote for þi mytigacion · mercy y by-seche.
253, 254. H *omits these lines.*
253. *on*] at TU. *for*] for þat TU.
254. *fel*] befel TU.
255. *But*] THU omit. *faste*] H omits.
256. *to—ȝit*] þerto H ; ȝit U.

<small>and vowed penitence.</small>

 þat *Penitencia* is [pike · he] schulde polissche newe,
 And lepe w*ith* him ouerlond · al his lyf tyme,
 For he haþ leiȝen bi *latro* · lucifers brother.

<small>Then a thousand men thronged together, weeping and wailing, that they might have grace to find St Truth.</small>

¶ A þousent of Men þo · þrongen to-geders, 260
 Weopyng and weylyng · for heore wikkede dedes,
 Criȝinge vpward to Crist · and to his clene moder
 To haue grace to seche seint treuþe · god lene þei so
  mote !

257. V *reads*, þat Penitencia is prest · schulde polissche him newe. *But this is probably wrong; cf.*
 þat penitencia his pike · he shulde pulsshe newe T;
 þat penaunce his piked staf shulde be polischid al new H;
 þat penitencia his pyke · schulde pulsche newe U.
258. *leep*] go H.
259. *haþ leiȝen*] hadde leiȝe TU; hadde leyn H. *brother*] hyne T; Aunte U.
260. *A*] And T. *of—þo*] of men T; men H; men & mo þo U. *þrongen*] þe wronge (!) T.
261. *weylyng*] wringing H. *heore—dedes*] here mysdedis H.
262. *Criȝinge*] Criede T; Cryden U. *olene*] dere T.
263. *seint*] THU *omit*. *god—mote*] god lene þat hy moten T; so god lene þat þei mote U.

PASSUS VI.

[Passus Sextus de visione, vt prius.]

NOw riden þis folk · & walken on fote
  to seche þat seint · in selcouþe londis].
BOte þer were fewe men so wys · þat couþe þe wei
  þider,
BOte bustelyng forþ as bestes · ouer valeyes *and* hulles,
[for while þei wente here owen wille · þei wente alle
  amys].   5
Til [hit] was late *and* longe · þat þei a Leod metten,
Apparayled as a Palmere · In pilgrimes wedes.
He bar a bordun I-bounde · wiþ a brod lyste,   8
In A weþe-bondes wyse · I-wriþen aboute.
A Bagge and a Bolle · he bar bi his syde ;
An hundred of ampolles · on his hat seeten,
Signes of Synay · and Schelles of Galys ;   12
Moni Cros on his cloke · and keiȝes of Rome,
And þe vernicle bi-fore · for men schulde him knowe,

Sidenotes:
They all set out on a pilgrimage to find Truth; but no one knows the way.
At last they met a Palmer in pilgrim's weeds, a staff in his hand, a bag and a bowl by his side, ampullæ in his hat, and marked with crosses and keys on his cloak.

Title from T; *also called* Passus Sextus *in* HUD.
1, 2. *These two lines are in* H *only.*
3. *were*] was T. *men*] U *omits.*
þat—þider] þat þei þider couþe T; þe wey þider coude U; þat þe wey couþen H.
4. *bustelyng*] blustrid T; blustren U; bolstride H. *forþ as*] as blynd H. *and*] or U.
5. *In* H *only.*
6. *(hit) was*] *So in* H; TU *omit*; V *omits* hit. *leod*] lede TU; man H.
7. *Palmere*] paynym TU. *wedes*] wyse THU.

8. He bar a burdun in his hond · bounde wiþ a lyste H.
9. U *omits.* *weþebondes*] wodebyndes H; way wendis T. *Iwriþen*] he bond hym T.
11. *seeten*] seten THU.
OBS. *In this l.* H₂ *has* apples (!) *for* ampolles.
13. *Moni cros on*] And many crouch in T; & many crosses on H; And many a cros on U.
14. *bifore*] to-fore H; hym byforn U. *hym knowe*] y-knowe H; knowe T

[fol. 398 b. col. 1.] And seo be his signes · whom he souht hedde.

They asked him whence he came;
¶ Þis Folk fraynede him feire · from whenne þat he coome ?   6

and he said, From Sinai, the sepulchre, Bethlehem, and Babylon.
"From Synay," he seide, · " and from the Sepulcre ;
From Bethleem and Babiloyne · I haue ben in boþe,
In Ynde and in Assye · and in mony oþer places.
Ȝe mouwe seo be my Signes · þat sitteþ on myn hat, 20
Þat I haue walked ful wyde · In weete and in druye,
And souht goode seyntes · for my soule hele."

"Knowest thou a saint named Truth; where dwells he?"
¶ "Knowest þou ouht A Corseynt · Men calleþ Seynt Treuþe ?
Const þou wissen vs þe wey · wher þat he dwelleþ ?" 24

He answers that he cannot.
"Nay, so God glade me ! " · seide þe gome þenne,
"Sauh I neuere Palmere · with pyk ne with schrippe
Such a seint seche bote now in þis place."

Enter PERS THE PLOUHMON.
"Peter ! " quod a Plouȝ-Mon · and putte forþ his hed,
"Peter!" quoth he, "I know him well.
"I knowe him as kuyndeliche · as Clerk doþ his bokes ;
Conscience and Common Sense told me where he lives.
Clene Concience and wit · [kende] me to his place, 30
And dude enseure me seþþe · to serue him for euere.
¶ Boþe to sowen and to setten · while I swynke mihte,
I haue ben his felawe · þis fiftene wynter ; 33
I have sown his seed, carried his
Boþe I-sowed his seed · and suwed his beestes,

---

16. *Expanded in U into two lines;*
Þis folk frayneth him faire · for hym þat hym made,
Fro whennes þat he come · & whiderward he schulde.
from whenne] whenis T.
18. at bedlem & at babilon · haue y ben also H. *From—Babiloyne*] At bedlem (bethlem U) at babiloyne TU.
19. *In—Assye*] In Armonye, in Alisaundre THU. *and*] TU *om.*
21. *ful*] wel T; U *omits*.
23. *ouht—corseynt*] · ouȝt a corseint, quod þei TU ; a seint, quoþ þei H. *Men—seynt*] þat men callen THU.
24. *wissen*] teche H. *he*] wy T. *dwelleþ*] walkeþ H.

25. *God—me*] god mote me helpe T; god me helpe H; me god helpe U. *gome*] man T; pilgrym H.
26. *Sauh I*] I sauȝ TH. *pyk—schrippe*] scrip ne wiþ pyk H.
27. *Such—seche*] Axen aftir hym TU ; aske after seint treuþe H. *bote*] er T; eer þan U.
30. *Clene*] kynde H. *and wit*] H *omits*. [*kende*] *So in* TU ; VH *read* tauȝte. *to*] riȝt to H.
31. *enseure—seþþe*] me to sure hym TU ; me assure H.
32. *to—setten*] sowe his seed T; now and sithe U.
33. *felawe*] folowere TU ; holdere H. *þis fiftene*] al þis fourty TU.
34. *suwed*] kepid U; folewid H.

And eke I-kept his Corn · I-caried hit to house,   corn, and
I-dyket and I-doluen · I-don what he hihte,   36
With-Innen and withouten.· I-wayted his profyt;   everywhere
Þer nis no laborer in þis leod · þat he loueþ more,   watched his
                                                                    profit; and I
For þauh I Sigge hit my-self · I serue him to paye.   please him well.
¶ I haue myn hure of him wel · and oþerwhile more;
He is þe presteste payere · þat pore men habbeþ;   41
He with-halt non hyne his huire · þat he hit naþ at
    euen.   He pays me well."
He is as louh as A lomb · louelich of speche,
And ʒif ʒe wolleþ I-wite · wher þat he dwelleþ,   44
I wol wissen ow þe wey · hom to his place."
" YE, leue pers," quod þis palmers · and profreden him   The pilgrims then
       huire.   offer Piers money,
                                                          which he refuses.
" Nai, bi þe peril of my soule," quod pers · and bigon
    to swere,
" I nolde fonge a ferþing · for seynt Thomas schrine!
Treuþe wolde loue me þe lasse · a gret while after!   49
¶ Bote ʒe þat wendeþ to him · þis is þe wei þider: But he tells them
                                                         to go through
ʒe mote go þorw mekenesse · boþe Mon and wyf,   Meekness, till
Til ʒe come in-to Concience · þat crist knowe þe soþe   they come to
                                                         Conscience.

---

35. *eke*] TH omit. *I-caried*] &
cariede THU.
36. I haue dichid & doluen · & do
what he bad H. *Idon*] and do THU.
37. *I-wayted*] waytide T; to
wayten U.
38. *nis*] is H. *laborer*] laboure H.
þis *leod*] his lordsshipe TU; lordschip
H. *he loueþ more*] he louiþ betere
T; hym likeþ betere U.
39. *paye*] plese U.
40. *I*] And T. *wel*] TH *omit*.
41. *presteste*] rediest H. *habbeþ*]
knowen TU; knowiþ H.
42. *with-halt*] ne halt TU. *hit naþ*]
ne haþ it TU. H *reads*, he with-holdiþ
no mannys huyre · he paieþ hem at
euen.
43. *louelich*] & loueliche TU.
44. *And ʒif*] ʒif þat H. ʒe-- *I-
wite*] þat ʒe wille wite U. *he*] wy T.

45. I shal wisse ʒow wel · þe riʒt
    way to his place T;
   I shal teche ʒou ful riʒt · home
    to his house H;
   I schal wisse ʒow þe wey · right
    to his place U.
46. *þis palmers*] þe pilgrimes THU.
47. *Nai*] H *om*. *pers*] he H.
bigon to] gan to T; gan for to U;
fast he dide H.
48. *fonge*] take H.
49. *Treuþe*] For treuþe TU. *lasse*]
wers THU. *a—after*] a longe time
aftir TU; a gret while here after H.
50. *wendeþ—him*] wilneþ to wende
TU; wole to hym wende H.
51. *mon—wyf*] men & wyues TU.
OBS. 52—Pass. VII. l. 2. MS. H *has
here lost a folio; the rest of the
Passus is collated with D*.
52. *knowe*] wyte TUD.

THE PLOUGHMAN DESCRIBES THE RIGHT WAY. [PASS. VI.

þat ȝe loueþ him leuere · þen þe lyf in oure hertes, 53
And þenne oure neiɦebors next · In none wyse apeire
Oþerweys þen þou woldest · men wrouȝten to þi-seluen.

"Next (says he) cross the brook called Be-buxom-of-speech by the ford called Honour-your-fathers.

¶ So Bouweþ forþ bi a brok · beo-boxum-of-speche,
[Forþ til ȝe fynde a forde · ȝour-fadres-honoureth] ; 57
Wadeþ in þat water · wasscheþ ow wel þere,
And ȝe schul lepe þe lihtloker · al oure lyf tyme.

¶ Sone schaltou þenne I-seo · swere-not-but-þou-haue neode- 60

Pass by Swear-not-in-vain and the croft called Covet-not;

And-nomeliche-In-Idel- · þe-nome-of-God-Almihti.

¶ þenne schul ȝe come bi a Croft · but cum ȝe not þer-Inne ;
þe Croft hette coueyte-not- · Mennes-catel-ne-heore-wyues-
Ne-non-of-heore-seruauns- · þat-nuyȝen-hem-mihte ; 64
Loke þou breke no Bouȝ þere · but ȝif hit beo þin owne.

also by the stocks named Slay-not and Steal-not.

¶ Twei stokkes þer stondeþ · but stunt þou not þere,
þei hetten, Sle-not, ne-stel-not · stryk forþ bi hem boþe ;
Lef hem on þi luft half · loke hem not aftur, 68
And hold wel þin haly-day · euere til euen.

Turn aside from the brook Bear-no-false-witness,

¶ þenne schaltou Blenchen at a brok · ber-no-fals-witnesse,

---

54. *apeire*] apeiriþ T ; to apeire UD.
56. *So bouweþ*] And so bouȝ T; And so boweþ U; And so bowe D. *brok*] banke T.
57. *From* U; *also in* TD. *Forþ til*] For to T; For D.
58. *Wadiþ*] Wades U. *wassheþ—þere*] & wassche ȝou þerynne U.
59. *lihtloker*] liȝtliere T.
60. *Sone—Iseo*] So shalt þou se TD ; So schul ȝe se U. *þou haue*] it be for TUD. *þe*] U *om.*
61. *In Idel*] an ydel T; on ydel D; on þe ydel U. *þe nome*] name U
62. *schul ȝe*] shalt þou TD. *but—ȝe*] ac come þou T ; but come D;

cometh U.
63. *þe*] þat T. *hette*] hattiþ T; hatte U ; hiȝte D.
64. *nuyȝen*] noiȝe T ; noye UD.
65. *Bouȝ*] bowis TUD. *ȝif hit*] it TD; þei U. *þin*] ȝour U.
66. *stunt þou*] stynte þou TD ; stynte ȝe U.
67. *hetten—not*] hote stele nouȝt ne sle nouȝt TUD. *stryk—hem*] but strike forþ by UT.
68. *þi*] þe U. *luft*] left TUD. *loke—aftur*] & loke nouȝt þere-aftir TUD.
69. U *omits. euer til*] heiȝ til þe T; eyliche to D.
70. *blenchen at*] see blenche U. *brok*] bourne T; bak U; berwe D.

He is frettet wi*th*-Inne*n* with Floreyns · and oþes wel
   monye;
Loke þou plokke no plonte þer · for *per*il of þi soule.
¶ Þe*n*ne schaltou [se] sei-soþ- · so-hit-beo-to-done-   *and then shall ye see Say-sooth.*
And-loke-þat-þou-lyȝe-not- · for-no-monnes-bidyng.   74

Þenne schaltou come to a Court · Cleer as þe Sonne,   *So shall ye come to a court, with*
   þe Mot is of Merci · þe maner al abouten,   76   *walls of Wit, and battlements of*
And alle þe walles beþ of wit · to holde wil þeroute ;   *Christendom,*
þe Carnels beþ of Cristendam · þe kuynde to saue,
Brutaget wi*th* þe bileeue · wher-þorw we moten beo   *with houses that are roofed with*
   sauet.   *Love-as-brethren.*
Alle þe houses beoþ I-hulet · Halles and Chaumbres,
Wiþ no led bote wi*th* loue- · as-Breþeren-of-o-wombe.
¶ Þe Tour þer treuþe is Inne · I-set Is aboue þe sonne,   *There is Truth's tower, set above*
He may do wi*th* þe day-sterre · what him deore lykeþ ;   *the sun.*
Deth dar not do · þing þat he defendeþ.   84

¶ Grace hette þe ȝate-ward · A good mon forsoþe,   *Grace is the gate-keeper, and his*
His Mon hette a-Mende-þou · for mony men hi*m* knoweþ ;   *man is called Amend-thou, to*
Tel him þis tokene · for treuþe wot þe soþe :   *whom give a*
'I p*er*formede þe penau*n*ce · þat þe prest me en-Ioynede ;   *token.*
¶ I am sori for my sunnes · and so schal I euere   89
Whon I þenke þer-on · þauȝ I weore a pope.'

---

71. *frettet withinnen*] frettid in T; frethid yn U; fryþed in D. *with floreyns*] white floures (!) D. *oþes wel*] oþere flouris TD; oþere feeȝ U.
72. *Loke*] And loke TD. *plonte*] plantis TUD.
73. *þenne*] And þanne TD. [*se*] *in* UD *only, yet required. sei*] D *omits. so hit*] V *has* so þat hit ; *but þat is best omitted, as in* TUD.
74. *And loke*] loke TD.
75. *cleer*] as clere U; as chere D.
76. *mot*] moot U; mote D.
77. *wil*] wel U.
78. *carnels*] kirnelis TU ; cornels D. *þe*] þat TD.
79. *Brutaget*] And bot*er*asid TD ; And briteschid U. *þe*] TUD *om. wherþorw—beo*] oþer þou worst not T; or elles þou best noght U; so elles þou worst nouȝt D.
80. *þe*] U *om. Ihulet*] helid TUD. *halles*] halle U.
81. *with loue*] loue & louȝnesse TD ; al wiþ loue U.
82. *is inne*] is hymselfe TD ; him-selue is U. *Iset—aboue*] is vp to TUD.
83. *him deore*] hym good U; þat hym D.
84. *not—þing*] do no þing D.
85. *ȝateward*] porter TD ; gate-ward U.
86. *amende þou*] amende ȝow TU ; amendes D. *him*] he T.
87. *for*] TUD *om.*
88. *þe—þat*] D *om.* þat] T *om.*
89. *I*] And TD ; And y U.
90. *þenke þeron*] þeron þenke U.

Ask Amend-thou to pray his master to open the wicket-gate of Paradise.	Bidde a-Mende [-þou] Meken him · to his Mayster ones, To wynne vp þe wiket-ȝat · þat þe wey schutte, 92 Þo þat Adam and Eue · eeten heore bone ; For he haþ þe keye of þe cliket · þauȝ þe kyng slepe. ¶ And ȝif grace þe graunte · to gon in in þis wyse,
[f. 398 b. col. 2.]	Þou schalt seo treuþe him-self · sitten in þin herte. 96
Take heed that ye love Truth, lest ye be driven out,	¶ Þenne loke þat þou loue him wel · and his lawe holde ; Bote beo wel I-war of wraþþe · [þat wykkide] Schrewe, For he haþ Envye to him · þat [in þyn herte sitteþ ;] And puiteþ forþ pruide · to preisen þi-seluen. 100
and the door be closed and locked against you	¶ Þe boldnesse of þi benfes · blendeþ þin eiȝen, And so worþestou I-driuen out · and þe dore I-closet, I-keiȝet and I-klikeded · to [kepe] þe þer-oute ; Hapliche, an Hundred ȝer · er þou eft entre. 104 ¶ Þus maihtou leosen his loue · to leten wel bi þi-seluen, Bote gete hit aȝeyn bi grace · and bi no ȝift elles.
But there are also seven sisters there at the gates,	Ak þer beoþ seuen sustren · þat seruen treuþe euere, And ben porters at posternes · þat to þe place longen.
called Abstinence, Humility, Charite, Chastity,	Þat on hette Abstinence · And Humilitie a-noþer, 109 Charite And Chastite · beoþ tweyne ful Choyse Maidenes,

91. *amende þou*] See *l.* 86 ; amende ȝow TU ; amendis D ; a-Mende V. *ones*] *Begins l.* 92 *in* TUD.
92. *wynne vp*] weue out TD. *wiket-ȝat*] wyket TUD. *þe—schutte*] he with shette TD ; þe wight schetteþ U.
93. *þo þat*] Þo TUD. *bone*] bane TUD.
94. *keye of*] keiȝes & TUD.
95. *þe graunte*] graunte þe TUD. *in in*] in on U ; in TD.
96. *sitten*] wel sitte T ; wil sette D.
97. *þenne—wel*] And lere þe for to loue TUD.
98. *Bote—wraþþe*] Ac be war þanne of wraþþe T ; Ac be war of wretthe noght U ; Ac bo waar þanne wraþe nouȝt D. [*þat wykkide* TUD] for he is a V.
99. [*in þyn herte sitteþ*] So in TUD ; sitteþ in þyn herte V.
100. *puiteþ forþ*] pokiþ þe for TD ; lokith for U.

101. *þi benfes*] þi bien fait T ; þat ben feet U ; þy benfet D. *blendeþ—eiȝen*] makiþ þe blynd þanne TUD.
102. *worþestou*] worst þou TUD. *out*] out as dew TUD.
103. [*kepe*] TD ; holden V ; holde U.
104. *Hapliche*] Happily TUD. ȝer] wynter TUD.
105. *maihtou*] miȝt þou TUD.
106. *Bote*] And TUD. *bi*] þoruȝ T ; þurw U ; with D ; (*in both places*). ȝift] þing D.
107. *sustren*] doutres U. *seruen*] T *om.* (*by mistake*).
108. *at posternes*] to þe posternis T ; at þe posterne U ; of þe posternes D.
109. *þat on*] þe ton U. *and*] U *om.* *humilitie*] meknesse TD. *anoþer*] a noþer T ; an oþer U ; þat oþer D.
110. *Charite— Chastite*] Chastite and charite U. *tweyne—choyse*] hire chief TUD. *maidenes*] U *om.*

PASS. VI.] THE DIFFICULTY OF OBTAINING ADMISSION. 73

Pacience and Pees · Muche peple helpen, *Patience, Peace*
Largesse þe ladi · ledeþ in ful monye. 112 *and Bounty.*

¶ Bote hose is sib to þis sustren · so me god helpe !
Is wonderliche wel-comen · and feire vnderfonge. *Without their aid it is hard to*
And bote ȝe ben sibbe · to summe of þeos seuene, *gain entrance at*
Hit is ful hard, bi myn hed ! · eny of ow alle 116 *that gate."*
To gete in-goynge at þat ȝat · bote grace beo þe more."

¶ "Bi Crist," quaþ a Cutte-pors · "I haue no kun þere !" *The cut-purse,*
"No," quaþ an Apeward · "for nout þat I knowe !" *the ape-ward, and wafer-maker*
"I-wis," quaþ a waferer · "wust I þis for soþe, 120 *declare they have no kindred there;*
Schulde I neuere forþere a fote · for no freres prechinge."

¶ "Ȝus," quaþ pers þe plouȝ-mon · and prechede hire to goode,
"Merci is a Mayden þer · and haþ miht ouer hem alle ; *but Piers tells them Mercy*
Heo is sib to alle synful men · an hire sone alse ; 124 *dwells there also, who is of kin to*
And þorw þe help of hem two · (hope þou non oþer), *all sinful men.*
þou maiȝt gete grace þer · so þat þou [go] bi-tyme."

111. U *omits. muche peple*] mekil folke þei T ; many folk þei D.
112. *Largesse*] Largite U. *þe*] þat UD. *ledeþ*] letith U ; let TD. *ful*] wel TUD.
113. *hose*] who so T ; ho so D ; sche U. *þis*] þe U.
114. *Is*] He is TUD. *wel-comen*] welcome T ; wolcome D ; vnwolcome (!) U. *feire*] vnfair (!) U.
115. *And—ȝe*] But ȝif ȝe T ; But ȝe D ; But if he U.
116. *Hit—hed*] He is wel hard to ben had D. *ful*] wel TUD.
117. *To—ȝat*] Gete ingate at eny U. *in-goynge*] ingange TD. *at þat*] at any T ; atte D.

118. *a*] þe D. *haue*] ne haue T. *kun*] kyn TUD.
119. *No*] Ne I TUD. *for nout*] be auȝt TUD.
120. *Iwis*] Wyte god TUD. *þis for*] þat for TD ; þat þe U.
121. *neuere*] no D.
122. *ȝus*] ȝis TU ; þus D. *prechede hire*] pukide hym T ; pokid hym U ; poked hem D.
123. *is*] haþ TD ; hadde U. *þer*] T *om. and haþ*] haþ TD ; þat U.
124. *Heo*] And she TUD. *men*] TUD *om. an*] and UTD.
125. *two*] TD *om.*
126. *þer*] TU *om. þat*] TUD *om.* [*go* TUD] come V.

PASSUS VII.

[Passus septimus de visione, vtprius.]

<small>The pilgrims say that they need a guide;</small>

"Þis weore a wikked wei · bote hose hedde a gyde,
Þat mihte folwen us vch a fote · forte þat we come þere."

<small>Piers says he will guide them, when he has ploughed his half-acre.</small>

Quaþ perkyn þe plouȝmon · "bi peter þe Apostel,
I haue an half Aker to herie · bi þe heiȝe weye ;   4
Weore he wel I-Eried · þenne with ou wolde I Wende,
And wissen ou þe rihte weye · til ȝe founden treuþe."

<small>"That were long to wait," said a lady; "and what shall we women do meanwhile?"</small>

¶ "Þat weore a long lettynge" · quaþ a ladi in a skleir,
"What schul we wimmen · worche þe while ? "   8
" Summe schul souwe sakkes · for schedyng of Whete,
And ȝe wyues þat habbeþ wolle · worcheþ hit faste,

<small>Piers tells them to sew, to spin, and to clothe the naked;</small>

[Spynneth it spedily · spareþ noght ȝour fyngres],
Bote ȝif hit beo haly day · or elles holy euen.   12
Lokeþ forþ or Linnene · And labereþ þer-on faste.
Þe Neodi and þe Nakede · nym ȝeeme hou þei liggen,

Title from T; *also called* P. Septimus *in* UD.
2. *vch a*] iche T; ech U. *forte—come*] til þat we were T; til we were U.
OBS. *Collation with* H *here recommences.*
3. *peter*] seint peter H; seint poule TU.
4. *herie*] ere H; erie U; ern T. *bi*] by-side H.
5. Hadde y herd þat halfe akir · so me god helpe T;
hadde y erid þat · þen wolde y wiþ ȝou wende H;
Hadde eryed myn halue acre · I schal brynge ȝou þere U.
6. U *omits. wissen ou*] teche ȝow

H. *founden treuþe*] come þere H. T *reads,* I wolde wende wiþ ȝow · til ȝe were þere.
7. *þat*] þis TU. *in a skleir*] in a scleire TU; wiþ a sleyre H.
8. *schul*] schulde T.
9. *souwe sakkes*] sewe þe sake TU. *of*] of þe THU.
10. *ȝe*] TU *om. wolle*] wollene T. *worcheþ—faste*] wurche it ȝe schulle U.
11. *From* U; *also in* TH.
12. *or elles*] oþer T.
13. *or*] ȝoure THU.
14. *Þe Neodi*] þer nedy ben U. *þe*] U *om. nym ȝeeme*] nymeþ hed T; nym hede U; takiþ kepe H. H *transposes* neodi *and* nakede.

And cast on hem cloþes for colde · for so wolde treuþe ;
For I schal lene hem lyflode · But ȝif þe lond fayle, 16
As longe as I liue · for vr lordes loue of heuene.
¶ And ȝe, loueli Ladies · with oure longe Fyngres,   to sew chasubles, and to help the poor labourers.
þat habbeþ selk, and sendel · souweþ, whon tyme is,
Chesybles for Chapeleyns · and Churches to honoure ;
And alle maner of Men · þat bi Mete liuen, 21
Helpeþ him worche wihtliche · þat winneþ oure fode."

"BI Crist," quaþ a kniht þo · "þou [kennest] vs þe beste !   A knight declares he will help Piers to labour.
Saue o tyme trewely · þus tauht was I neuere ! 24
Bote [kenne] me," quod þe kniht · "and I-chul conne erie ;
[I wol helpe þee to labore · whil my lyf lastiþ."]
"Bi seint peter," quod Pers · "for þou profrest þe so lowe,   Piers says he will work for both, if the knight will guard the church from wasters,
I schal swynken and sweten · and sowen for us boþe,
And eke labre for þi loue · al my lyf tyme, 29
In Couenaunt þat þou kepe · Holi chirche and my-seluen
From wastors and Wikkede men · þat Wolden vs destruyen.
And go þou hunte hardily · to Hares and to Foxes, 32   and hunt hares and foxes, and

15. And] THU om. on] TU om. wolde] wile T; wole HU.
16. lene] fynde H.
17. vr] our U ; þe T. loue] U om.
18. oure longe] ȝour louely TU.
19. souweþ] sewiþ it TU.
20. Chesybles] chesiples H. Chapeleyns] chapellis TU ; churchis H. and] T om. Churches] chapels H.
21. of] H om. bi] by þe HTU.
22. him] hem TU. worche] forþ H. oure] ȝoure THU.
23. þo] U om. [kennest HU] techist V; techist T; the allit. requires kennest.
24. Saue—tyme] but o tyme H; Ac on þe tem TU. þus] so H ; TU om.
25. H omits. [kenne TU] tech. V; see l. 23. Ichul—erie] I wile lerne to eren T; y wol lere to erye U.
26. From H; in H only; perhaps redundant; see l. 29.
27. peter] poule TU. Pers] perkyn THU.
28. swynken—sweten] swete and swynke U.
29. eke] U om. labre] labore H; laboure T; labouren U. Spelt labore in l. 117; but see U 221, 259.
30. kepe] kepe wel U. and myseluen] right And me (the two last words in next line) U; And myself (in next line) T.
31. wastors] watris (sic) U. and—men] T om. vs] me TU.
32. þou] THU om. to—Foxes] þe hare & þe fox TU.

kill the small birds with falcons.	To Beores and to Bockes · þat brokeþ menne hegges,
	And fecche þe hom Faucuns · þe Foules to quelle ;
	For þei comen in-to my croft · And Croppen my Whete.'
The knight gladly consents.	¶ Ful Curteisliche þe kniht · conseiued þeose wordes ;
	"Be my pouwer, pers · I plihte þe my troupe 37
	To folfulle þe Foreward · while þat I may stonde !"
Piers further bids him to harm no tenant, to take no gifts from the poor,	¶ "But ȝit O poynt," quod pers · " I preye þe no more;
	Loke þou teone no tenaunt · bote treuþe wol assente :
	And ȝif pore men profreþ ou · presentes or ȝiftes, 41
	Takeþ hem not, in auenture · ȝe mouwen hem not de-
	seruen ;
	For þou schalt ȝelden hit a-ȝeyn · at one ȝeeres ende,
	In a wel perilous place · þat Purgatorie hette. 44
to injure no labourer, to be true of tongue,	And mis-beode þou not þi bonde-men · þe beter þou
	schalt spede,
	And þat þi-self be trewe of tonge · and tales þou hate,
	Bote hit beo wisdam or wit · þi werkmen to chaste.
and to avoid ribalds.	Hold not þou with harlotes · here not heore tales, 48
	And nomeliche atte Mete · suche Men eschuwe ;
	For þei ben þe deueles disours · I do þe [to] vndurstonde."
[f. 399 a. col. 1.] The knight again assents.	¶ " Ich a-sente, be seint Iem !" · seide þe kniht þenne,
	" For to worche bi þi word · while my lyf dureþ."

33. *To Beores*] to beris H; And þe boris T ; And to brokkys U. to *Bockes*] þe bukkes T ; to bukkes U. *menne*] mennys H ; myn TU.
34. *þe Foules*] foules U. *quelle*] kille THU.
35. *þei*] þise TU. *in-to*] to TH. *Croppen*] crepen in H.
36. *Ful*] THU *om. conseiued*] comsed H ; compsiþ T. *þeose*] his U.
38. *folfulle*] folewe H. *þe*] þis H ; þat U. *þat I*] I T ; my lyf H.
39. *But—O*] ȝe, ȝit a H ; ȝa, & ȝet a T; And a U. *pers*] perkyn THU. *no*] sire H; TU *om*.
40. *assente*] Accorde U.
41. *ȝif*] þei T; þeiȝe U. *profreþ ou*] profre þe TU ; *presentiþ* þee H. *presentes or*] wiþ H.

42. *Takeþ*] Nyme TU. *in auenture*] an aunter TU. *ȝe mouwen*] þou mowe TU ; þou maist H.
45. *þou*] TU *om. þou schalt*] þou miȝt HU; shalt þou T.
46. *And—þiself*] And þat þou TU; & H. *of*] of þy HU. *and*] H *om*.
47. *beo*] be of TU. *or*] or of TU ; & H. *þi*] H *om. werkmen*] wicked men H.
48. *not—with*] wiþ none TU. *þou*] H *om. here*] ne here TU
49. *atte*] at þe HU ; at T. *suche*] for suche T (*badly*). *Men*] men þou U.
50. *þei ben*] it arn TU ; it beþ H. [*to* THU] V *om*.
52. *word*] wordis H.

¶ "And I schal A-paraile me," qu*o*d pe*r*kin · "In pilgrimes wyse, 53
And wende wi*th* ou þe rihte wei · til ȝe treuþe fynde."
He caste on his cloþes · I-clouted and I-hole,
His Cokeres and his Coffus · for Colde of his nayles,
He heng an Hoper on his Bac · In stude of a Scrippe,
A Busschel of Bred corn · he bringeþ þer-Inne : 58
"For I wol souwen hit my-self · and seþþen wi*th* ou wende.
For hose helpeþ me to heren · or eny þing to swynken,
He schal haue, beo vr lord · þe more huyre in heruest,
And make him murie wi*th* þe Corn · hose hit euere bi-grucccheþ.
And alle ku*n*nes Craftus men · þat cunne lyuen wi*th* treuþe, 63
I schal fynden hem heore fode · þat Feiþfuliche lyuen ;
¶ Saue Iacke þe Iogelour · And Ionete of þe stuyues,
And Robert þe Ribaudour · for his Rousti wordes.
Treuþe tauhte hit me ones · and bad me telle hit forther,
Deleantur de libro · [I ne shulde not dele wiþ hem,] 68
Holi churche is holden of hem · no tiþe to taken ;

Piers gets ready to go, and takes with him corn to sow,

promising that all who help him shall have the more hire in harvest,

and that he will find all their food,

except Jack the Jongleur, and Janet of the stews, and Robert the tale-teller, a worthless set.

53. *me*] U *om. pilgrimes*] pilgrym T ; a palme*r*ys H.
54. *wende*] U *om. ou—rihte*] ȝow þe TU ; þee on þe H. *ȝe—fynde*] ȝe fynde treuthe U ; we fynde treuþe TH.
55. *I-hole*] hole TU. H *reads*, He cast on his cloutid cloþis & his olde cokeris.
56. *His cokeres*] H *om.* (see l. 55). *coffus*] coffis also H ; cuffis T ; cuffes U.
57. *He*] And T. *an*] his THU. *on—bac*] at his hals T ; on his rugge H. *stude*] stede THU. *a*] his U.
58. *busschel*] boyschel H. *he bringeþ*] brouȝte he T ; he brouȝte H ; bryng me U.
59. *myself*] my-self, quoþ he H. *with ou*] wile I THU.
60. *For hose*] And who-so THU. *heren*] eren T ; erie HU. *to*] TU *om.*
61. *He*] TU *om. huyre*] here T ; mede U. *in*] at U.

62. *with—corn*] þerwith U. *euere*] THU *om.*
63. *kunnes craftus*] manere craftis H ; kyne crafty TU. *with*] in THU.
64. *heore*] THU *om. þat*] H *om. Feiþfuliche*] skilfulliche U. *lyuen*] to lyuen H.
65. *Ionete*] Ienot H. *of*] at U. *stuyues*] styves H ; stywes U ; stewis T.
66. *Robert*] Robyn TU.
67. *tauhte hit*] tolde THU. *me*] me þus U. *telle*] teche H. *forther*] forþ T.
68. *I have made this an allit. line, as it stands in* T ; V *has only* Deleantur de libro viuencium ; H *has the whole quotation* Deleantur—scribantur, *and omits* 69, 70; U *has* deleantur de libro viuencium y schulde noght dele with hem ; *which is too long.*
69. H *omits. Holi*] For holy TU.

78 PIERS MAKES HIS WILL AND TESTAMENT. [PASS. VII.

Et cum Iustis non Scribantur ;
þei ben a-scaped good þrift · god hem amende !"

Piers' wife is named Work-when-time-is, his daughter is Do-as-you-are-bid,

Dame [werche]-whon-tyme-is · Hette Pers Wyf,
 His douhter hette do-riht-so- · or-þi-dame-wol-þe-
 bete,   72

and his son is Obey-your-king.

His sone hette Soffre-þi-souereyns- · for-to-han-heor-
 wille-
And-deeme-hem-not-for-ȝif-þou-do- · þou-schalt-hit-deore-
 abugge.
[" Let god worþe wiþ al · for so his woord techiþ ;]

Piers says he is old, and must make his will.

For nou Icham old and hor · and haue of myn owne,
To Penaunce and to pilgrimage · I wol passe with þis
 oþure.
For-þi I wole, ar I Wende · write my Testament.
In dei nomine, Amen · I make hit mi-seluen.

THE TESTAMENT. "I bequeath my soul to Him that best deserves it,

He schal haue my soule · þat best haþ deseruet,   80
And defende hit from þe fend · for so I beo-leeue,
Til I come to myn A-Countes · as my Crede me telleþ,
To ha Reles and Remission · on þat Rental I be-leeue.

and my body to the church, that takes tithe of my corn.

þe Chirche schal haue my Careyne · And kepe mi
 Bones ;
For of my Corn and Catel · heo Craueþ þe Tiþe.   85
I Payede him prestly · for peril of my soule,

---

tiþe] tiþes T.   taken] asken T ; axen U.
 70. H omits.   þrift] Auntir T ; auntour U.   god] now god T.
 71. [werche THU] V om.   Hette—wyf] piers wyf hatte THU.
 72. so] T om.   wol] shal TU.
 73. for to] to TU.
 74. do] doist H ; dost TU.   deore abugge] dere abigge TH ; sore abie U.
 75. From T; also in HU.   worþe] wurche U.
 76. nou] now HU ; T om.   Icham] I am THU.   and hor] and hoor U; H om.   haue] y-now haue H.
 77. I wol] wile I T.   þis] TU om.
 78. Forþi] For U.   ar] er TU; or H.   write] do writen U ; do wyte (sic)

T. testament] bequest T ; byquestes U.
 79. In—amen] In þe name of god H (which has here in margin, In dei no.).
 80. He] For he TU.
 81. I] is my U.
 82. myn] his THU.   me telleþ] me techiþ TU ; techiþ H.
 83. ha] haue THU.   reles] a relese H.   and] and a H.   on] of H.   I beleeue] I leue T; for euer H.
 84. kepe] kepe þer H.
 85. corn—catel] catel & my corn H.   heo craueþ] I crauide T.   tiþe] tiþes TU.   heo] I T; he HU.
 86. I payede] I haue paied H ; It payd it U ; And payede T.   him] U om.

[PASS. VII.] MANY SET TO WORK IN EARNEST.

He is holden, Ich hope · to haue me in Muynde,
And munge me in his memorie · Among alle cristene. 88
¶ Mi wyf schal haue þat I won · with treuþe, and no more, *My wife shall have my lawful winnings, for my debts are all paid.*
And dele A-mong my Frendes · and my deore children.
For þauh I dye þis day · my dettes beoþ I-quit ;
I Bar hom þat I Borwede · er I to bedde eode, 92
And with þe Residue and þe Remenaunt · by þe Rode of Chestre ! *With the residue will I worship Truth, and be His pilgrim."*
I wol Worschupe þer-Wiþ · Treuþe in my lyue,
And ben his pilgrym atte plouȝ · for pore Mennes sake.
Mi plouh-pote schal be my pyk · and posshen atte Rootes, 96
And helpe my coltre to kerue · and close þe vorwes."
Now is Pers and þe pilgrimes to þe plouh I-fare ; *Piers and the pilgrims set about ploughing, and many workmen help him.*
To heren þis half-Acre · helpen him ful monye.
Dykers and Deluers · Dikeden vp þe Balkes ; 100
þer-with was perkyn a-payed · And preisede hem ȝerne.
Oþur werk-men þer weren · þat Wrouȝten ful monye,
Vche Mon in his maner · Made him to done ;
And Summe, to plese perkyn · pykeden vp þe weodes.
¶ At heiȝ prime perkyn · lette þe plouȝ stonde, 105 *At high prime Piers looked at*
While þat he ouer-seȝe him-self · ho þat best wrouhte ;

87. *in*] in his U. *muynde*] mynde TU.
88. *munge*] monewe T ; mynwe H ; menewe U.
89. *with treuþe*] trewliche U.
90. *Frendes*] children H. *deore children*] frendis boþe H.
91. *dye—day*] deiȝe to day TU ; deied to day H. *Iquit*] quyt TH ; yquytte U.
92. *to—eode*] went to bedde H. *eode*] ȝede TU.
93. *with þe*] wiþ U. *Remenaunt*] remelaunt H.
94. *in*] be U.
95. *atte*] at his U ; at þe T.
96. *plouh-pote*] plowbat H ; plow U. *pyk*] pykstaf U ; pilgrimstaf H. *and—atte*] & putte at þe T ; picche vp þe U ; to posse at þe H.
97. *vorwes*] forewis T ; forwis H ; furwes U.
98. *and—pilgrimes*] þe pilgryme H. *Ifare*] faren THU.
99. *heren*] erien TU. *þis*] þe U ; his H. *ful*] THU om.
100. *dikeden*] dykeþ T ; dyggen U ; diȝten H. *balkes*] baukis H.
101. *hem*] hem ful H.
102. *þat*] & T. *monye*] faste THU.
103. *Vche*] Eche TH ; Euery U. *in*] on TU. *him*] hymself T.
104. *vp*] out U.
105. *At—prime*] At hye prime of þe day U ; An hast þen H. *perkyn*] piers U ; peris T.
106. *While—ouerseȝe*] To ouersen hem TU ; to ouerse H.

He schulde ben huyred þer-aftur · whon heruest tyme come.

¶ Þenne seten summe · And songen atte ale, 108
And holpen him to herien · wiþ "Hey! trolly-lolly!"

¶ "Now, be þe prince of paradys" · quaþ pers þo in wraþþe,

"Bote 3e Rysen þe raþer · and Rape 3ow to worche,
Schal no greyn þat heer groweþ · gladen ow at neode,
And þauh 3e dyen for de-faute · þe deuel haue þat Recche!" 113

¶ Þenne weore þe faytors a-ferd · And feynede hem blynde,
And summe leiden þe legges a-liri · as suche losels cunne,
And playneden hem to pers · with suche pitouse wordes:
"We haue no lymes to labore with · vr lord we hit þonken, 117

Bote we preyeþ for ou, pers · and for oure plouh boþe,
þat God for his grace · oure greyn multiplye,
And 3elde ow for oure Almus · þat 3e 3iuen vs here! 120
For we mowe nouþur swynke ne swete · such seknes vs eileþ."

¶ "3if hit beo soþ þat 3e seyen," quod pers · "sone I schal a-spye!
3e beoþ wastors, I wot · and treuþe wot þe soþe!

---

107. *He*] þei H; TU *om.*
108. *atte ale*] at þe ale T; at þe nale HU.
109. *him*] TU *om. to herien*] ere þe half akir T; to erye þe halue acre U. *hey—lolly*] dieu sa dame emme U.
110. *Now*] TU *om.*
111. *þe*] vp þe H.
112. *heer*] H *om.*
113. *þauh*] 3if U. *defaute*] þe defaut H; doel T; dool U. *haue*] hange U.
114. *þe*] þer H; TU *om. aferd*] fele H. *and*] þat H.
115. *And*] TU *om. þe legges*] here lege T; þe leg U. *aliri*] a lery TH; a lyry U. *losels*] lorellis T.

116. *hem*] U *om.*
117. *no lymes*] none hondis T. *vr*] oure H. *vr—þonken*] lord, ygracid be 3e T; lord, y-graced be þe U.
118. *ou*] 3ow TU; þee H. *oure*] 3oure TU; þy H.
119. H *omits. for*] of T. *oure*] 3oure TU.
120. H *omits. for*] of TU. *oure*] 3oure TU. *almus*] almesse T; almes U.
121. *nouþur*] not T. *swynke ne swete*] swete ne swinke U. *seknes*] feblesse U.
122. *soþ*] so U. *þat 3e seyen*] HU *om. sone—schal*] I shal it sone TU.
123. *wot*] wot wel TU.

PASS. VII.] ONE OF THE IDLERS IS CONTUMACIOUS. 81

Icham his holde hyne · and ouȝte him to warne 124
Whuche wastors In world · his werk-Men distruyȝen.
Ȝe eten þat þei schulden eten · þat [heren] for vs alle ;
Bote Treuþe schal techen ow · his Teeme for to dryue, "Truth shall teach you to drive his team, to sow, and to scare crows ;
Boþe to sowen and to setten · and sauen his tilþe, 128
Gaste Crowen from his Corn · and kepen his Beestes,
Or ȝe schulle ete Barly Bred · and of þe Brok drynke.
Bote heo beo blynde or broke-schonket · or bedreden liggen, [f. 399 a. col. 2.] but those who are really blind I will help.
þei schul haue as good as I · so me god helpe, 132
[Til god of his grace · gare [hem] to arise].
¶ Ancres and Hermytes · þat holdeþ hem in heore Celles Anchorites and hermits I will feed, but only once a day,
Schulen habben of myn Almus · Al þe while I liue,
I-nouh vche day at Non · but no more til a morwe, 136
Leste þe Fend and heore flesch · fouleden heore soules ;
Ones at Noon Is I-nouȝ · þat no werk ne vseþ, for once is enough."
He abydeþ wel þe bet · þat Bommeþ not to ofte."

Þ Enne wastours gunne arise · *and* wolden han I-fouhte ; Then the wasters began to resist, and one of them threatened Piers,
To Pers þe plouh Mon · [one] profrede his gloue,
A Brutiner, A Braggere · A-Bostede him Alse, 142
And bad go pisse him w*ith* his plouh · pillede screwe !

124. *Icham*] And I am TU. *holde*] olde TU. *and*] I U.
125. *Whuche*] Suche TH; Whiche U. *In*] in þis TU; in þe H.
126. *þei*] I T. *[heren] Such should be the reading ;* eren T; erien HU; V *has* swynken. *See* ll. 60, 99. *vs*] ȝow H.
128. *to—setten*] to setten & to sowen TH; setten & sowe U. *tilþe*] telþe TH.
129. *Gaste crowen*] Chase gees TU. *from his*] fro þe HU.
130. *Brok*] brod T (*wrong*).
131. *heo*] he TU; ȝe H. *broke-schonket—liggen*] bedrede or ellis broke-shankid H.
132. *þei—haue*] þei shuln ete T; ȝe schul eten U; þen shulle ȝe haue H. *good—I*] I seie U.
133. *In* T *is here an extra line,* Til god of his grace · gare hym to arise ; *where* hym *should be* hem.
135. *Al—while*] while þat H.
136. *but*] & H. *til a*] til on þe T; til þe H; er U.
137. *þe—flesch*] his flessh & þe fend T; þe feend and his flesche U. *fouleden—soules*] foulide his soule T; folewen here soulis H; folewed togidre U.
138. *ne*] U *om*.
139. *Bommeþ*] ne bommeþ H.
140. *wastours gunne*] gan þe wastour T; gan wastour U; bygan wastour to H.
141. [*one* H] he TU; V *has* And.
142. *Brutiner*] bretoner T; brytoner UH. *A-Bostede*] he bostide T; bostide U. *alse*] also THU.
143. *bad*] bade hym H. *with*] & H. *pillede*] olde pilede H. *screwe*] shrewe TH; schrewe U.

	" For we wolen habbe of þi Flour · wol þou so nulle þou,
	And of þi Flesch fecche · whon þat vs lykeþ, 145
	[And make vs merye þerwiþ · maugre þi chekes !"]
who prayed the knight to keep his promise.	¶ Þenne Pers plouh-mon · playnede him to þe kniht,
	To kepen him as Couenaunt was · from cursede schrewes,
	From wastors þat wayten · winners to schende. 149
The knight sternly warns them.	Curteisliche þe kniht · as his kuynde wolde,
	Warnede wastors · and wissede hem do betere ;
	" Or ȝe schul a-bugge hit bi [þe] lawe · bi þe Ordre þat
	I bere ! " 152
But one of them cared nothing for Piers or the knight, and threatened them.	¶ " I was not wont to worche," quod a wastour · " ȝit
	wol I not biginne ! "—
	And lette luytel of þe lawe · and lasse of þe kniht,
	And countede pers at a peose · and his plouh boþe,
	And Manasede him and his men · whon þat þei next
	metten. 156
Piers swears he will punish them yet, and calls in Hunger.	" Nou be þe peril of my soule," quaþ Pers þe plouh-Mon,
	I schal a-peiren ow alle · for oure proude wordes !"
	And hoped aftur hunger þo · þat herde him atte furste:
	" A-wrek me on þis wastors," quod pers · " þat þis world
Hunger caught Waster, and	schendeþ ! " 160
	¶ Hongur in haste · hente [wastor] bi þe mawe,

144. Wilt þou, nilt þou, we wile haue · oure wil of þis flour T ;
Woltou, neltou, we wole haue · y-now of þy floure H ;
Wil þou, nyl þou, we wol · haue of þi floure U.
145. of] T om. fecche] fecche awey TU ; & þy fysch H. whon þat] whanne T; whan so U.
146. From U; also in TH.
150. þe] þo þe H. kniht] kniȝt þanne TU.
151. wastors] þe wastour T ; wastour U. wissede] bade H. hem] hym TU. do betere] betere TU ; go werche H.
152. ȝe schul] þou shalt TU ; þei shulde H. a-bugge hit] abigge TH ;

abye U. [þe THU] V om. ordre] lord (!) U. I bere] he bere H ; I welde U.
153. a] THU om. ȝit] nowe TU.
154. luytel] liȝt THU.
155. peose] pese TH. countede—peose] bad piers go pisse U.
156. þat] THU om.
157. þe plouhmon] I shall appeire ȝow alle THU.
158. THU omit ; see l. above.
159. hoped] houpide T; howpide U ; huntid H. þo] THU om.
160. Awrek] Wreke UH. þis (1)] TH om. þis (2)] þe U. schendeþ] apeiriþ T.
161. Hongur] & hunger U. haste] haste þanne T. [wastor] wastour THU ; V has wastors.

And wrong hi*m* so be þe wombe · þat boþe his eȝen _{wruug and buffeted him so,}
watreden,
And Buffetede þe [brutiner] · aboute boþe his chekes ;
He lokede lyk a Lanterne · al his lyf After.   164
He Beot so þe Boyes · he barst neih heore Ribbes,
Nedde Pers wiþ a peose lof · I-preyed him to leue ;   _{that Piers had to interfere, and}
And wi*th* a Benene Bat · I-bot hem by-twene,   167   _{beat Hunger off.}
And hutte hongur þer-wi*th* · A-midde boþe his lippes,
And he bledde in-to þe Bodiward · a Bolleful of gruwel ;
Nedde þe Fisicien furst · defendet him water
To Abate þe Barli bred · and þe Benes I-grou*n*de,
þei hedden beo ded bi þis day · and doluen al warm.

Enne Faytors for fere · flowen to Bernes,   173   _{Then the shirkers flew to the barns}
And flapten on wi*th* fleiles · from morwe til euen,   _{to thrash ;}
þat Honger nas not hardi · vp for to loke,
For A potful of peosun · þat pers hedde I-mad.   176
An Hep of Hermytes · henten heom spades,   _{Hermits seized spades and dug.}
And doluen drit *and* donge · to dutte honger oute.
¶ Blynde and Bedraden · weore Botned a þousent,   _{The blind, bedridden, and}
þat lyȝen for blynde · and for broke-legget   180

162. *And—wombe*] U *om*. *boþe—watreden*] al watride his eiȝen TU.
163. [*brutiner* (see l. 142)] bretoner TH; brytoner U; V *has* boye (*by mistake*); *see l*. 165. *boþe his*] þe TU.
164. *He*] þat he THU.
165. *He—boyes*] He beet hem so boþe TH; And beet hym boþe U. *he—neih*] þat he brast ner T; and brak ner*e* U. *ribbes*] mawis THU.
166. *Nedde*] Ne hadde HU; Nhadde T. *wiþ*] but T. *I-preyed—leue*] ypreied hem to lyue H; þei preyede hym beleue T; prayed hym by-lyue U.
167. *benene bat*] bene batte T; beny batte U. *I-bot hem*] he hadde TU ; ȝede hem H.
168. *hutte*] hitte THU. *þer-with*] U *om*. *boþe his*] hise T ; þe U.
169. *he—bodiward*] bledde in-to þe bodyward TU ; made hym blede

inward H. *gruwel*] growel TU ; gruel H.
170. *Nedde*] Ne hadde TU ; Nadde H. *furst*] U *om*.
173. *þenne*] THU *om*. *fere*] ferde þen H. *to*] into THU.
174. *flapten*] flappid H ; flappe U ; flatte T. *morwe*] morne UH.
175. *nas*] was TU. *not*] noght so U. *vp for*] on hem for T ; on hem H ; ones on hem U.
176. *potful*] potel THU. *peosun*] pesen H ; pesyn U ; pecis T. *hedde I-mad*] let make H.
177. *An Hep*] & an hepe H ; In helpe T. *heom*] hem TU ; here H.
178. *dutte—oute*] ditte out hunger TH ; dryuen hungir out U.
179. *bedraden*] bedrede T ; blereeyȝed U. *botned*] botind T ; aboute U.
180. T *omits*. *for broke-legget*] brokelegged by þe lıye weie U.

lame received assistance.	Vppon softe sonenday · bi þe heiȝe weye; Hungur hem helede · wiþ an hot Cake.
Lame men asked to keep Piers' beasts,	¶ Lome mennes limes · weore lyþet þat tyme, 183 And bi-come knaues · to kepe pers beestes, And preyeden for Charite · with pers for to dwelle, [Al] for Couetyse of his corn · to caste a-wey hunger.
for which he gave them meat.	¶ Pers was proud þer-of · And put hem in offys, 187 And ȝaf hem mete and moneye · as þei mihte deseruen.
Then had Piers pity, yet fears they will do ill when Hunger departs,	¶ Þenne hedde peers pite · and preiede hunger to wende Hom to his oune hurde · And holden him þer for euere. ¶ "And ȝit I preye þe," quod pers · "er þou passe henne, Of Bidders and of beggers · what is best to done? 192 I wot wel whon þou art I-went · þei wol worchen ful ille;
though they are meek enough now.	And Mischef hit makeþ · þei beoþ so meke nouþe, And for de-faute of foode · þus faste þei worchen; And heo beoþ my blodi breþeren · for god bouȝte vs alle. Treuþe tauhte me ones · to louen hem vchone, 197 And helpen hem of alle þyng · aftur þat hem neodeþ.
So he asks Hunger to give him advice.	¶ Ȝit wolde I witen ȝif þou wustest · what were þe beste, And hou I mihte A-Maystren hem · and maken hem to worche." 200

181. T *omits*; U *omits part (see l.* 180). *sonenday*] sonedaies H.
182. *hot*] oten H; ote U.
183. *Lome*] And lame THU. *lyþet*] liþnid T; liþed HU.
185. *for*] hym for U; pur T. *pers*] hym U.
186. [*Al* THU] V *has* And, *repeated from* 184, 185. *caste*] chase TU.
187. *Pers*] & pieris THU. *þer-of*] þerfore H.
188. *deseruen*] asserue TU.
190. *Hom to*] Hom into TU; into H. *hurde*] erþe TH; ȝerde U. *for*] TU *om.*
191. *And ȝit*] Ac ȝet T; but H. *henne*] ferþere THU.

192. *bidders—beggers*] beggeris & bidderis T; beggeres and of bydderis U; bedreden & beggeris H. *is best*] best is T.
193. *I—I-went*] For I wot wel, be þou ywent T; I woot, be þou went H; For I wot wel by ȝe went U. *ful*] TU *om.*
194. *And*] TU *om. And—makeþ*] þy-self makiþ it iwis H. *þei*] hym T.
196. *And—breþeren*] þei boþ myne breþeren of one blood H. *heo beoþ*] it ben TU. *bouȝte*] made H.
198. *aftur—hem*] þat hem of T; what þat hem U.
199. *ȝit—I*] now wolde I HU; I wolde T. *wustest*] wistest THU.
200. *And*] H *om.*

PASS. VII.] BEGGARS OUGHT TO HAVE ONLY COARSE FOOD. 85

"HEre nou," quod hunger · "and holde hit for wisdam,   *Hunger tells him to feed the able-bodied beggars with horse's bread and beans,*
Bolde Bidders and Beggers · þat mowen her mete bi-swinke,
With houndes bred and horse bred · hold vp heor hertes,
And Bamme hem with bones · for bollyng of heore wombes ;   204
And ȝif þe gomes grucchen · bidde hem go swynke,   *and to make them work.*
And þei schule soupe þe swettore · whon þei han hit deseruet.
And ȝif þou fyndest eny Freik · þat fortune haþ a-peiret   *Men who have been unfortunate should be comforted.*
With fuir, or with fals folk · fonde suche to knowe ;
Cumforte hem with þi Catel · for cristes loue of heuene,
Loue hem, and lene hem · so þe lawe of kuynde wole.
And alle manere of Men · þat þou mayȝt aspye,   211   *The needy and naked should be helped with meat and money.*
þat neodi ben, or naket · and nouȝt haue to spende,
With Mete or with Moneye · mak hem fare þe betere,   [f. 399 b. col. 1.]
Or with word or with Werk · while þat þou art here.
Mak þe Frendes þer-with · for so Seint Matheu techeþ,   Luke xvi. 9.
Facite vobis amicos de mammona iniquitatis."

¶ "I wolde not greue god," quod pers · "for al þe gold on ground ;   216   *Piers wants to know if it is right*

---

201. *for*] for a THU.
202. *bidders—beggers*] beggeris & bigge TU. *mete*] breed T. *biswinke*] swynke U.
203. *houndes bred*] houndes U. *hold—hertes*] holde þow here mawes H.
204. *And bamme*] And bane TU ; a-bane H. *bones*] benys U. *bollyng*] bolluynge TH ; swellynge U.
205. *And—þe*] ȝif eny H. *gomes*] gromes THU.
206. *þe*] T *om. swettore*] betere U. *han hit*] it haþ T ; haue H ; it han U.
207. *fyndest*] fynde THU.
208. *fuir*] fure H ; fyre U. *folk*] men THU. *to*] T *om. ;* forto H ; men to U.
210. *lene*] lone U. *so þe*] & so þe T ; for so H ; for so þe U. *wole*] wolde TU.

211—216. *These lines are in* U *made into only four lines, with omissions and false arrangements.*
211. *of*] H *om. mayȝt*] miȝte TH.
212. *neodi—or*] ben nedy & H. *nouȝt haue*] naue not H.
213. *or—moneye*] or mone T. *mak*] lete H. *mak—betere*] let make hem at ese T.
214. TU *omit.* H *has,* wiþ werke oþer wiþ wordis · whils þou art here.
215. H *puts the Lat. quotation before this line. mak þe*] And make þe T ; lat make þi U. *þerwith*] þermiþ T ; þermyde U. *seint—techeþ*] matheu vs techiþ TU ; seiþ þe gospel H.
216. TU *here corruptly arranged. greue*] wraþþe H. *gold—ground*] good-on erþe H. *on*] on þis T.

to make men work
Hunger refers him to Gen. iii. 19;

Miht I su*n*noles don as þou seist ?" · seide pers þenne.

¶ " ʒe, I be-hote þe," q*uo*d hu*n*ger · " or elles þe Bible lyʒeþ ;

Go to Genesis þe Ieaunt · e*n*gendrure of vs alle ;

In Sudore and swynk · þou schalt þi mete tilie, 220

And labre for þi lyflode' · for so vr lord hiʒte.

¶ And Sapie*n*s seiþ þe same · I saih hit in þe Bible ;

and to Prov. xx. 4.
' *Piger propter frigus* · no feld nolde he tilie,

He schal go bidde *and* begge · *and* no mo*n* beete his hu*n*ger.' 224

The slothful servant, Mat. xxv. 28; Lu. xix. 22, 24.
¶ Matheu þe Mo*n*nes face · he Mommeþ þeose wordes,

.1. talentu*m*
' *Seruus n*e*quam* hedde npnam · an*d* for he nolde hit vsen,

He hedde Maugre of his Maister · euere more aftur ;

Auferte ab illo mnam, & date illi, &c.]

besaunt
¶ He bi-nom hi*m* his npnam · for he nolde not worche,

And ʒaf hit hi*m* in haste · þat hedde ten bi-fore ; 229

And seþþen he þus seide · his seruau*n*s hit herden,

Mat. xxv. 29; Lu. xix. 26.
¶ He þat haþ schal haue · to helpe þ*er* neod is,

And he þat nouʒt haþ, nouʒt schal haue · ne no mon him helpe ; 232

---

217. *Miht*] May U. *I—don*] y do synles H.
218. *be-hote þe*] hote þe T; hote god U. *Bible*] book H.
219—221. H *arranges in the order* 220, 221, 219.
219. *Go to*] So i*n* TU ; V *has* Go to þe ; so seiþ H. *Ieaunt*] geaunt TU ; gent H. *engendrure*] gendrer H.
220. *sudore—swynk*] sudore &c., & swynke T ; *sudore uultus tui* swynke U ; sweting & swinking H. *tilie*] *begins next line in* TU
221. *hiʒte*] biddith UH.
222. H *omits. saih*] saiʒ T ; seic U.
223. *he*] TU *om. no—tilie*] *arare noluit* H ; no feld wolde tilie TU
224. *He—go*] þerfore he shal H. *bidde—begge*] begge and bidde U. *beete*] bete TU.
225. *þe*] wiþ þe T. *he mommeþ*] mowþed H ; nempniþ T. *he—wordes*] mouthith vs þe same U.
226. H reads, *Serue nequam, sciebas quia, &c.* þe wicked *s*eruaunt made a couenaunt, & for he nolde it vse. *npnam*] a *n*am TU.
227. *maugre*] a maugre T. *euere*] for euere T. *aftur*] þeraftir UH. *The Latin is in* H *only.*
228. *He bi-nom*] And benom TU ; & byraft H. *npnam*] nam TU ; besaunt H. *not*] TU *om.*
229. U *omits. hit*] T *om. ten*] ten þere T.
230. *þus*] THU *om. seide*] seide hym to þat H. *seruauns—herden*] *s*eruaunt it hadde T. *After this line* H *has* Omni habenti dabitur.
231. *neod is*] it nediþ H.
232. *nouʒt schal*] shal nouʒt TU. *no mon*] none shal H.

And he þat hopeþ forte haue · hit him beo bi-reuet.'
For kynde wit Wolde · þat vche mon wrouhte
Wiþ techinge or with tilynge · or trauaylynge of hondes,
Actyf lyf or Contemplatyf · Crist wolde hit alse.   236
For so seiþ þe Sauter · In Psalm of *beati omnes*,
    [*Labores manuum tuarum quia manducabis, &c.*]
¶ He þat get his fode her · with trauaylinge in Treuþe,
God ȝiueþ him his blessyng · þat his lyflode so swynkeþ."

"Yit I preye þe," quod pers · " par Charite, ȝif þou
    Conne   240
Eny lyf of leche Craft · lere hit me, my deore.
For summe of my seruauns · beoþ seke oþer-while,
Of alle þe wike heo Worcheþ not · so heor wombe akeþ."
¶ "I wot wel," quod Hungur · " What seknesse hem
    eileþ,   244
þei han I-Maunget ouur muche · þat makeþ hem grone
    ofte.
¶ Ac Ich hote þe," quod Hungur · "and þou þin hele
    wylne,
þat þou drynke no dai · til þou haue dynet sumwhat;
¶ Ete not, Ich hote þe · til hunger þe take,   248
And sende þe sum of his sauce · to sauer þe þe betere;

Marginalia:
Common sense tells men to work.
Ps. cxxvii. 2; (Vulg.)
Piers complains that some of his men are always ill.
Hunger says it comes from their over-eating.
They should not eat till they are hungry.

233. And þat he (he þat H) weniþ wel to haue · I wile it be hym bereuid T H U.
234. *For*] T H U *omit. mon*] wiȝt T. *vche mon*] euery man for his fode U.
235. U *omits. Wiþ*] oþer wiþ T H. *or—tilynge*]oþer tellinge T. *trauaylynge*] wiþ trauel H.
236. *Crist*] so crist H. *hit alse*] it were H; it were so U.
237. *For—In*] The sauter seiþ in þe T; þe sauter seith it in a U; H reads, as þe sauter hymself seiþ in a psalme. *The Latin is from* T H; *also in* U, *which adds*, beatus es, & bene tibi erit.
238. *get*] getiþ H U. *trauaylinge —Treuþe*] trauaile of his hondis T H U.
239. *him*] T *om. his lyflode*] here liflode here T; so his lyuelood H. *so swynkeþ*] so wynneþ T U; wynneþ H.
240. *þe*] U *om. Conne*] canst H; cunne U; kenne T.
241. *lyf*] life T; leef U; lessoun H. *lere*] lerne H; teche U. *hit*] H *om. my*] H *om.*
242. *oþer-while*] som tyme U.
243. *wike*] wyke T; weke H; wowke U. *heo*] T *om.*; þei H U.
245. *I-maunget*] mangid T H U. *muche*] mykil U. *hem*] U *om. grone ofte*] oft grone H.
246. *hote*] bidde U. *and*] as T U; ȝef H. *wylne*] wilnest T H; desirest U.
247. *til*] er T. *haue—sumwhat*] dyne sumwhat T U; haue ydyned H.
248. *Ete not*] And ete nouȝt T; And noght U. *hote*] bidde U. *til*] er T U.
249. *þe*] U *om. sum*] T H U *om.* þe þe betere] þi lippes T H; wiþ þi lippes U.

TEMPERANCE STARVES THE DOCTORS. [PASS. VII.

Keep sum til soper tyme · And [sit] þou not to Longe,
A-Rys vp ar appetyt · habbe I-ȝeten his Fulle.

They should not let Sir Surfeit sit beside them.
¶ Let not sir Surfet · sitten at þi Bord ; 252
Loue him nót, for he is a lechour · *and* likerous of Tonge,
And aftur mony Metes · his Mawe is a-longet.

Were men thus moderate, Physic would sell his cloak, and turn farm-labourer.
And ȝif þou diȝete þe þus · I dar legge boþe myn Eres,
þat Fisyk schal his Forred hod · for his [foode] sulle,
And eke his cloke of Calabre · wi*th* knappes of Gold,
And beo Fayn, be my Feiþ · his Fisyk to lete, 258
And leorne to labre wiþ lond · leste lyflode Faile ;
þer beoþ mo lyȝers þen leches · vr lord hem amende !
þei don men dyȝen þoruȝ heor drinke · er destenye wolde."

Piers thanks Hunger for such advice.
"BI seint Poul !" q*uo*d pers · "þeos beoþ p*r*ophitable wordes ! 262
þis is a loueli lesson · vr lord hit þe for-ȝelde !
Wend nou whon þi wille is · Wel þe beo for euere !"

Hunger says he must dine ere he goes away.
"I beo-hote þe," q*uo*d hungur · "heonnes nul I wende
Er I haue I-dynet bi þis day · and I-dronke boþe."

Piers says he has no geese or pigs, only cheese, curds,
¶ "I haue no peny," q*uo*d pers · "Poletes to bugge,
Nouþer gees ne grys · bote twey grene cheeses, 268
And a fewe Cruddes and Craym · and a þerf Cake,

---

250. *Keep*] And kep THU. *sum*] som-what U. [*sit* TU] V *and* H *have* faste, *which is clearly wrong.* þou] THU *om. to*] U *om.*
251. *vp*] U *om. habbe I-ȝeten*] haþ eten T ; haue eten HU. *Fulle*] fille THU.
253. *Loue*] Leue TU.
254. *mony*] many maner of T ; many maner U. *a-longet*] alongid TU *is a-longet*] H *om.*
255. *diȝete*] diete U ; vsest H. *legge—Eres*] ley myn armes T ; leye my lyf H ; leyn myn eres U.
256. [*foode* THU] V *has* lyflode, *which spoils the metro ; see* l. 259.
257. *his—of*] his cloke wiþ T ; his clokis of H ; þe clokis of U. *with knappes*] & þe knoppis TU ; & his coppis H.

258. U *om. Fayn—my*] ful fayn in H.
259. *lond*] hondes U. *lyflode*] liflode hym TU ; his lyuelode H.
260. *beoþ—lyȝers*] arn mo liȝeris TU ; ne beþ no*n* more losels H. *vr lord*] oure lord H ; lord T ; god U.
261. *þoruȝ*] with U. *drinke*] drynkes T. *wolde*] it wolde TU.
262. *Poul*] pe*r*nel TH. *pers*] pe*r*kyn U. *beoþ*] arn TU.
263. *vr lord*] lord T ; crist U. *hit*] H *om.*
264. *nou*] H *om. wel—beo*] þat wel be þou T ; þat wel be þe U. *for*] THU *om.*
265. *beo-hote*] hote U. *þe*] god T.
267. *I haue*] & y naue H. *peny*] penyes U. *Poletes*] pulettis T ; pultys U. *to*] with to U.
269. *And*] T *om. a—Cake*] non

And a lof of Benes and Bren · I-Bake for my Children. *cream, an oat-cake, and a loaf of beans and bran,*
¶ And I sigge, bi my soule · I haue no salt Bacon,
Ne no Cokeneyes, bi Crist · Colopus to maken.   272
¶ Bot I haue porettes *and* percyl · and moni Col- *also leeks, parsley, and cabbages,*
plontes
And eke a Cou, and a Calf · and a Cart-Mare
To-drawe a-feld my donge · Whil þe drouhþe lasteþ.
¶ Bi þis lyflode I mot lyuen · til lammasse tyme ; 276 *which must last out till harvest.*
Bi þat, Ich hope forte haue · heruest in my Croft ;
þenne may I dihte þi dyner · as þe deore lykeþ."
¶ Al þe pore peple · pese-coddes fetten, *The poor people brought peascods, beans, and cherries to feed Hunger.*
Bake Benes in Bred · þei brouhten in heor lappes, 280
Chibolles, Cheef mete · and ripe chiries monye,
And proferde pers þis *present* · to plese wi*th* hungur.
¶ Honger eet þis in haste · and asked aftur more. *Hunger wanted more, and they brought peas and leeks,*
þenne þis folk for fere · fetten him monye 284
Poretes, and Peosen · for þei him plese wolden ;
From þat tyme þat þulke weore eten · take he schulde *to keep him away till harvest.*
his leue
Til hit to heruest hiȝede · þ*a*t newe corn com to chep-
ynge. 287

oþer cake T ; an hauir cake U ; two hauere cakis H.
270. *And*] T *om.* *And—Bren*] al of benys & of bran H.
271. *And*] And ȝit U. *haue*] naue H.
272. *cokeneyes*] cokenay T ; cokeney U. *colopus*] colopis T ; colhoppis H ; colopes with U.
273. *porettes—percyl*] persile & poret T ; per*s*il, porrette U ; per*s*ely & poretis H. *col-*] cole- T ; caul- H.
274. *eke*] H *om.*
275. *afeld my*] on feld my T ; on felde U ; a-feld þe H.
276—278. U *omits.*
276. *mot*] most H.
278. *þenne*] And þanne T.
279. *fetten*] þei fetten HU.
280. H *reads*, benys & bacoun wiþ hem þei brouȝten. *Bake—bred*] Benes & blake (*sic*) applis T ; Benys and baken apples U. *lappes*] lappe T.
281. *Inserted by* H *after* 284. *Chibolles*] chibollis T ; chibols H ; chybolys U. *Cheef mete*] & *v*hirinell*is* T ; chernelys U ; chesteyns H. *ripe*] riche T. *monye*] also H.
282. *proferde*] offriden H. *þis*] a T. *with*] þerewiþ TU.
283. *Honger*] And hungir T. *eet þis*] hente þis T ; eet hit H ; ete al þis U.
284. *þenne þis*] & þe H. *fere*] ferd H.
285. T *omits.* H *reads*, Poretis & peris · applis & plowmes ; U *reads*, Grene porret and pesen · to poysen him þei þouȝte.
286. THU *omit.*
287. Be þat it neiȝide ner herues newe corn com to chepynge (towne U) TU ; by þat it neiȝed heruest, þat newe corn riped H.

But in harvest-time they fed Hunger plentifully,	Þenne was þat folk fayn · and tedde hunger ȝeorne With good Ale, and glotonye · and gart him to slepe. And þo nolde þe wastor worche · but wandren aboute, Ne no Beggere eten Bred · þat Benes Inne coome,
[f. 399 b. col. 2.] and beggars would eat only the finest bread.	Bote Coket and Cler Matin · an of clene whete ; 292 Ne non halfpeny Ale · In none wyse drynke, Bote of þe Beste and þe Brouneste · þat Brewesters sullen.
Labourers were dainty,	¶ Laborers þat haue no lond · to liuen on Bote heore honden, Deyne not to dyne a day · niht-olde wortes. 296 Mai no peny Ale hem paye · ne no pece of Bacun,
and wanted fresh flesh and fried fish,	Bote hit weore Fresch Flesch · or elles Fisch I-Friȝet, Boþe chaud and pluschaud · for chele of heore Mawe.
and grumbled about wages,	¶ Bote he beo heihliche I-huret · elles wol he chide, Þat he was werkmon I-wrouȝt · warie þe tyme, 301 And Corse ȝerne þe kyng · and al his Counseil aftur, Suche lawes to loke · laborers to chaste.
except when hungry.	¶ Ac while hunger was Mayster heer · wolde þer non chyde, 304 Ne striue aȝeyn þe statues · so steorneliche he lokede.

288. *was*] were H. *þat*] THU *omit*. *ȝeorne*] with þe beste TU ; fast H.
289. *and gart*] he gart T ; & made H ; þei dyden U.
290. *nolde—wastor*] nolde wastour not T ; wolde wastour not H ; wolde no wastours U. *wandren*] wandrite T ; wandriden U ; wandrid H.
291. *Beggere*] lengere U. *eten*] ete no U. *Inne coome*] comen ynne U.
292. *and*] or TU. *an*] or TU ; & H.
293, 294. H *omits*.
293. *none*] no T.
294. *and þo*] and of U.
295. *haue*] hadde U. *to—honden*] but lyue on here handis T ; but lyue by hemsilue H ; to lyue by but here handes U.
296. *Deyne*] Deyneþ T ; Deygned U. *not*] H *om*. *dyne—day*] dynen wiþ U.
298. *hit weore*] ȝif it be T ; it be UH. *Fresch*] rostid U. *elles*] T *om.*; fresch H.
299. *Boþe*] And TU. *chele*] chillyng THU. *heore mawe*] his mawe T ; here mawes H ; here chekys U.
300. H *reads*, but þei be hiȝely y-huyred, ellis wollen þei chide. *he*] ȝif he T. *heihliche*] lyliche U (*wrong*).
301—304. U *omits*.
301. *he was*] þei were H. *Iwrouȝt*] bycome H.
302. *Corse ȝerne*] þanne curse T ; curse H. *his*] þe T.
303. *chaste*] chastise T.
304. *mayster heer*] here maister T *þer non*] þei not H.
305. *statues*] statut T ; statutes UH.

¶ I warne ȝou, alle werk-men · winneþ while ȝe mowe, A warning to workmen,
Hunger hiderward aȝeyn · hiȝeþ him ȝeorne.   307
¶ He wole a-wake þorw watur · þe wastours alle,   and a prophecy of famine.
Er Fyue ȝer ben folfult · such Famyn schal a-Ryse
þorw Flodes and foul weder · Fruites schul fayle ;
And so seiþ [Saturne] · and sent vs to warne.   311

U *reads*, And stryue aȝens þe statutes · and sternely loken.
306. *alle*] THU *omit. winneþ*] wercheþ H.
307. *Hunger*] For hungir THU. *aȝeyn*] THU *om. hiȝeþ—ȝeorne*] hastiþ hym faste T ; hastiþ ful fast H ; hyeth hym faste U.
308. *wole—watur*] shal awake þis water T ; wol wade þurȝ watris H ; schal awake ȝour wele U.   þe] his U ; TH *om. alle*] to chaste THU.
309. *fyue*] fewe H. *schal*] wol H.
310. *flodes*] flood T ; tempestes U. *and*] oþer þoruȝ T. *weder*] wederis TU. *fruites*] flodis U. *fayle*] falle TU.
311. [*Saturne*] satourne T ; saturne HU ; V *has* Saturnes. *sent vs*] sente ȝow T ; sende ȝow H ; sendith ȝow U.

PASSUS VIII.

[Passus Octauus de Visione, vt prius.]

<small>Truth bids Piers labour before the famine comes,</small>

TReuþe herde telle her-of · And to Pers sende,
To taken his teeme · and tilyen þe eorþe;
And purchasede him a pardoun · *A pena et a culpa*
For him, and for his heires · euer more aftur.   4
And bad holden hem at hom · and heren heore leyȝes,

<small>and promises pardon to all who help him to work.</small>

And al þat euere hulpen him · to heren or to sowen,
Or eny maner mester · þat mihte Pers helpen,
Part in þat pardoun · þe Pope haþ I-grauntid.   8

<small>Just kings and knights pass lightly through purgatory.</small>

¶ Kynges and knihtes · þat kepen holi churche,
And Rihtfuliche Rulen · þe Reame and þe peple,
Han pardoun þorw Purgatorie · to passen ful sone,
Wiþ patriarkes in paradys · to pleyen þer-aftur.   12

<small>Bishops who observe the commandments,</small>

¶ Busschops þat blessen · and boþe þe lawes cunnen,
Lokeþ on þat on lawe · and lereþ men þat oþer,

Title; from T. Also called P. octauus *in* HUD.
2. *tilyen—eorþe*] his erþe tilien T.
3. *purchasede*] purchace TH; purchasen U. *a*] U *om*.
4. *for his*] his U. *euer*] for euere T. *aftur*] þeraftir U.
5. *holden hem*] hym holde hym THU. *heore leyȝes*] his laiȝes TU; here leies H.
6. *al*] þo T. *euere*] THU *om*. *him*] T *om*. *or*] & H.
7. *or eny*] & alle H. *maner*] maner of T. *mester*] myster men H. *mihte Pers*] piers myghte U.

8. *in*] of H. *þat*] þe T. *Igraunted*] hem grauntid TU.
9. *kepen*] helpen U.
10. *Rihtfulliche*] rewfulliche (!) T. *rulen—þe*] in reaum rewliþ þe T; in here rewme rewlen here U; reulen þe rewmes & þe H.
11. *ful*] wel TU.
12. *pleyen*] pleyen hem U.
13. *þe*] TU *om*. *cunnen*] kenne TU; knowen H.
14. *þat on*] þat o T; þe to U. *lereþ*] lere T; leren H; lerne U. *þat oþer*] þe tothir U.

And bereþ hem boþe on heore bac · as heore baner scheweþ,
And precheþ heore persouns · þe peril of sunne,   16   *and preach to their parsons the peril of sin,*
Hou heore schabbede schep · schal heore wolle saue,   *sit with the Apostles at doomsday.*
Han Pardoun with þe Apostles · whon þei passen hennes,
And atte day of dom · with hem on deis setten.

¶ Marchau[n]s in þis Margin · hedden mony ȝeres,   20   *Merchants have not plenary pardon,*
Bote non *A pena et a culpa* · þe pope nolde hem graunte,
For þei holdeþ not heore haly-day · as holy churche techeþ,   *because they keep not holidays and swear.*
And for þei sworen bi heore soule · —"so God hem moste helpe !"—
Aȝeyn heore clene Concience · heore catel to sulle.   24

Bote vndur his secre seal · Treuþe sende a lettre,   *Truth bade them trade fairly and build hospitals,*
And Bad hem Bugge Boldely · what hem best lykede,
And seþþen sullen hit a-ȝeyn · And saue þe wynnynge,
And make *Meson deu* þer-with · Meseyse to helpe,   28
And wikkede wones · wihtly to amende ;
¶ Beete Brugges a-Boute · þat to-Broke were,   *repair broken bridges, and dower maidens,*
Marie Maydens · or Maken hem Nonnes ;
¶ Pore widewes þat wolde beo · none wyues aftur,   32
Fynde suche heore foode · for Godes loue of heuene ;

15. *baner scheweþ*] dedis shewyn H.
16. *persouns*] paryschens U.
17. *heore*] þat TU; þat here H. *schabbede*] shabbide TH ; scabbide U. *schal*] schulde H.
19. *And atte*] And at þe T ; On þe U ; at þe H. *with—deis*] at here deis to TU ; on hiȝe deis to H.
20. *þis*] þe THU. *mony ȝeres*] ȝeris many H.
21. *nolde hem*] wolde hym T ; wolde U.
22. *holdeþ*] helde T. *heore haly-day*] here haly-dayes TH ; þe haly-day U.
23. *sworen*] swere THU. *soule*] soulis H. *so*] & so T. *hem moste*] muste hem TU ; shulde hem H.
24. *heore*] THU *om*. *catel*] ware U.
25. *sende*] sente hym T ; sente U.

26. *hem* (1) hym] T. *hem best*] þat hym T. *lykede*] likeþ TU.
27. U *omits*.
28. *make*] þe U (*wrong*). *meson deu*] mesonis deux T ; mesoun dieux H. *meseyse*] myseises T ; mesels H ; þe myseyse U.
29. U reads, Wightliche wikkide weyes · for to don amende. *And—wones*] Wykkide weyes T ; & also wicked weies H.
30. U *omits*. *Beete Brugges*] And bynde brugges T ; & bigge brigges H.
31. *Marie*] & marien H. *or*] also & T ; or ellis H. *nonnes*] wyues U.
32. Wydewis þat wiln not be wyues · helpe hem þer aftir T ; þat pore wydewes wol ben · and none wyues aftir U. *none*] no more H.
33. *Godes*] oure lordis THU.

THE LAWYERS GET LEAST PARDON. [PASS. VIII.

and assist widows and poor scholars.
¶ Sette scolers to scole · or to sum oþer craft,
Rule Religion · and Rente hem Betere;
"And I schal sende ow my-self · seint Mihel myn
  Aungel,   36
þat no deuel schal ȝou dere · whon ȝe dye schulle,

Then they would reach heaven.
þat I ne schal sende ȝor soules · saaf in-to heuene,
And bi-foren þe Face of my Fader · fourmen or seetes.
Vsure And Auarice · and oþes I defende,   40
þat no gile go with ou · Bote þe grace of treuþe."

Then the merchants wept for joy, and rewarded William for copying the bull.
Þ<small>E</small>nne were Marchaundes Murie · þei wopen for Ioye,
  And ȝeeuen wille for his writynge · wollene cloþes;
For he Copiede þus heore Cause · þei couden him gret
  þonk.   44

Lawyers had least pardon; for they take bribes.
Men of lawe hedden lest · for heo beoþ [loþ
To mote for mene men · but ȝif þei hadde money;]
So seiþ þe sauter · and sapience boþe,
  Super Innocentes munera non Accipiunt. A Regibus

Ps. xiv. 5 (Vulg.)
  [*et principibus erit merces (eorum).*]
Of [princes] and Prelatus · heor pencion schulde aryse,
And of þe pore peple · no peneworþ to take.   49

---

34. *Sette*] & sett HU. *to—craft*] summe skynes craftis T; to somme kynne crafte U.
35. *Rule*] Releue T; Reule wel U; & releue H. *Religion*] religiouse HU. *Rente—betere*] rede hem þe beste U.
36. *ow*] ȝow UH; T *om.* *myself*] selue U. *Mihel*] Michel TU; myȝhel H.
37. *whon—schulle*] diȝe whan ȝe diȝe TU; when ȝe beþ dede H.
38. *þat I*] for I H; þat he U. *ne*] H *om.* *ȝor soules*] his soule T. *saaf into*] sauely to H.
39. *And*] H *om.* *þe—Fader*] my fadir face U. *fourmen—seetes*] frely ȝow sette H.
40. *I*] y ȝou H.
41. *grace of*] graiþ T; grete HU.
42. *þei wopen*] many wepe T; & wepten H; and wepyn U.
43. *ȝeeuen*] ȝaf TH. *wille*] william H. *wollene*] wel newe H.
44. *For*] And for T. *he copiede*] to copie H. *hoore cause*] here clause TU; þis clause H. *þei—þonk*] þei ȝeue hym gret mede T; þei couþe hym gret þank H; cowde hym gret mede U.
45. *Men*] And men U. *hedden lest*] were laft oute H; þei haddyn lest U. *heo—loþ*] lewid þei ben alle T; þey beþ loþ H; lettrid þei ben alle U; heo beoþ lettred alle V.
46. *This line, and the word* loþ *preceding, are from* H. *The other MSS. omit it, and are hardly intelligible.*
47. *So*] For so T; as H; And so U. *seiþ*] in H follows sauter. *and*] & þe H. *Innocentes*] innocentem TU. *Accipiunt*] accipies TU. *Regibus*] V *has* Regibus, &c.; T *has down to* principibus; U *down to* erit; eorum *I have supplied.* H *quotes loosely.*
48. [*princes* THU] V *has* Parisches (*wrong*).
49. *þe*] no TU. *peneworþ*] penyworþ HU; peny T.

¶ Ac he þat spendeþ his speche · and spekeþ for þe pore
þat is Innocent and neodi · and no mon haþ apeyret,
Cumforteþ him in his caas · Coueiteþ not his goodes, 52
Bote for vr lordes loue · lawe for him scheweþ,
Schal no deuel at his deþ-day · deren him worþ a Myte,
þat he ne worþ siker saaf · and so seiþ þe psauter,
[*Qui facit hec, non mouebitur in eternum.*]

¶ Ac to bugge water, ne wynt · [ne] wit, (is þe þridde),
Nolde neuer holy writ · God wot þe soþe! 57
¶ þeos þreo for þralles · beo þriuen a-mong vs alle,
To waxen or to wonien · wheþer God lykeþ.
His pardoun In purgatorie · is petit, I trouwe, 60
þat eny Meede of mene Men · for Motynge receyueþ.
¶ ȝe Legistres and lawyers · ȝe witen wher I lyȝe;
Seþþe ȝe seon þat hit is so · serueþ to þe Beste.

L ibbinde Laborers · þat libben bi heore hondes, 64
þat treuliche taken · and treuliche tiþen,
And liuen in loue and in lawe · for heore lowe hertes,
Hedde þe same Absolucion · þat sent was to pers.
¶ Bidders and Beggers · Beoþ not in þe Bulle, 68
Bote þe suggestion be soþ · þat schapeþ hem to Begge.

But he that pleads the cause of the poor—

no devil shall harm him at his death-day.

Ps. xiv. 5 (Vulg.)

Water, air, and wit ought never to be bought,

being servants common to all men.

[fol. 400 a. col. 1.]

Ye lawyers, serve men well.

Labourers that are true, loving, and meek had the same pardon as Piers.

Beggars are not pardoned if they feign.

50. *Ac*] For U; but H. *pore*] pore peple U.
51. *þat—neodi*] Also for an Innocent H; þat *innocentis* ben and nedy U. *and*] þat HU. *haþ apeyret*] apeiriþ TH; hem apeire U.
52. *him*] hem U. *his caas*] þat cas TH; þat caas U. *his*] here HU.
53. *loue*] loue of heuen H. *him*] hem HU.
54. *worþ*] TU *omit*.
55. *siker saaf*] saufe sykirly T; sikerly sauf U. [*Qui, &c.*] *In* H *only*.
56. *ne wynt*] ne wynd T; or wind H; wynd U. [*ne*] *Supplied from* T; or. H; V *om*. U *reads*, Ac to bigge water, wynd or wit · is ydel, y rede (*which gives the sense*).
57. *Nolde*] Ne wolde THU. *writ*] cherche U.

58. *þriuen*] þrowe T; throwen U; y-ȝeuen H. *amony*] H *om*.
59. *or—wonien*] & wanyen T; or to wanye H; and wanyn U. *wheþer*] where þat TU; wheþer þat H.
60. *is petit*] ful litel is H; wel litel is TU.
62. *lawyers*] lawisteris T. *ȝe*] T *om. wher*] ȝif TU.
63. *þat—so*] it is þus TU. *serueþ*] sewiþ T; sueth U.
64. *Libbinde*] Alle libbyng T; Alle lyuynge HU. *libben*] lyuen THU.
65. *tiþen*] wynnen THU.
66. *hertes*] herte TU.
67. *Hedde*] shul haue H. *same*] H *om. sent—pers*] was sent to pers plowman U.
68. *and*] ne U. *þe*] þat U.
69. *Bote*] But ȝif TU. *þe—soþe*]

For he þat beggeþ or biddeþ · bote he habbe neode,
He is Fals wi*th* þe Fend · and defraudeþ þe neodi,
And eke gyleþ þe ȝiuere · al aȝeyn his wille. 72

Such are loveless and lawless, and seducers of women.
Þei libben [not in loue · ne] no lawe holden ;
Þei weddeþ no wom*m*on · þat þei wi*th* deleþ ;
Bote as [wilde] Beestes, [wiþ] wo · worcheþ to-gedere,
And bringeþ forþ Barnes · þat Bastardes beon holden.

Some break a bone, and beg ever after.
¶ Or his Bac, or his Bon · heo brekeþ in heore ȝouþe, 77
And goþ, Fayteþ wi*th* heore Fau[n]tes · euer-more after.

They are always meeting with accidents.
Þer ben mo mis-happes among*us* hem · hose takeþ heede,
Þen of alle oþ*ur*e men · þat on Molde wandren. 80
Þei þat lyuen þus heore lyf · mouwe loþe þe tyme,
Þat eue*re* þei weore Men I-wrouȝt · whon þei schul henne fare.

But the old and feeble, women with child, blind and maimed, that are meek,
BOte olde Men *and* hore · þat helples beoþ of strengþe,
And wymmen wi*th* childe · þat worchen ne mowen,
Blynde and Bedreden · And Broken heore membres, 85
Þat taken Meschef Mekeliche · as Meseles or oþere,
Han as pleyn p*ar*doun · as þe plouh-mon him-seluen ;

have their purgatory on earth.
For [loue of] heore lowe hertes · vr lord haþ hem graunted 88

---

here destenye be so U.   þat—Begge] þat þei fore begge TH.
70. biddeþ] bit T ; byt U.   bote—habbe] til he haue H.
71. *with*] as U.   defraudeþ] kiliþ T.
72. eke] T *om.*   ȝiuere] kende U.   al —his] ageyns his TH ; ageyn godis U.
73. [*not—ne* UT] not in loue þat H ; V *has (by mistake)* in no lawe · þat.
74. weddeþ—wommon] ne wedde no wom*m*an T ; wedde none wyues U.
75. [*wilde—wo*] wilde bestis wiþ wehe T ; wilde bestis wiþ woo H ; wilde bestes þat wiþ wo U ; V *reads*, Beestes þat wo; *but we should insert* wilde *and* wiþ (THU) ; *and omit* þat (*not in* TH). worcheþ] & worþ vp T ; worþen H ; wurchen vp U.
76. Barnes] children U.   Bastardes] bois T.
77. or his] oþer here H.   his bon]

here boonys H.   heore] his TU.
78. goþ] gon & TH ; U *om.* fautes V (*wrongly*)] fauntis THU.   euer] for euere T.
79. mishappes] mysshapen TU.
80. of—oþure] of alle oþer maner T ; of alle manere H ; oþer maner of U.   on molde] on þis molde T ; in þis world U.
81. loþe] curse U.
82. þei—weore] he was TU.   þei] he TU.
83. & hore] trewly U.
85. blynde] Blynde men U.   bedreden] blereyed U.   heore] of here H ; þe U.
86. þat] & þo þat H.   meschef] his meschiefe T ; meschefs H.   or oþere] & oþere T ; oþer ellis H ; & siche oþere U.
88. [loue of THU] V omits. hertes]

Heore penaunce and heore purgatorie · is her vppon
    eorþe.
¶ "Pers," quod a prest þo · "þi pardon most I reden,   *A priest asks to see Piers' pardon.*
For I wol construe vch a clause · and knowen hit in
    Englisch."
¶ And Pers at his preyere · þe pardon vnfoldeþ,   92   *Piers shows it; it had but two lines.*
And I bi-hynden hem boþe · bi-heold al þe Bulle.
In two lynes hit lay · and not a lettre more,
And was I-writen riht þus · In witnesse of treuþe :
    ¶ *Et qui bona egerunt, Ibunt in vitam eternam;*   *quoted from Mat. xxv. 46.*
    Qui vero mala, in ignem eternum.
"Peter!" quod þe preost þo · "I con no pardoun fynde,   *The priest says it is no pardon at all.*
    Bote dowel, and haue wel · and god schal haue þi
    soule,   97
And do vuel, and haue vuel · hope þou non oþur,
Þat aftur þi deþ day · to helle schaltou wende!"
¶ And Pers, for puire teone · pollede hit a-sonder,   100   *Piers, for pure vexation, tears it asunder,*
[& siþþe he seide to hem · þese semely sawis,]
    "*Si Ambulauero in medio vmbre mortis, non timebo*   *quoting Ps. xxii. 4 (Vulg.).*
    [*mala, quoniam tu mecum es.*]
¶ I schal sese of my sowynge," quod pers · "*and* swynke
    not so harde,
Ne aboute my lyflode · so bisy beo no more!
Of preyere and of penaunce · my plouh schal ben her-   *Piers says he shall give himself*
    aftur   104

herte TU.   *vr lord*] oure lord TH ;
þat god U.
   89. *Heore*] þe H.   *and heore*] of
here H.   *is—vppon*] upon þis pur
TU ; here vpon H.
   90. þo] T *om.*
   91. *For—wol*] For I shal T ; & H.
vch a] it iche T ; it euery HU.
knowen hit] kenne it þe TU ; vndo
it H.
   92. *vnfoldeþ*] vnfeld H.
   93. *I*] U *om.*   *biheold*] he hylde U.
in ignem eternum] H *om.*
   OBS. H *inserts this quotation after
l.* 98.
   94. *not a*] no H.

   96. þo] HU *om.*
   98. *hope þou*] & hope þou T ; &
hope to H.
   99. *schaltou*] ne shalt þou T ; þou
schalt U ; shalt þou H.
   100. *And*] þo H.   *puire*] T *om.*
   101. *In* H *only; in place of it,*
VTU *have* and seide, at end of l. 100.
[*mala—es*] *From* T ; V *has* m. q. t.
m. es ; U *has* mala, &c. ; H *ends at*
mortis, *and inserts the quotation after*
l. 103.
   102. *quod pers*] HU *om.*   *not*] no
more H.
   104. *preyere*] preieres UTH.   *of*]
H *om.*

up to prayer and penance.	And bi-loure þat I beo-louh · er my lyf fayle.
"David ate his bread with weeping,	¶ þe [prophete his payn eet] · In penaunce and wepyng;
	As þe psauter vs seiþ · so dude moni oþere,
	þat loueþ God lelly · his lyflode is wel muche : 108
Ps. xli. 4 (Vulg.)	*Fuerunt michi lacrime mee panes, die ac nocte.*
	¶ And bote [ȝif luke] lyȝe · he lereþ vs a-noþer ;
	þat to bisi we ne schulde beo · her vppon eorþe,
	While we woneþ in þis world · to make vs wombe Ioye.
Mat. vi. 25.	¶ *Ne soliciti sitis* · he seiþ in his godspel, 112
	And scheweþ hit by ensaumple · vr soules to wisse.
Who feeds the birds in winter? they have no garner."	¶ þe Foules in þe Firmament · [who fynt] hem in winter ?
	Whon þe Forst freseþ · foode hem bi-houeþ ; 115
	Haue þei no gerner to go to · ȝit God fynt hem Alle."
The priest asks Piers who taught him all this.	"What ?" quod þe prest to Perkyn · "peter ! as me þinkeþ,
	how art lettret a luyte · ho lered þe on Boke?"
"Abstinence and Conscience," he replies.	"Abstinence þe Abbesse · myn A-b-ce me tauȝte, 119
	And Concience com aftur · and [kennide] me betere."
	¶ "Weore þou a prest," quod he · "þou mihtest preche whon þe luste,

105. *biloure*] lowren U; *by-loure* H. *beolouh*] louȝ T; *by-louȝ* H; *er by-lowhe* U. *er—lyf*] þeiȝ liflode me TU; or lyuelode me H.

106. *Thus in* U (*cf.* quot. below); other MSS. wrong; we find þe prophetes peyneden hem V; þe prophet his peyned T; þer is profyt in peyne H. *and*] & in THU.

107. *As*] By þat UTH. *seiþ*] techith U. *so dude*] & so dede T; & doþ H.

108. *lelly*] wel U. *his*] H *om. wel muche*] þe moré T; myche H.

109. [ȝ*if luke* UT; *luk* H] þe Bok V. *lereþ*] lerneþ HU. *anoþer*] non oþer H.

110, 111. þat we ne schuln nouȝt be besy · aboute þe bely ioye T ; he biddeþ vs we shuld not · here be to besy In no maner wise · aboute oure wombe ioiȝe H; By fowles he vs techith · þat we schulde besy ben For to make wombe ioye · in þis wonynge here U.

112. *in*] it in T. *he—godspel*] H *omits*.

113. *hit by*] it vs be T; vs by U; vs by an H. *vr soules*] oure selue T· vs selue U.

114. [*who fynt* THU] heo feedeþ V (*see* l. 116).

115. *forst*] frost THU.

116. *Haue þei*] þei haue U. *gerner*] berne U. *to go to*] þerto T; greiþ H. ȝ*it*] but THU.

118. *lettret*] lernid T. *luyte*] litel THU. *lered*] lernide THU. *on*] in H.

119. *After Abbesse* H *inserts* quod he. *A-b-ce*] a.b.c THU.

120. *aftur*] aftirward U. [*kennide* TU] tauȝte VH. *betere*] moche more U.

121. *prest*] prest, piers TU. *luste*] likiþ T; liked HU.

Quoniam literaturam non cognoui · mihte be [þy] Teeme!"   "You should take Ps. lxx. 15 [Vulg.] for your text," says the priest.

"Lewede lorel!" qu*o*d he · " luite lokestou on þe Bible,
On Salamones sawes · [seldom] þou bi-holdest;   124
[slynge awey þese scorners, he seiþ · wiþ here shrewid fliting,   "I refer you to Prov. xxii. 10," quoth Piers.
for wiþ hem redely · y kepe not to rest;]
[*Ejice*] *derisores et Iurgia cum eis*, [*ne crescant*]."

¶ Þe Prest and Perkin þo · Apposeden eiþer oþer,   They disputed so, that I awoke.
And þorw heore wordes I a-wok · and [waitide] a-boute   128
And sauh þe sonne sitte souþ · euene þat tyme
Meteles and Moneyeles · on Maluerne hulles,   Wandering over Malvern hills, I mused on this dream.
[Musyng] on þis Meeteles · A myle wei Ich ȝeode.
Mony tyme þis Metels · han made me to studie   132
For pers loue, þe plouh-mon · ful pensyf in myn herte;
For þat I sauh slepynge · ȝif hit so be mihte.
¶ Bote Catou*n* construweþ hit nay · An Canonistres boþe,   Cato (Dist. ii. 31) bids us despise dreams.
And siggen bi hem-seluen · *Sompnia ne cures*.   136
Ac for þe Bible · bereþ witnesse hou

122. H *reads*, For þou knowist no lettrure miȝt be þy teme, *and then adds the Latin.* mihte] þat miȝte TU. [þy HTU] V *wrongly has* my.
123. lorel] losel H. he] peris T. luite] litel THU. lokestou] lokest þou THU.
124. [*seldom* U] luitel V; litel TH; *but the alteration is clearly right.*
125, 126. *In* H *only.* [*Ejice*] Ecce VTHU (*all wrong*). Iurgia] uirga *or* iurga U; virga H. [*ne crescant*] So *in* TU; nunc crescunt V; non quiescam H.
127. þe] And þe T; þus þe U. þo] THU *om.* þo—oþer] eiþer apposid oþer U.
128. [*waitide* THU] lokede V.
129. sitte—tyme] euene souþ sitte þat tyme TU; þat tyme sitte euen souþ H.
130. *and moneyeles*] on merueilles (!) T.
131. [*Musyng* THU] Mony elynge V. Meeteles] metelis T; mat*e*re U; meting H. wei] weies U.
132. metels] meting H; metelis T. han] haþ HU.
133. For] And for THU. pers] peris his H. loue þe] lyf U. ful] wel T; U *om.* pensyf] pitously U. myn] THU *om.*
134. ȝif] if þat U.
135. construweþ] construed U. nay] T *om.* canonistres] catonistris U.
136. *The readings are*, Sompnia ne cures T; And by hem selue Sompnia ne cures (*sic*) U; Sompnia ne cures nam mens est humana quod (?) optat, & seiþ þat we shulde charge no sweucnys H.
137—139 V *is here misdivided, and omits part of l.* 139, *having for it only* þat Nabugodonosor hette.

[fol. 400 a. col. 2.] Daniel deuynede · þe Dremels of a kyng,

Yet Daniel interpreted that of Nebuchadnezzar (Belshazzar),

þat Nabugodonosor · [nempne þese clerkes.]

Daniel seide, " Sir kyng · þi sweuene is to mene, 140
þat vnkouþe knihtes schul come · þi kin[g]dam to clayme ;

Among lower lordes · þi lond schal be departet."

which turned out quite true.

As Daniel diuinede · hit fel in dede after, 143
þe kyng laste his lordschupe · and lasse men hit hadden.

Joseph too had a dream,

¶ And Ioseph Mette Metels · ful Meruilous alse,

How þe sonne and þe Mone · and enleuene sterres

which his father interpreted,

Falden bi-fore his Feet · and heileden him alle. 147

¶ " *Beu fiz,* quod his Fader · for defaute we schulle,

I my-self, and my sones · seche þe for neode."

and so it came to pass.

¶ Hit fel as þe Fader seide · In Pharaones tyme,
þer Ioseph was Iustise · Egipte to kepen.

Wherefore I often mused upon Piers and the priest,

¶ Al þis makeþ me · on Metels to þenken 152

Mony tyme at Midniht · whon [men] schulde slepe,

On Pers þe plouh-mon · and whuch a pardoun he hedde,

And hou þe preost inpugnede hit · al bi pure Resoun,

and concluded that Do-well

And diuinede þat Dowel · Indulgence passede, 156

Bienals and Trieuals · and Busschopes lettres

---

137. *After*] how U *has* daniel þe prophete. H *reads*, but daniel dampneþ it, & þe bible boþe (!)

138. *Daniel*] Dauid T. *dewynede*] demide T. *dremels*] drom T; dremys U. *kyng*] kyng onys U. H *has,* & beriþ witnes þer of a kingis dremyng.

139. *þat*] H *om.* [*nempne—clerkes*] *from* U; *also in* T; þese clerkis hym nempneþ H.

141. *vnkouþe knihtes*] an vnkynde knizt T; vncouthe kynges U. *kingdam*] kindam V; kingdom THU.

142. *lower*] lewide T. *lond*] londis THU.

143. *diuinede*] demide T; deuysed H. *hit—dede*] in dede it fel T; in dede it byfel UH.

144. *kyng*] lord U. *laste*] les T; lost HU. *lordschupe*] lond H. *lasse*] lesse T; false U. *men hadden*] lordis hadden it H. Obs. H *ends here.*

145, 6, 7. *In* T *and* U *only two lines.* And Iosep mette meruicillously · how þe mone & þe sonne And þe enleuene sterris · halsiden hym alle T; And Ioseph mette merueilousliche · how þe mone & þe sonne And seuene sterres · hailsede hym al abowtyn U.

150. *fel*] befel TU. *þe*] his TU.

151. *þer*] þat TU. *Egipte*] al egipte U.

152, 153. *Transposed in* U.

152. *me*] me mochil U.

153. *Mony tyme*] Manye tymes T. [*men*] T; VU *have* I.

154. *and—a*] whiche a T; & whiche a U. *hedde*] hauiþ T.

155. *bi pure*] before T.

156. *diuinede*] he leuide T. *passede*] passiþ T.

Dowel on Domesday · Is digneliche I-preiset, *surpassed indulgences.*
He passeþ al þe pardouns · of seint Petrus churche.

Now haþ þe pope pouwer · pardoun to graunte, 160
þe peple with-oute penaunce · to passe to Ioye.
The pope, I fully believe, can grant pardon.
þis is a lef of vre bileeue · as lettret men vs techeþ,
   Quodcunque ligaueris super terram, erit ligatum et in *Mat. xvi. 19.*
   celis.
And so bileeue I lelly · (vr lord forbeode hit elles!) 163
þat pardoun and penaunce · and preyers don sauen
Soules þat han sunget · seuen siþes dedlich.

¶ Bote trustene to Trienals · treuly me þinkeþ
Is not so syker for þe soule · sertes, as do-wel. 167
But to trust to Triennials is very unsafe.

¶ For-þi I rede ȝow Renkes · þat Riche ben on eorþe,
Vppon trust of oure tresour · Trienals to haue,
Beo ȝe neuer þe Baldore · to Breke þe ten hestes;

¶ And nomeliche, ȝe Meires · and ȝe Maister Iuges,
þat han þe welþe of þis world · for wyse men ben holden, 172
Ye mayors, and wealthy judges, who purchase pardons,

To purchasen pardoun · and þe popes Bulles.
At þe dredful day of dom · þer dede schullen a-rysen,
And comen alle bi-fore crist · and a-Countes ȝelden,
when ye stand before Christ at doomsday,
How þou laddest þi lyf · and his lawe keptest, 176

---

158. *on Domesday*] at þe day of dome TU. *digneliche*] ferforþliche U. *I-preiset*] vndirfongen TU.
159. *pardouns*] pardoun TU. *of*] at T. *churche*] chirche at rome U.
OBS. U *here inserts the Latin line,* Quodcunque, &c.; *see* l. 162.
161. *to—Ioye*] a pena & a culpa T.
162. *a lef*] þe lif T; a leef U. *techeþ*] shewiþ T.
163. *so—lelly*] so I leue lelly T; y byleue it wel U. *vr*] TU *omit.* *hit*] T *omits.*
164. *don sauen*] do salue T; to-gidres Mown saue U, (*the last two words being in* l. 165.)
165. *sunget*] ysynned T; synned U.
166. *Bote—to*] And to triste on þis T; Ac to traste on þese U. *treuly*] certes U.

167. *Is*] It is T. *sertes*] trewly U (*see* l. 166). *as*] as is TU.
168. *Forþi—Renkes*] þerfore y rede þat lordes U.
170. *Beo ȝe*] Be þou UT.
171. *Meires—Iuges*] maistris, as meiris & iuggis T; maistres, þat men þat Iuggeȝ holden U.
172. *þat—for*] þat han þe world at wille & T; þei to haue welthe of þis world U.
173. T *omits this line.* *To*] For to U.
174. *day—dom*] dom day T. *þer*] whanne þe T; whan U.
175. *alle*] T *omits.* *and acountes*] acountes to TU.
OBS. U *omits to end of Passus, leaving a small blank space.*
176. *lyf*] life here T.

> and your deeds are rehearsed;

What þou dudest day bi day · þe Doom þe wol rehersen;

> though you had a sackful of provincial letters,

¶ A powhe ful of pardoun þer · with Prouincials lettres,
þauh þou be founden in Fraternite · a-mong þe foure Ordres,   179

> I will give little for your pardon unless Do-well help you!

And habbe Indulgence I-doubled · bote Dowel þe helpe,
I nolde ȝeue for þi pardoun · one pye hele!

FOrþi I counseile alle cristene · to crie crist merci,
And Marie his Moder · to beo mene bi-twene,

> God give us grace to work such works, that Do-well at doomsday will say we did God's will.

þat God ȝiue vs grace · er we gon hennes,   184
Such werkes to worche · while þat we ben here,
þat aftur vr deþ day · Dowel reherce,
þat atte day of dom · we duden as he us hiȝte.

[*Explicit hic visio willelmi de Petro de Plouȝman. Eciam Incipit Vita de do-wel, do-bet, & do-best, secundum wyt & resoun.*]

177. *day—day*] day T (*by mistake*). þe *wol*] wile T.
178. *powhe ful*] pokeful T. *with*] ne þe T.
179. *in*] in þe T.
180. *I doubled*] double-fold T.
181. *nolde*] ne wolde T. *pardoun*] patent T.
182. *to—crist*] criȝe god T.
185. *while þat*] whiles T.
187. *atte*] at þe T. *us*] T *omits*.
[*Explicit, &c.*] *From* T; *so also* UH₂D; *see* Critical Notes *and* Preface.

PASSUS IX.

Incipit hic Dowel, Dobet, and Dobest.

¶ [þ]us I-Robed in Russet · Romed I a-boute
Al a somer sesoun · For to seche Dowel,
And [fraynide] ful ofte · of [folk] þat I mette
[ʒif any wiʒt wiste · where do-wel was at Inne,   4
And what man he miʒte be · of many man I askide].
Was neuer wiht as I wente · þat me wisse couþe
Wher þis ladde loggede · Lasse ne more ;
¶ Til hit fel on a Friday · twei Freres I mette,   8
Maistres of þe Menours · Men of grete wittes.
Ich heilede hem hendeli · as Ich hedde I-leorned,
And preiede hem, par Charite · er þei [passede furre,]
"ʒif þei [knewen any] Cuntre · or Coostes a-boute   12
Wher þat Dowel dwelleþ · do me to wisse."
¶ " Mari," quod [þe] Menour · " A-mong vs he dwelleþ,

Everywhere I wandered, to find Do-well.

None knew where he dwelt.

One Friday, I met two Minorites,

and asked them to tell me where Do-well dwelt.

" With us, at times," said one.

Incipit hic, &c. *This is the only title that occurs in* V. *The large initial* þ *is omitted by mistake, and a blank space left for it.*

OBS. H₂ *is collated with the rest to the end of the volume.*

1. *Romed I*] I rombide T ; y romyd al U ; I rome H₂.
3. [*fraynide* TH₂; y frayned U] askede V; *see l.* 5. [*folk* TUH₂] Men V ; *see l.* 5.
4, 5. *From* T; *also in* UH₂ ; V *omits.*
5. *he*] it U. *askide*] fraynud U.
6. *wente*] wene TUH₂.
7. *loggede*] lengide TH₂ ; lengith U.

Lasse ne more] þe lesse ne þe more TH₂.
8. *fel*] befel T ; byfel U ; befil H₂.
9. *wittes*] wyt T ; witte UH₂.
10. *heilede*] hailside TU ; halside H₂.
11. *par*] for U. [*passede furre*] furre passede V ; passide ferþere TUH₂.
12. [*knewen any* T] knewe ony U ; knewen ony H₂; V *has* knewe, *omitting* any.
13. *dwelleþ*] dwellide TH₂.
14. V *has a* Menour ; TH₂ þe maistris ; U þese maistres ; *cf. ll.* 22, 24. *Among*] at hom wiþ U; *see l.* 20.

And euer haþ, as Ich hope · and euer schal her-after."

"Nay," said I, "even the righteous man sins seven times a day,
(Prov. xxiv. 16.)

¶ "*Contra*," qu*o*d I as a Clerk · and comsede to dispuite, 16
["*Sepcies in die cadit iustus ;*"]
Seue siþes a day, seiþ þe Bok · sungeþ þe rihtful mon ;
And hose sungeþ," I seide · "certes, as me þinkeþ,
þat Dowel and do vuele · mowe not dwelle togedere.

so he cannot *always be with you."*

Ergo, he nis not alwey · [at hom] among ow Freres, 20
He is or while elles-wher · to wisse þe peple."

"I'll explain that about the righteous man," said he.

¶ "I schal seie þe, my sone" · seide þe Frere þenne,
"Hou seuen siþes þe sadde mon · sungeþ in a day ;
Bi [a forebisene]," seide þe frere · "I schal þe feire schewe. 24

"Put a man in a boat in open sea,

¶ Let bringe a Mon In A bot · A-midde a Brod water,
And þe wint *and* þe wat*ur* · *and* þe waggyng of þe Bot

and the wagging of the boat will make him stumble, though he is safe.

Makeþ þe Mon Mony tyme · to stomble and to falle ;
(For stonde he neu*e*re so stif · he stumbleþ in þe waggyng) ; 28
And ȝit he is saaf and sound · and so him bi-houeþ ;

Yet if he neglects the helm, he will be upset by his own fault.
[fol. 400 b. col. 1.]

For ȝif he ne rise þe raþer · and rauhte to þe steorne,
þe wynt wolde w*ith* þe water · þe Bot ouer-þrowe ;
þer weore þe Monnes lyf I-lost · þorw [lachesse] of himselue. 32

Even so on earth.

Riht þ*us* hit fareþ," qu*o*d þe Frere · "bi folk her on corþe ;

15. *as*] TH₂ omit.
16. V *omits the Latin quotation;* TUH₂ *give it.*
17. *a day*] on þe day U ; TH₂ *omit. sungeþ*] falliþ TUH₂. *mon*] TUH₂ *omit.*
18. *I seide*] I seiȝe TH₂ ; he seiþ U. *as*] TUH₂ *omit.*
19. *þat*] TH₂ *omit.*
20. [*at hom* TH₂] a tom V ; U *omits ; see l.* 14.
21. *or while*] oþer while TH₂ ; som tyme U.
22. *sone*] sawe U. *seide*] seiþ U.
23. How seuen sithes on þe day · þe sadde man synnes U.

24. [*a forebisene* TUH₂] ensaumple V. *seide*] quod TUH₂.
25. *a Brod*] the brode H₂
26. *And þe wint*] þe wynd TUH₂. *waggyng—Bot*] wawes eke H₂.
27. *þe—tyme*] many tyme þe man U. *to—falle*] to falle & to stande TUH₂.
29. *and sound*] U omits.
30. *rise*] arise TUH₂. *and—steorne*] & ariȝt sterede TH₂ ; and raughte þe stere U.
31. *ouerþrowe*] ouertorne H₂.
32. *þorw*] for TUH₂. [*lachesse* TUH₂] sleuþe V.
33. *hit*] TH₂ *omit.*

¶ þe watur is liknet to þe world · þat wonieþ and waxeþ;
þe goodes in þis world · ben lyk þis grete wawes,
Riht as wyndes and watres · waleweþ aboute.   36
¶ þe Bot is liknet to þe Bodi · þat Brutel is of kuynde;
And þorw þe fend and his Flesch · and þe False world
Sungeþ þe sadde Mon · seuen siþes in þe day.   39
¶ But dedly sunne doþ he not · for Dowel him helpeþ,
þat is charite þe Champion · cheef help aȝeyn sunne ;
For he strengþeþ þe to stonde · he stureþ þi soule,
þat þauȝ þi bodi Bouwe · as a Bot in þe Water,
Euer is þi soule saaf · Bote ȝif þi-self wolle.   44
¶ Folewe þi Flessches wil · and þe fendes aftur,
And do dedlich sunne · and drenche þi-seluen,
God wol soffre þe dye so · for [þi-self hast þe maistrie]."
¶ " I haue no kynde knowyng," quod I · " to conceyue
        þi wordes,   48
But ȝif I may liuen and loken · I schal go lerne betere.
I beo-take ȝou to crist · þat on [þe] Crois diȝede."
And þei seiden þe same · " God saue þe from mischaunce,
And ȝiue þe grace vppon grounde · In good lyf to ende."
þus I wente wyden wher · Dowel to seche ;   53
    And as I wente bi a wode · walkyng myn one,
Blisse of þe Briddes · made me to Abyde,

Marginalia:
- The waves are this world's fluctuating riches.
- The boat is the frail body.
- Yet the just man doth no *deadly* sin, and is safe.
- If thou do *deadly* sin, thou art justly drowned."
- "I can't follow that," said I ; "so farewell."
- Again I wandered wide, seeking Do-well, and came to a grove,

34. *liknet*] lyk U. *wonieþ*] waniþ T ; wanyeth UH₂. *Also,* U reads waxeth and wanyeth.
35. *in þis world*] of þis ground TUH₂. *ben—grete*] arn lyk to þe U.
36. *Riht*] That H₂T ; And U. *waleweþ*] wawen TH₂ ; wawes U.
37. *liknet*] like TU ; liken H₂. *Brutel*] britel TUH₂.
38. *And*] That H₂TU. *his*] þe TUH₂.
39. *siþes*] tymes TH₂. *in*] on U.
41. *þat*] And þat TH₂. *is*] H₂ om. *aȝeyn sunne*] of alle U.
42. Aȝens synne for to synne · he stireth þe soule U (*corruptly*). *he stureþ*] & steriþ TH₂.
43. *a Bot*] bot doþ TH₂ ; a boot doþ U.
44. *Euer*] Ay TUH₂. ȝif] þou TH₂ ;

U omits. *wolle*] wilt TH₂ ; wolt U.
45. *fendes*] feend U ; fende H₂.
46. *þi-seluen*] þi soule U.
47. *dye so*] to deiȝe so TH₂ ; to dey U. *þiself—maistrie*] so in TH₂ ; þou hast þe maistry U ; þou art þin owne Mayster V.
48. *quod I*] U omits.
50. *beotake—to*] bekenne þe TUH₂. [þe TUH₂.] V omits.
51. *God*] TUH₂ omit.
52. *vppon grounde*] on þis erþe TUH₂.
53. *wyden wher*] wyde where TH₂ ; wide whare U.
54. *And*] T omits. *myn one*] me alone U.
55. *to*] TUH₂ omit.

And vnder A Lynde, vppon A launde · leonede I a
 stounde,   56
For to leorne þe layes · þat louely foules maden.
Blisse of þe Briddes · Brou3ten me a slepe;
þe Meruiloste Meetynge · Mette I me þenne
þat euere dremede driht · In drecchynge, I wene.   60
¶ A Muche Mon, me þouhte · lyk to my-seluen,
Com and clepede me · be my kuynde nome.
¶ "What art þou," quod I · "þat my nome knowest?"
"þat þow wost wel," quod he · "and no [wi3t] betere."
"Wot I," quod I, "ho art þou?" · ["thought," seide he]
 þenne,   65
"I haue suwed þe þis seuen 3er · se3e [þou] me no raþere?"
¶ "Art þou þou3t?" quod I þo · "const þou me telle,
Wher þat dowel dwelleþ · do me to wisse?"   68
¶ "Dowel," quod he, "and Dobet · and Dobest þe
 þridde
Beoþ þreo faire vertues · and beoþ not fer to fynde.
H[o] is Meke of his Mouþ · Mylde of his speche,
 Trewe of his tonge · and of his two hondes,   72
And bi his labur or bi his lond · his lyflode wynneþ,
And trusti of his taylende · takeþ bote his owne,

Side notes: and listened to the sweet birds' lays. Then I slept again, and had a wondrous dream. One like myself came, and called me by name, who said, he was Thought. "Thought," said I, "tell me where is Do-well." "Whoever is meek, mild, and true," said he,

---

56. *leonede I*] lenide I me TH₂; y lened me U.
57. *For to leorne*] To lerne TH₂; To lithen U. þat] þe U. foules] briddis TUH₂.
58. þe] þise T. a slepe] on slepe UH₂.
59. *I*] TUH₂ omit.
60. þat euere dright in doute · drempte, as I wene U. *In drecchynge*] in doute as TH₂.
61. *Muche*] muchel TH₂; mykil U.
62. *clepede*] callide TUH₂. kuynde] kynde T; righte UH₂.
63. *I*] I þo TH₂.
64. þow wost] wost þou U; thou H₂ (by mistake). [wi3t TUH₂] bodi V.
65. *Here* V *is corrupt, having* þhou3te I me seide I þenne; T reads, þou3t, I-seide he þanne; H₂ has, thou3t, seyde he than; *the reading given is from* U; *see note.*
66. *suwed*] swyed U. þis] TH₂ om. se3e] sei3e þou TH₂; seye þou U; V omits þou.
67. *quod I þo*] þo quod I TH₂; þo, quod he U (*wrongly*). const þou] þou couþest TH₂; coudest þou U.
68. *Wher þat*] Where TUH₂. do] & do H₂.
70. *fer*] for TH₂ (*wrongly*).
71. *Ho*] V *has* He, *by mistake;* Who-so TUH₂.
72. *Trewe*] Treuthe H₂ (*corruptly*).
73. *And—lond*] And þoru3 his labour or his lond TH₂; And þurw þe laboure of his handes U.
74. U *omits.* And] TH₂ *omit.*

PASS. IX.] AN ACCOUNT OF DO-WEL, DO-BET, AND DO-BEST. 107

And is not dronkeleuh ne deynous · Dowel him folewe þ. "him Do-well follows.
Dobet do þ þus · bote he do þ muche more ;   76
He is as louh as a lomb · louelich of speche ;   Do-bet does even more, and gives
While he ha þ ouȝt of his owne · he helpe þ þer neod is, to the needy, and hath rendered the
þe Bagges and þe Bi-gurdeles · he ha þ broken hem alle Bible,
þat þe Auerous hedde · or eny of his heires ;   80
And wi þ Mammonas moneye · ha þ maked him frendes,
And is Ronnen in-to Religiun · And ha þ Rendret þe
  Bible,
And preche þ þe peple · seint poules wordes,   and preaches from the text, 2 Cor. xi. 19.
  Libenter sufferte.

¶ ' Ȝe wyse, soffre þ þe vn-wyse ' · wi þ ow for to libbe,
And *with* glad wille do þ hem good · for so god him-
  self hiȝte.   85
Dobest is a-boue bo þe · And Bere þ A Busschopes cros, Do-best is above both, and bears a
Is hoket atte ende · to holden [hem] in good lyf. bishop's crosier.
A pyk is in þe [potent] · to punge a-doun þe wikkede,
þat wayten eny wikkednesse · Dowel to teone.   89
And as Dowel and Dobet · duden hem to vnderstonde, Do-well and Do-bet have crowned
þei han I-Corouned A kyng · to kepen hem Alle, a king,
þAt ȝif Dowel or Dobet · dude aȝeyn Dobest,   92
  [And were vnbuxum at his biddinge · and bold to
  don ille],

75. *is not*] nouȝt TH₂. *deynous—foleweþ*] deignous of speche U (*see* l. 77), *omitting* l. 76, *and part of* l. 77.
76. U *omits.* *do þ þus*] þus do þ TH₂.
78. *ouȝt*] U *omits.* *helpe þ þer*] delith þer moste U.
79. *Bigurdeles*] bygirdles U; breigerdlis T ; breigu[r]delis H₂. *broken hem*] *so in* TUH₂; V *has* hem broken, *which spoils the line.*
80. þat þe Erl Auerous · hadde, or his eires TUH₂.
81. *ha þ maked*] he ha þ mad TH₂ ; ha þ mad U.
82. *into*] to TH₂.
83. *sufferte*] *so in* TH₂ ; U *omits this quotation;* V *is indistinct.*

84. *ȝe*] The TH₂.
85. *glad*] good U. *god—hiȝte*] our lord highte U ; god bit hym TH₂.
86. *bo þe*] hem bo þe TUH₂.
87. *atte*] at þat on TH₂ ; at þe ton U. [*hem* U] him V ; men TH₂.
88. *in—potent*] in þat potent TH₂ (*but* H₂ *omits* in) ; in þe potente U ; V *has* in þe ende, *copied by mistake from* l. 87. *punge*] pynche U.
89. *wayten*] haunte þ U.
90. *duden hem*] dede hem T ; don hem H₂ ; do þ him U.
91. *A*] o T.
92. *þat*] And U. *or*] and TH₂.
93. *From* T ; *also in* UH₂.

	þen schulde þe kyng comen · And casten hem in prison,
	And puiten [hem] þer In penaunce · with-outen pite or grace,
with consent of Do-best."	Bote ȝif Dobest beede for [hem] · a-byde þer for euere!
	¶ þus Dowel and Dobet · And Dobest þe þridde 97
	Crounede on to beo kyng · And bi heor counseil worche,
	And Rule þe Reame · bi Red of hem Alle,
	And oþerwyse elles not · bute as þei þreo assenten."
I thanked him, and asked him where these three dwelt.	¶ I þonkede [þouȝt þo · þat] he me so tauȝte, 101
	" But ȝit saureþ not me þi siggynge · so me God helpe,
	More kuynde knowynge · I coueyte to here,
	Hou Dowel and Dobet · and dobest beþ on eorþe." 104
"Only Wit can tell thee," said he.	¶ " But wit con wisse þe," quod þouȝt · " wher þeos þre dwelleþ,
	Elles not no Mon · þat nou is alyue."
So Thought and I went on till we met Wit.	¶ þus þouȝt and I also · þroly we eoden
	Disputyng on Dowel · day aftur oþer, 108
	And er we weoren war · with Wit conne we meeten.
	¶ He was long and lene · to loken on ful symple,
	[Was no pride on his apparail · ne no pouert noþer],
	Sad of his semblaunt · and of softe speche. 112
I asked Thought	I durste meue no mateere · to make him to Iangle,

94. *þen*] þat þanne TH₂. *schulde—kyng*] þe kyng schulde U.
95. *puiten*] putten TUH₂. [*hem* TUH₂] him V. *þer—penaunce*] in prisone U.
96. *Bote ȝif*] But TH₂; & but ȝif U. *beede*] bede TU; bidde H₂. [*hem* TUH₂.]
98. *heor*] his TUH₂; him V.
99. *bi Red*] be red T; be rede H₂; for reed U.
100. *oþerwyse elles*] oþere wise & ellis TUH₂. *þei*] þese U. *assenten*] assentide T.
101. [*þouȝt—þat*] *so in* TH₂; þouȝte so · þat U (*where so is an error for* þo); V *has* him feire · þo.
102. *not me*] me nouȝt TH₂; me not U.

103. *here*] lere TH₂; lerne U.
104. How do-wel, do-bet, & dobest · don on þis erþe TH₂; How dowel and do-bet · don on þis erþe U.
105. *quod*] U *omits (by mistake)*. þeos] þo TUH₂.
106. *not*] wot T; woot UH₂.
107. þouȝt & I þus · þre dayes we ȝeden TUH₂. *eoden*] V *really has* eodem, by mere mistake.
109. *weoren war*] ywar were T; I-war were H₂. *with*] U *om.* *conne*] gonne TH₂; gunne U.
110. *to—simple*] lyk to non oþer TUH₂.
111. *From* T; *also in* H₁; VU *omit*.
112. *softe*] a softe TH₂; a sad U.
113. *durste*] ne durste TH₂.

Bote as [I bad þouȝt] þo · to beo mene bi-twene,
To putte forþ sum purpos · to preuen his wittes.
¶ þenne þouȝt þat tyme · seide þeose wordes,   116
"Wher Dowel and Dobet · and Dobest beoþ in londe,
Oure wille wolde I-witen · ȝif wit couþe [hym] techen."

[fol. 100 b. col. 2.]
to ask him a
question for me,
and he asked him
where Do-well,
Do-bet, and Do-
best dwelt.

114. But as I bad þouȝt þo · be mene betwene TH₂U ; but U *has* to be me bytwene ; V *has* þouȝt bad, *omitting* I.
115. *to preuen*] & prouen T.
116. þouȝt] H₂ *om*. þat] in þat TUH₂.
117. *Wher*] Where þat TUH₂.
118. *Oure wille*] Here is wil TUH₂. [*hym* TH₂U] V *omits*.

PASSUS X.

[*Passus primus de dowel, &c.*]

<small>"Do-well dwells," said Wit, "in a castle made by Kind of four things,</small>

"SIre Dowel dwelleþ," quod wit · "not a day hennes,
In A Castel, of kuynde I-mad · of foure kunne þinges,

<small>earth, air, wind, and water.</small>

Of Erþe and Eir hit is mad · I-medelet to-gedere,
Wiþ wynt and wiþ watur · ful wittiliche I-Meint.   4
Cuynde haþ Closet þer-In · Craftiliche wiþ alle,

<small>Within the castle Kind has enclosed the lady *Anima*,</small>

A loueli lemmon · lyk [to] him-self,
Anima heo hette ; · To hire haþ Envye

<small>whom 'the prince of this world' hates.</small>

A proud prikere of Fraunce · *Princeps huius mundi*,   8
And wolde wynnen hire a-wei · with wiles ȝif he mihti.
Bote kuynde knoweþ hit wel · and kepeþ hire þe betere,

<small>Do-well, Do-bet, and Do-best are her appointed keepers.</small>

And haþ I-don hire to Sire [Dowel · duke of þese marches.
Dobet is hire damysele · sire] Doweles douȝter,   12
And serueþ þat ladi lelly · boþe late and raþe

Passus, &c.] *so named in* TUH₂.
OBS. *Throughout this Passus the readings of* H₂ *agree with those of* T, *except where specially given*.
1. *dwelleþ*] U *omits*.
2. *of—Imad*] þat kynde made TU. *foure kunne*] foure skenis T ; foure skynnes H₂.
3. *Eir*] of eyr UH₂.
4. *ful—Imeint*] wiȝtliche enioynede T ; wittyly enioyned U.
6. *A—lemmon*] A lemman þat he louiþ TU. [*to*] *in* TUH₂ ; V *omits*.
7. U *resembles* V ; TH₂ *are corrupt ;* Anima · he haþ to hire enuye T ; Anima he hath to hem enuye H₂.
8. *Princeps*] sire princeps H₂.
10. *hit*] þis U ; hire T.
11. 12. V *omits the words within brackets by mistake, owing to the repetition of* sire ; *they are supplied from* U ; l. 11 *is alike in* TH₂, *but in* l. 12 TH₂ *have* sistir *instead of* douȝter.
13. *þat*] þis TU.

þus Dowel and Dobet · and Dobest þe þridde
Beoþ Maystres of þis Manere · þat Mayden to kepen.
¶ But þe Cunstable of þe Castel · þat kepeþ hem alle, 16
Is a wys kniht wiþ alle · Sire Inwit he hette,
And haþ fyue feire sones · bi his furste wyf;
¶ Sire seowel and seywel · And herewel þe [h]ende,
Sire worche-wel-with-þin-hond · A wiht mon of strengþe,
And sire Godfrei Gowel · grete lordes alle.   21
¶ Þeose sixe ben I-set · to saue þe Castel;
To kepe þis wommon · þis wyse men ben Charget,
Til þat kuynde come or sende · And kepe hire him-
   seluen."   24
¶ "What calle ȝe þe Castel," quod I · "þat kuynde haþ
   I-maket,
And what cunnes þing is kuynde · con ȝe me telle?"
¶ "Kuynde," quaþ he, "is C[r]eatour · of alle kunne
   [beestes],
Fader and Foormere · þe furste of alle þing;   28
Þat is þe grete God · þat bigynnyng hedde neuere,
Þe lord of lyf and of liht · of [lisse] and of peyne.
Angeles and alle þing · [arn] at his wille,
Bote Mon is him Most lyk · of Marke and of schap;
   For wiþ word þat he warp · woxen forþ Beestes, 33
And alle þing at his wille · was wrouȝt wiþ a speche,
   Dixit et facta sunt;

The constable of the castle is In-wit [Conscience], whose sons are See-well, Say-well, Hear-well, Work-well, and Go-well."

"What is the castle's name?" said I, "and who is Kind?"

"Kind is the great Creator, who made all things;

man being most like Himself.

Ps. cxlviii. 5, (Vulg.)

15. *þis*] þe U. *þat*] þis T; þe U.
17. *Inwit*] þouȝt T (*wrongly*).
18. *And*] He U.
19. *and*] sire U (*twice*). *hende*] so in TUH₂; V has ende.
20. *A*] and UT (*wrongly*); a H₂.
22. *sixe*] vij U (*owing to* and *in* l. 20).
23. *þis wyse*] wise U.
24. *Til þat*] Til TU. *And*] to T.
25. *þe*] þat T; þis U; þe H₂. *haþ*] so in TUH₂; V *really has* haþ þus, *but* þus *is best omitted.*
26. T *omits;* U *has,* Of what kynne thinge · cunne ȝe me telle; H₂ *agrees* with V.
27. *Creatour*] creatours U. *kunne beestes*] kenis bestis T; kynne bestis U; V *has* best, *but see* l. 33.
28. *þe*] U *omits.* *alle*] H₂ *omits.*
29. *þat*] And þat TU. *is þe*] he is U. *bigynnyng*] gynnynge TU.
30. *liht*] liþ T. [*lisse* TH₂] Blisse VU. *peyne*] pyne U.
31. [*arn* TUH₂] ben V.
33. *wiþ*] þoruȝ TU.
34. *þing*] TUH₂ *om.* *dixit—sunt*] Faciamus hominem ad ymaginem et similitudinem nostram U; *see* l. 41.

Saue Mon þat he Made · Ymage to him-seluen,
ȝaf him goost of his Godhede · and grauntede him Blisse,
Lyf þat euer schal lasten · and al his lynage aftur.   37

The castle is called Caro.
¶ þat is þe castel þat kuynde made · *Caro* hit hette,
And is as muche to mene · As Mon wiþ a soule,
þat he wrouhte with Werk · and wiþ word boþe;   40

Gen. i. 26.
Þorw miht of his Maieste · Mon was I-maket,
 [*Faciamus hominem ad ymaginem et similitudinem nostram.*]
Inwit and alle wittes · ben closet þer-Inne,
For loue of þat ladi · þat lyf is I-nempnet;

The lady is Life, or Anima, and dwells in man's heart;
þat is *Anima* þat ouer al · in þe Bodi wandureþ,   44
But in þe herte is hire hom · hiȝest of alle;
Heo is lyf and ledere · and a lemmon of heuene.
Inwit is þe help · þat *Anima* desyreþ;
After þe grace of God · þe gretteste is Inwit.   48

In-wit is in his head, and rules Caro and Anima.
¶ Inwit in þe hed is · and helpeþ þe soule,
For þorw his connynge he [kepeþ] · *Caro et Anima*
In Rule and in Reson · bote Recheles hit make.

¶ He eggeþ þe [eiȝe-siht · and herynge] to goode,   52
Of good speche and of cunnynge · he is þe biginnere,

He is most in the brain, and
In Monnes Brayn he is most · and mihtiest to knowe,
þer he is Bremest · But ȝif blod hit make.

---

37. *euer*] ay TU.   *al*] U *om*.
38. *hette*] hatte TU; hattith H₂.
39. *And is*] Is U; TH₂ *omit*. *to*] forto H₂. *As*] þat T. *a*] his T; þe U.
40. U *omits*.   *werk*] werkis T. *word*] wordis T.
41. *his*] þe TU.   *Mon*] whan (!) U. Faciamus, &c.] *From* U *above, at* l. 34; TH₂ *insert it here, but omit et* similitudinem.
42. *ben closet*] enclosid ben T; bien I-closid H₂.
44. *in*] U *omits*.
46. *and a*] and U; a T.
47. *help*] halle T.
48. *þe—Inwit*] Inwyt is þe grettest TU.
49. *and helpeþ*] & an help to T;

an help to UH₂.
50. *he kepeth*] is kept TU; *hence the reading of* V, *viz*. he clepeþ, *is a mere mistake for* he kepeþ; *see* l. 16.
52. *The readings are,*
   He eggeþ þe iþe siht · and Bringeþ to goode V;
   He (It H₂) eggiþ eiȝe-siȝt · & herynge to gode TH₂;
   He eggide eye to sighte · and herynge to gode U.
In V, *iþe is probably written for* iye *or* eiye.
53. *Of*] Ofte H₂. *good—cunnynge*] speche & of goynge U.
55. *he is*] is his bour TU.   *ȝif*] hoot U.

PASS. X.]   THE HOME OF "INWIT" IS IN THE BRAIN.   113

For whonne Blod is Bremore þen Brayn · þen is Inwit   *contends against the passions.*
   I-bounde,   56
And eke wantoun and wylde · withouten eny Resoun.
IN ȝonge Fauntes and Fooles · with hem Fayleþ Inwit,   *Children, idiots, and sots have but little In-wit.*
   And eke in [sottes] þou miht seo · þat sitteþ atte Ale;
þei heldeþ Ale in heore hed · til Inwit beo a-dreynt,   60
And [ben] Brayn-wode as Beestes · so heore Blod waxeþ.
¶ Þenne haþ þe Pouke pouwer · Sire *Princeps huius*   *Over sots the devil has power,*
   mundi,
Ouer suche Maner Men · Miht in heore soules.
Bote In Fauntes ne in Fooles · þe Fend haþ no miht   *but not over children and idiots,*
For no werk þat þei worchen · wikked or elles ;   65
Bote þe Fadres and þe Frendes · For Fau[n]tes schul be   *whose guardians are responsible for them,*
   Blamet
Bote þei witen hem from wantounesse · whil þat þei ben
   ȝonge.
¶ And ȝif þat þei ben pore or Catelles · to kepen hem
   from ille,   68
Þenne is holy chirche a-signet · to helpen hem and sauen   *or else the Church protects them.*
From Folyes, and Fynden hem · til þat þei ben
   wysore.
¶ Bote vche [wiȝt] in þis world · þat haþ wys vnder-   *Each man who is sane has charge over himself, and is responsible.*
   stondinge,
Is Cheef souereyn [of] him-self · his soule for to ȝeme,

---

56. *Bremore þen*] brent in U. *Inwit*] þe wit U.
58. *ȝonge*] U om. *with*] in U.
59. [*sottes*] UTH₂ ; V *has* wrecches. *atte ale*] at þe nale TU ; at þe ale H₂.
60. *heldeþ*] helde T ; heeld U ; holde H₂. *adreynt*] drenchit TU.
61. [*ben*] *So in* TU ; bien H₂ ; V omits. *Braynwode*] brayned U.
62. *princeps—mundi*] *omitted in* U ; *see note*.
63. *men*] of men T. *in*] is in U.
64. *ne in*] and U. *Fend*] deuil T. *miht*] wit U.
65. *no*] to U (*wrongly*).

66. *Faderes*] fadir TU. *Fauntes* TU] V *has* Fautes.
67. *Bote*] But ȝif T. *witen*] wone U. *ȝonge*] ȝouþe T (*sic*) ; ȝonge H₂.
68. *And ȝif*] And H₂ ; ac if U. *þat*] TU *om. to*] and U.
69. *asignet*] owynge T ; awynge U.
70. *Fynden*] fende H₂. *þat—wysore*] þei ben wise T. U *reads*, And for to fynde hem forþ · til þei ben wisere.
71. *Bote*] And TU. [*wiȝt* T ; *wight* U] mon V. *þis*] þe U. *haþ*] H₂ omits *by mistake*.
72. [*of* H₂] ouer TU ; V *omits. for to*] to TU.

8

And Cheuesschen him from charge · whon he childhode
  passeþ, 73
Saue him-self from sunne · for so him bi-houeþ;
For worche he wel oþer wrong · þe wit is his oune.

[fol. 401 a. col. 1.]
Do-well destroys vices, and saves the soul.

Þene is Dowel a Duyk · þat distruieþ vices, 76
  And saueþ þe soule · þat sunne haþ no miht
To Route ne to Reste · ne to Rooten in þe herte ;
And þat is drede of God · for Dowel hit makeþ,
Hit is biginnynge of goodnesse · God for to drede ; 80
[Salamon it seide · for a soþ tale],

Prov. ix. 10.

Innicium sapiencie, timor domini.
For doute, Men doþ þe Bet ; · drede is such a Mayster
þat he makeþ Men Meoke · and Mylde of heore speche,
And alle kunne scolers · In Scoles forte lerne ; 84

Do-bet is to beware of punishment; see Ps. xxii. 4 (Vulg.)

Þenne is Dobet to beo war · for betynge of ȝerdes,
And þerof seiþ þe Sauter · þi-seluen þou miht reden,
  Virga tua [et baculus tuus, ipsa me consolata sunt.]
[Ac ȝif clene consience acorde · þat þi-selfe dost wel],
Wilne þou neuere in þis world · forte Dobetere ; 88
  For, *Intencio [indicat hominem].*

Act always by advice of Conscience.

¶ Bi Counseil of Concience · a-Cordynge with holy
  churche,
Loke þou wisse þi wit · and þi werkes aftur ;
For ȝif þou comest aȝein Concience · þou Cumbrest þi-
  seluen,

---

73. *cheuesschen*] cheuisshiþ TU. *from*] for any TU.
74. *Saue*] To saue U. *bihoueþ*] behouid H₂.
75. *wit*] wyte U.
76. *þat*] and U.
77. U *omits.*
78. *To*] Ne U. *to—þe*] roren in þin T.
79. *for*] TU *omit.*
80. And is þe begynnynge · god for to doute U. *drede*] douten TU.
81. *From* T ; *also in* UH₂. *timor*] est timor T.
83. *þat he*] And þat U.
84. *kunne*] kynne U ; kynde T.

scoles—lerne] scole to lerne T ; scole to lere U.
85. *Dobet—war*] do-bet to ben ywar T ; do-bet ywar H₂ ; dowel to drede U. *ȝerdes*] þe ȝarde TU.
86. *þerof*] þere U. *þiseluen*] þe salme TU. *The Latin is from* TU ; V *has only* virga tua, &c.
87. *From* T ; *so also* UH₂ ; V *has a corrupt line,* Bote Clene Concience a-Corde · Bote þi-self Dowel. *clene*] þi clene U.
88. *forte*] why for to UH₂. [indicat hominem TUH₂] V *indistinct.*
89. *Bi*] Wiþ U. *with*] of H₂ ; T *omits.*

And so witnesseþ Godes Word · And holiwrit boþe ; 92
[*Qui agit contra conscientiam, edificat ad iehennam.*]
Bote ȝif þow worche bi god*us* word · I warne þe for þe
   beste,
What so men worden of þe · wraþþe þe neuere ;
Catou*n* Counseileþ so · tak [kepe] of his teching,   <small>Cato (Dist. iii. 3) advises us to despise calumny.</small>
   Cum recte viuas, ne cures verba malorum ;
¶ Bote suffre and sitte stille · And sech þou no furre,
And beo glad of þe grace · þat God haþ þe I-sent ;   97
For ȝif þou cumse to Clymbe · and Coueyte herre,
þou miht leose þi louhnesse · for a luitel pruyde.
¶ I haue lerned hou lewede men · han lered heore   <small>Men say, the stone men oft tread on gathers no moss;</small>
   children,   100
þat selden Moseþ þe Marbelston · þat men ofte treden ;
¶ And Riht so walkers · þat walken A-bouten
From Religion to Religion · Recheles ben þei eue*re*.
And men þat Cunne mony Craftes · Clergie hit telleþ,   <small>and he who is Jack of all trades, is master of none.</small>
þruft or þeodam wi*th* hem · selden is I-seye ;   105
   Qui circuit omne genus, [*nullius est generis.*]
Poul þe Apostel · In his pistel wrot   <small>Remember Paul's advice,</small>
   In ensaumple of suche · Rennars a-boute,
And for wisdam Is writen · as witnesseþ Clerkes,   108

92. T *omits, but not* H². *holiwrit boþe*] holi chirche aftir U. *The Latin quotation is from* U ; TH₂ *have only the first four words of it.*
93. *for þe*] þe T.
94. *worden*] seyn U.
95. *so*] T *omits.* [*kepe* UTH₂] hede V. Catoun conseileþ þe · to take kepe on þis þinge U.
96. *And*] U *om. furre*] ferþere TU.
97. *þe Isent*] I-sent þe T ; þe sent U.
98. *herre*] to ben heiere U ; hiȝere H₂.
100. *lerned*] herd TU. *how*] ȝou H₂. *lered*] lernid T.
101. þat selde men seþ þe marbil ·
   þat men ofte dreden T ;
   (*corrupt*) ;
   þat seelde men seen þe marbil
   mose · þat men ofte mouen U ;

That selde men seth the
   marbul · that ofte men
   tredith H₂.
102. *walkers*] be romberis T ; by renneres U. *walken*] rennen TU.
104—162. *Omitted in* H₂.
104. *And*] Ne T. *mony*] alle U. *Clergie—telleþ*] clergie techiþ eue*re* T ; and clergie boþe U.
105. *þeodam*] þedom TU. *hem*] þo TU. *selden is*] is seldom U. [*nullius—generis*] *in* U ; &c. T ; V *omits.*
106. *wrot*] wrot it TU.
107. *of—Rennars*] of suche · schulde not renne T ; þat siche · schulde not renne U.
108. U *omits. as—Clerkes*] & witnessid in chirches T. *The Latin is from* U ; T *has,* In eadem vocacione qua vocati estis, state, &c. ; V *omits.*

116 BE CONTENTED WITH THY LOT. [PASS. X.

1 Cor. vii. 20.   [*In ea vocacione qua vocati estis, in eadem permaneatis*].

Ȝif þou beo Mon I-Mariet · Monk, oþur chanoun,
Hold þe stable and studefast · And strengþe þi-seluen
To beo blesset for þi beryng · ȝe, Beggere þauh þou weore!

Murmur, not against God, but be content.
¶ Loke þou grucche not on god · þauȝ he þe ȝeue luytel,
Beo payed wiþ þi porcion · porore or Ricchore.   113
Þus in drede lyþ Dowel · And Dobet to soffren,
For þorw soffraunce seo þou miht · hou souereyn[es] Ariseþ;

Luke xiv. 11.
Qui se humiliat, [*exaltabitur, &c.*];
And so lerede vs luc · þat lyȝede neuere.   116
And þus of drede and his dede · Dobest aryseþ,
Whuch is Flour and Fruit · I-fostred of Boþe.

As the sweet red rose grows on a rough briar,
¶ Riht as þe Rose · þat Red is and swote,
Out of a Ragged Roote · and of Rouwe Breres   120
Springeþ and spredeþ · þat spicers desyreþ.

or wheat grows from a weed, so Do-well, Do-bet, and Do-best
¶ Or as whete out of a weod · waxeþ vppon eorþe,
So Dobest out of Dowel · and Dobet doþ springe   123
A-Mong men of þis [molde] · þat Meke ben, or kuynde;

spring out of the lowly.
For loue of heore louhnesse · vr lord ȝiueþ hem grace
Such werkes to worche · þat he is wiþ apayet.

110. *þiseluen*] þi soule U.
111. *ȝe—þou*] þe biggere þeiȝ þou T; ȝif þou a beggere U.
112. *ȝeue*] gyue þe T.
113. *porore—ricchore*] pore oþer riche T; be it pore or riche U.
114. *And*] T *omits.*
115. *þorw*] þus þurw U. *souereyn* V.] soueraynes TU. U *has a blank space for the Latin;* exaltabitur, &c., *is from* T.
116. U *omits this line, and* T *inserts it before the quotation.* lerede] leriþ T.
117. *his*] here T; of our U.

118. *Flour—Fruit*] þe flour & þe fruyt TU. *of*] on U.
119—121. *Wrongly made into two lines in* TU. *þe Rose*] a Rose TU. *þat—and*] T *omits.*
120. *of—Breres*] as a rowhe brere U; a rouȝ brere T.
121. *Springeþ*] þat springeþ U.
122. *a*] TU *omit.* vppon] out of þe TU.
123. TU *transpose* Dowel *and* Dobet. *doþ*] gynneþ TU.
124. [*molde* TU] World V. *or*] & TU.
126. *þat*] as T.

Furst and foreward · to folk þat ben I-weddet, *They that keep wedlock please God.*
And libbeþ as heore lawe wole · hit likeþ God
    almihti;   128
For þorw wedlac þe world stont · hose wol hit I-knowe.
Þei ben Ricchest in Reame · and þe Rote of dowel;
For of heore kuynde þei come · þat *confessours* beþ *Of such come confessors, martyrs, monks, &c.*
    nempned,
Boþe Maydens and Martires · Monkes an Ancres, 132
Kynges and Knihtes · and alle cunne Clerkes,
Barouns and Burgeis · and Bonde Men of tounes.

¶ Fals folk and Feiþles · þeoues and lyȝers *False folk are conceived in an ill hour, like Cain,*
Ben Conseyuet in Curset tyme · as Caym was on Eue,
After þat Adam and Eue · hedden eten of þe Appel 137
Aȝeyn þe heste of him · þat hem of nouȝt made.
¶ An Angel in haste · þennes hem tornde
In-to þis wrecchede world · to wonen and to libben *who was conceived just after the Fall.*
[In tene & in trauaile · to here lyues ende];   141
In þat Corsede Constellacion · þei knewen to-gedere,
And Brouȝten forþ [a barn] · þat muche bale [wrouȝte.]
¶ Caym men cleped him · In Cursed tyme engendret,
And so seiþ þe sauter · seo hit whon þe likeþ, 145
    Concepit in dolore, [*et peperit iniquitatem, &c.*] Ps. vii. 15 (Vulg.)
And alle þat come of þat Caym · Crist hem hatede Aftur,
And Mony Milions mo · of Men and of Wymmen

---

127. *Ferst—forward*] And formest & ferst T; Formest and first U.
128. *lawe wole*] lawis wiln T. *hit*] þat U.
129. *For*] þat T; And U. *hose*] whoso TU.
130. *Ricchest—Reame*] þe riccheste of reaumes TU.
131. *kuynde*] kynde T; kyn U.
132. *martires*] nonnes TU.
134. *tounes*] towne U.
135. *Fals*] Ac fals TU. *þeoues*] as þeuis TU.
136. *on*] and U (*wrongly*).
137. *Eue*] she T. *hedden*] TU omit. *of*] TU omit.
138. U *omits.*

139. *haste*] angir T. *þennes—tornde*] hiȝte hym (hem U) to wende TU.
141. *From* U; *also in* T. *in trauaile*] trauaille T.
142. *þei*] þat þei U.
143. [*a barn* TU] Barnes V. [*wrouȝte* TU] wrouȝten V; *cf. next line.*
144. *men—him*] þei hym callide TU.
145. *Part of the Latin is from* T; U *here inserts a wrong quotation,* Quare via, &c.; *for which see* Pass. XI. l. 23.
146. *And*] TU *omit.* *hem hatede*] hatide hem U; hatid T.

Seth's kindred inter-married with Cain's,

þat of Seth and his Suster · seþþen forþ coome; 148
For þei Marieden to corsed Men · þat comen of Caymes kuynde.
For alle þat comen of þat Caym · A-Cursed þei weren,
And alle þat couplede hem to þat kun · crist hem hatede dedliche.

though God warned Seth against it.

Forþi he sende to [Seth] · And seide him bi an Angel,
To kepe his cun from Caymes · þat þei coupled not to-gedere.   153
¶ And seþþen [Seth] *and* his suster sed · weren spoused to Caymes,
A-ʒeyn Godes heste · Gurles þei geeten,

God was wroth with them.

þat God was wroþ with heor werk · And suche wordes seide,   156

Gen. vi. 7.

Penitet me [fecisse hominem];
And is þus muche to Mene · A-monges ʒou alle,

[fol. 401 a. col. 2.] þat I makede Mon · nou hit me for-þinkeþ;
¶ And com to Noe Anon · And bad him not lette

Wherefore He bade Noah build the ark,

Swiþe to schapen A schup · of schides and Bordes;   160
Him-self and his sones þre · And seþþen heore wyues,
Bringen hem to þe Bot · And byden þer-Inne,

for the flood should destroy Cain's seed.

Til Fourti dawes ben folfuld · [þat] þe flod haue I-wassche
Clene awey þe cursede blod · þat Caym haþ I-maket.

148. þat] And TU. seþþen] sitthe þei U.
149. to] hem wiþ T; hem wiþ þe U. þat—kuynde] of caymes kyn TU.
150. acursed—weren] crist hatide hem euere U; *see next line.*
151. U *omits.* to] with T. hem] T *om.* dedliche] euere T.
152. he—Seth] he sente hym to seyn T; y sente hem to scye U. [Seth] V *has* Sem *by mistake; see* l. 148.
153. cun] kynrede TU. Caymes] caym U. þat] T *omits.* coupled] couple U.
154. [Seth] Seeþ U; Sem VT; *see* ll. 148, 152. sed] TU *omit.* to Caymes] wiþ caymes kynne U.
156. þat] And U. werk] werkis TU. suche—seide] seide suche wordis T; seide þese wordis U. *The quotation is in* TU; V *has only* Penitet me, &c.; *occurring after* l. 158.
157. And] þat U. þus] as TU. ʒou] vs TU.
158. makede Mon] man makide T; man made U. nou] sore U.
159. Noe] nowel U.
160. schapen] schapen him U. schides] shidis T; sides U.
161. heore] alle here U.
162. Bringen hem] Buskide T; Buskide hem U. þe] þat T. And byden] to abide U.

OBS. *Here collation with* H₂ *recommences; see note to* l. 104.

163. dawes] dayes T; U *omits.* [þat] TH₂ *have* þat, *but omit* þe. Iwassche] y-waschide U.

¶ 'Beestes þat now ben · mouwen [banne] þe tyme 165   "All the beasts must die for
þat euere þat Cursede Caym · Com vppon eorþe;   Cain's sin,
Alle schulen dye for his dedes · Bi Dounes and hulles,
Boþe Fisch and Foules · forþ wiþ oþer beestes, 168
Out-taken Eihte soules · And of vche beest A Couple,   save 8 souls, and of each kind a
þat in þe schynglede schup · schullen ben I-saued;   couple."
Elles schal al dye · and to helle weende.'

Þus þorw Cursede Caym · Com Care vppon alle; 172   This was all because Seth's
For [Seth] and his suster children · spouseden eiþer   seed married Cain's.
   oþer,
Aȝeyn þe lawe of vr lord · lyȝen to-gedere,
And weoren Maried at Mischef · as Men doþ now heore
   children.
For summe as I seo nou · soþ for to tellen,   176
For Couetise of Catel · vnkuyndeliche beoþ maried,   Now, some marry for money,
And Careful Concepcion · comeþ of such weddyng,
¶ Also bifel of þat folk · þat I beo-fore schewede.
Hit is an vn-Comely Couple · be Cryst, as me þinkeþ,
To ȝeuen a ȝong wenche · to an old feble Mon,   181   or a young wench is wedded to an
Or to wedden an Old widewe · for weolþe of hire   old feeble man.
   goodes,
þat neuer schal Child bere · bote hit beo in hire Armes.
¶ In Ielesye Ioyeles · and Ianglynge in Bedde   184

165. *mouwen*] shuln TU. [*banne* TUH₂] curse V.
166. *þat cursede*] curside T; þe curside U. *vppon*] on þis T; to þe U.
168. *Fisch*] fisshis TU. *forþ*] for H₂. *wiþ*] miþ T; with H₂. *oþer*] þe U.
169. *Eihte*] þe eiȝte T; þe souen U. *And*] þat U (*wrongly*).
170. Put þat in þe same ship · þat shal ben ysauid T;
   þat in þe sengle schyppe · þat tyme schal be saued U.
171. *schal*] schulde U.
172. *þus—caym*] þoruȝ curside caym þus T.
173. *For*] And al for TU. [*Seth*] seeth U; Sem VT; *see* l. 148. *children*] U om. *spouseden*] spousid here U.

174. *lyȝen*] ley hem T; leyen U.
175. *weoren maried*] mariede T.
176. U omits.
177. *For*] þat for U.
178. *And*] A TU.
179. *Also bifel*] As fel TU. *þat*] þe T; þis U. *þat I*] as T.
180. *me þinkeþ*] I wene TU.
181. *mon*] TU omit; retained in H₂.
182. Or wedde any wydewe · for any wele of godis TU.
183. *child bere*] bere child TU. *hire*] TU omit.
184. V *inserts* and *before* Ioyeles, *but it is best omitted, as it is in* TUH₂. *in Bedde*] of bedde T; abedde U.

THE GREAT EVIL OF UNEQUAL MARRIAGES. [PASS. X

Many, since the pestilence, have married ill,

Mony peire seþþen þe pestilence · han pliht hem to-
gedere ;
þe Fruit þat þei bringen forþ · ben mony foule wordes,

and have no children but strifes.

Han þei none children bote chestes · and choppes hem
bitwene. 187

Though they go to Dunmow, they never fetch the flitch.

¶ þauȝ þei don hem to [donmowe · but þe deuel helpe]
To folewen aftur þe Flucchen · fecche þei hit neuere ;
Bote ȝif þei boþe ben forswore · [þat bacoun þei tyne].

Then wed not for money, but marry well, and God bless you!

¶ Forþi I Counseile alle Cristene · coueite not ben I-
weddet
For Couetyse of Catel · ne of kun Riche ; 192
Bote Maydens and [Maydens · maccheþ ou ysamme,]
Widewers and widewes · [wercheþ riȝt] also,
And þenne glade ȝe god · þat alle goodes sendeþ !

None but the pure should live together,

¶ For in vn-tyme treweli · bi-twene Mon and wommon
Schulde no Bed-bourde be · bote Boþe weore clene 197
Of lyf and eke in loue · and in lawe alse.
þat deede derne · do no mon scholde,

and each man

As is vset, bi-twene · sengle and sengle ; 200

185. *þe*] þis T. *pliht*] piȝt T.
186. *ben mony*] arn manye T ; arn but U.
187. *chestes*] chidinge T ; cheste U. *hem bitwene*] togidere T ; by-twene U.
188. *þeiȝ þei don hem to dunmowe · but ȝif þe deuil helpe* T ; *þei hiden hem to donmowe · but þe deuel helpe* U ; *þauȝ þei don hem to done · al þat þei mowen* V ; *where done and mowen are corrupted from donmowe.*
189. *Flucchen*] flicche TU.
190. *Bote ȝif*] but U. [*þat—tyne* TUH₂] *and Cursen þat tyme* V.
192. *ne—kun*] or of kynrede T ; or for kynrede U.
193, 194. V *is here apparently corrupt ; see various readings below.*
198. [*maydens—ysamme*] maidenis · macche ȝow ysamme T ; maydenis · marie ȝou to-gyderis H₂ ; maydenes ·

ȝou to-same take U ; V *has* vn-Maydens · clene ow save.
194. [*wercheþ riȝt*] werchiþ riȝt T ; wurche ȝe U ; V *has* worschupeþ ; H₂ *ends the line with* werchith *the same.*
195. *And*] U *om.* *þenne*] T *om.* *goodes*] good T.
196. *vntyme*] my tyme TU (*also* U *omits* in). *mon—wommon*] men & wommen T.
197. *Bed-bourde*] bedborde U. *Boþe weore*] þei were boþe TU ; if thei were bothe H₂.
198. *eke in*] of TU. *in*] of TU.
199. *deede derne*] derne dede U. *scholde*] ne shulde T.
200—202. *Only two lines in* TUH₂, *thus :*
  As betwyn sengle & sengle · siþþe lawe haþ y-grauntid
  þat iche man haue a make · in maner of wedlak TH₂ (*where* H₂ *omits* As];

Seþþen lawe haþ I-loket · þat vche mon haue a make
In Mariage and Matrimoyne · I-Medlet to-gedere, 202
And worche þat with his wyf · and with no wommon elles. *should keep to his own wife.*

¶ þat oþer-gates ben I-geten · [for gadelynges ben holden, þat ben false folke and false heires] · fyndlynges and lyȝers, *Bastards are commonly false, liars, ungracious, and wasters.*
Vn-Gracios to gete loue · or eni good elles, 206
¶ Bote wandren as wolues · and wasten ȝif þei mouwen.
A-ȝeyn Dowel þei don vuele · and þe deuel plesen,
And aftur heore deþ day · schul dwelle wiþ þe schrewe,
Bute God ȝiue hem Grace · heer to A-Mende. 210
¶ þenne is Dowel to dreden · and Dobet to suffren, *Thus, Do-well is, to fear God; Dobet, to suffer, and Dobest, to be lowly of heart.*
And so comeþ Dobest aboute · And bringeþ a-doun Modi,
And þat is wikkede wil · þat Mony [werke] schendeþ."

Ac bytwene sengle and sengle ·
   siþþe lawe haþ y-graunted
þat euery man haue a make · in
   mariage of wedlok U.
203. *worche—with*] do þat werk on T; wurche on U. *with no*] on no T; no U.
204, 205. V *has only one line*, þat oþergates ben I-geten · ben fyndlynges and lyȝers; *I give* l. 204 *as it stands in* TUH₂; *for* l. 205 *we find*,
   þat ben false folke · and false
     heires also U.
   And þat ben fals folke & fals
eires · alse foundlynges & folis TH₂.
OBS. *The vellum (better) portion of* U *ends here; the rest is on paper; and begins at* l. 48 *of* Passus XI.
207. But wandriþ & wastiþ · what þat þei mowe T.
209. þe schrewe] þe same T; þat same H₂.
210. *Bute*] But ȝif T. *hem*] hym T.
212. *modi*] mody TH₂.
213. *is*] H₂ *omits*. [*werke* H₂T] men V.

PASSUS XI.

[Passus secundus de dowel, &c.]

<small>Then had Wit a wife named Study,</small>

þEnne hedde wit A wyf · was hoten dam Studie,
  þat [lene was of lich] · and of louh chere.
Heo was wonderliche wroþ · þat wit me þus tauhte,

<small>who sternly said to him, "Thou art wise to teach fools!"</small>

And al starinde Dam Studie · steorneliche seide,   4
¶ " Wel artou witti," quod heo · " wisdom to telle
To Fayturs or to Fooles · þat Frentik ben of wittes !"
And Blamede him for his Beere · And Bad him beo stille
Wiþ suche wyse wordes · to wisse eny fooles.   8

<small>Cast not pearls before swine (Mat. vii. 6).</small>

¶ And seide, " *Noli mittere* · Margeri perles
Among hogges þat han · hawes at heore wille ;
þei don hot drauele þeron · draf weore hem leuere
þen al þe presciouse Peerles · þat in paradys waxen. 12

<small>I speak of those that prefer riches to wisdom.</small>

¶ I sigge hit bi þulke," quod heo · " þat bi heore werkes
    schewen
þat hem weore leuere lond · and lordschupe on corþe,
Richesse, Rentes · or Reste at heore wille
þen Al þe soþ sawes · þat Salamon seide euere.   16

Passus, &c.] *so in* TH₂.
OBS. *The readings of* H₂ *are the same as those of* T, *except when specially given as different.*
1. *was hoten*] þat hatte T.
2. [*lene—lich*] *so in* TH₂ ; V *has* euer was I-liche. *louh*] loþly T.
3. *me þus*] so me H₂ ; so T.
4. And sterneliche staringe · dame studie seide T.
5. *artou witti*] art þou wys, wyt T. *wisdome*] any wisdomis T.

6. *Fayturs*] flatereris T.
7. *for his Beere*] bitterly T.
9. *Noli mittere*] *Nolite mittere.* man T.
10. *heore*] T omits.
12. *presciouse Peerles*] precious perrie T. *waxen*] wexiþ T ; wexit H₂.
13. *hit—þulke*] be þo T. *bi— schewen*] shewen be here werkis T ; schewen here werkis H₂.
15. Or ricchesse or rentis · & reste at here wille T.

¶ Wisdam and wit nou · is not worþ a Russche
But hit beo [cardet] with Couetise · as cloþers doþ heor wolle,
þat Cunterfeteþ disseites · and Conspiret wronges,
And ledeþ forþ A loueday · to lette þe trewethe ;   20
þat suche craftes cunnen · to counseil beoþ I-clept,
And ben serued as syres · þat serueþ þe deuel.
¶ Iob þe Ientel · in his Ieestes seide,
   Quare via impiorum prosperatur, bene est omnibus
     qui praue et inique agunt ?
¶ Ac he þat holy writ haþ · euer in his mouþe,   24
And con tellen of Tobie · And þe Twelue Apostles,
And prechen of þe penaunce · þat Pilatus wrouhte
To Iesu þe Ientil · þat Iewes to-drowe
On Cros vppon Caluarie · as Clerkes vs telleþ ;—   28
¶ Luytel is he loued or leten bi · þat such a lessun Redeþ,
Or Daunseled or Drawen forþ · þis Disours witen þe soþe ;
For ȝif Harlotrie ne Holpe hem þe bet · (haue God my soule !)
More þen Musyk · or Makyng of Crist,   32
Wolde neuer kyng ne kniht · ne Canoun of Seynt poules
ȝeuen hem to heore ȝeres-ȝiue · þe value of a grote !
Bote Munstralsye and Murþe · A-Mong Men is nouþe ;
Lecherie and losengrie · and loseles tales,   36
And geten gold with grete oþes · beoþ gamus nou A dayes.

Wisdom is worth nothing now-a-days, unless it is carded with Covetousness, like wool.

Jer. xii. 1.

[fol. 401 b. col. 1.]

Teachers of holy things are now little loved.

But minstrelsy and mirth are now the games best liked.

---

18. [*cardet*] cardit TH₂ ; carket V.
19. *Conterfeteþ*] can construe þe T ; *conspiret*] conspire T.
20. *ledeþ*] lede T.
21. *to—Iclept*] ben yclepid to counseil T.
22. *þat*] and H₂.
23. *seide*] seide it T. *bene*] ve TU. *praue*] peruerse U. (*This quotation occurs in U elsewhere ; see note to* Pass. X. l. 145.)
24. *holy—euer*] haþ holy writ ay T.
25. *And þe*] & of þe T.
26. *And*] Or T. *Pilatus*] pilatis T.
28. *telleþ*] techiþ T.
29. *Redeþ*] techiþ T.
30. *Daunseled*] dauntid T.
31. *þe bet*] betere T. *soule*] trouþe T.
32. *Crist*] god almiȝt T ; god almyȝty H₂.
35. *Bote*] T omits.
37. *And—with*] Glotonye & T. *beoþ*] þise arn T.

If they speak of Christ, it is to make a mock of the Trinity.	But ȝif þei Carpen of Crist · (þis Clerkes and þis lewede) Atte Mete in heor Murþe · whon Munstrals beoþ stille, ¶ þenne telleþ þei of þe Trinite · hou two slowen þe þridde, 40 And Bringeþ forþ Ballede Resouns · tak Bernard to witnesse, And puyteþ forþ presumpciun · to preue þe soþe.
Thus they talk at the daȝs, and are full;	¶ þus þei drauelen on heore deys · þe Deite to knowe, And demeþ God in-to þe gorge · whon heore Gottus follen. 44
but the needy man is driven from their gate like a dog.	But Carful Mon may crien · and clepen atte ȝate Boþe of hungur and of þurst · and for chele quake; Nis no Mon him neih · his nuy to Amende, Bote honesschen him as an hound · and hoten him go þennes! 48
	Luyte loueþ he þat lord · þat leneþ him þat Blisse, þat þus parteþ with þe pore · A parcel whon him noodeþ.
Were not the poor kinder than the rich, many would want a meal.	Neore Merci In Mene Men · More þen in Riche, Wiþ Mony defauti Meeles · Mihte þei go to bedde. 52 God is muche in þe gorge · of þeose grete Maystres, Bote A-Mong Mene Men · his Merci and his werkes; And so seiþ þe psauter · sech hit In "Memento,"
See the Psalm Memento Domine, Ps. cxxxi. 6 (Vulg.).	Ecce Audiuimus eam in effrata, inuenimus [eam] in campis silue. ¶ Clerkes and kete men · Carpen of God ofte, 56

39. *Atte—murþe*] At þe mete & at murþe T.
41. *Ballede—tak*] a ballid resoun · toke T.
42. *puyteþ*] putte T.
43. *drauelen on*] dryuelen at T.
44. And gnawen god in here þrote · whanne here guttis fullen T.
45. *But—Mon*] Ac þe carful T. *clepen atte*] carpe at þe T.
46. *of*] for T. *of*] for T. *quake*] quakiþ T.
47. Is non to nymen him In · ne his anguyssh amende T; H_2 omits him.
OBS. *Here collation with U recom-*

mences.
48. *honesschen*] honysche U; hunsen T.
49. *þat blisse*] al þat blisse T.
51. *Neore*] Ne were U.
52. Manye men meteles · miȝte go to bedde T; Manye mendinaw[n]tes meteles · myȝte go to bedde U.
53. *þe*] his U. *gorge*] þrote T; gorge H_2.
54. U *omits.* *mene*] TH_2 *omit.*
55. *seoh*] seek U; se T. [*eam* TUH_2] eum V.
56. *kete*] kid T; kedde U; kyd H_2. *ofte*] faste TU.

And han him muche in heore Mouþ · bote Mene men in herte. *Clerks have Christ in the mouth, but poor men in the heart.*
Freres and Faytors · han founden suche questions
To plese with þis proude men · seþþe pestilence tyme ;
Þei de-Foulen vre Fey · at Festes þer þei sitten.   60

For nou is vche Boye Bold · Broþel an oþer, *Now every boy talks about the Trinity, and cavils against God,*
To talken of þe Trinite · to beon holden A syre,
And fyndeþ forþ fantasyes · vr feiþ to Apeyre ;
And eke de-Fameþ þe Fader · þat vs alle made,   64
And Craken aȝeyn þe Clergie · Crabbede wordes.

¶ 'Whi wolde God vr saueour · suffre such a worm *asking why God let the serpent deceive Eve;*
In such a wrong wyse · þe wommon to bi-gyle ?
Boþe hir hosebonde and heo · to helle þorw him wenten,
And heore seed for þat sunne · þe same wo drien.'   69

¶ Suche Motyues þei meuen · þis Maistres in heor glorie, *and the men who believe them, disbelieve.*
And makeþ Men Misbileeue · þat [musen on] heore wordes.

But Austin þe Olde · for alle suche precheþ,   72 *Augustine refers us to Rom. xii. 3.*
And for suche tale tellers · such a teeme scheweþ,
Non plus sapere quam oportet sapere.
Þis wilneþ ȝe neuer to wite · whi þat God wolde
Soffre Sathan · his sed to bi-gyle ;

57. *him*] TU *omit* ; H₂ *retains*.
58. *founden*] founden vp TU ; fonden H₂.
59. *þis*] TU *omit*. *seþþe*] siþen þe T ; siþ þe U.
60. *þei*] þat TU. *Fey*] false (!) T ; feyth U. *festes*] þe feste T.
61. *Broþel—oþer*] & he be riche TU.
62. *talken*] tellen TU.
64. *eke defameþ*] defame T ; to defame U.
65. *craken—þe*] carpide aȝens T ; carpen of U.
66. *God*] TU *omit*. *worm*] worm in his blisse TU.
67. *þat he gilide þe womman · & þe wy aftir* T ; *þat begyles þe womman · & þe man after* U.
68. *þoruȝ whiche a werke & wille · þei wenten to helle* TU.
69. *And*] And alle TU. *þat*] here T. *drien*] suffride TU.
70. *motyues*] motifs T ; motes U.
71. [*musen on* T] mousen on U ; leeuen in V ; H₂ *torn away*.
72. *precheþ*] prechide T ; prechet U.
73. *scheweþ*] shewide T. *Non*] Nolite U. *oportet*] V *really has* oporteþ, *of course by mistake*.
74. That is to seyn ne wilneþ neuere · for to wyte why TU ; *see next line, and* l. 81.
75. *Soffre*] That god wold suffre TU.

Believe and pray.	¶ But leeueþ on þat lore · þat lereþ holichirche,	76
	And preye him of pardoun · and penaunce in þi lyue,	
	And for his muchele Merci · to amenden vs heere.	
Evil be to him who blames God's ways.	For alle þat wilneþ [to wite · þe] weyes of god Almihti,	
	I wolde his eȝe weore in his ers · and his heele aftur ;	
	þat euer eft Wilneþ to wite · whi þat God wolde	81
	Soffre Sathan · his seed to bi-gyle,	
	Or Iudas þe Ieuȝ · Iesu bi-traye ;	
Praised be Thou, O God! Thy will be done!	Al was as he wolde · lord, I-heried be þou !	84
	And al [worþ] as þou wolt · what so we tellen !	
And now—here is a fellow who wants to know Do-well from Do-bet!	¶ And nou comeþ a Conioun · and wolde cacchen of [my] wittes,	
	What is Dowel from Dobet ! · nou daffe mot he worþe,	
	[Siþen] he wilneþ to wite · whuche þei ben alle !	88
Let him seek Do-well, and the rest follows."	Bote he liue in þe leste degre · þat longeþ to Dowel,	
	I dar ben his borw · þat Dobet nul he neuere,	
	þauȝ Dobest drawe on him · day aftur oþur."	
Wit, hearing Study so talk, was confounded,	And whon þat wit was I-war · hou his wyf tolde,	92
	He bi-com so confoundet · he couþe not [mele],	
	And as doumbe as a dore · drouȝ him asyde.	
	Bote for no Craft þat I couþe · ne knelyng to grounde,	
	I mihte gete no greyn · of [his] grete wittes,	96
and signed to me to beseech her.	But al lauȝwhinge he loutede · and lokede vppon Studie,	
	In signe þat I schulde · bi-sechen hire of grace.	

76. Ac beleue lelly of lore · of holy chirche T ; And be-leef lely on þe lord · of holy chyrche U.
77. him] H₂ omits. of] of his U. in] be TU.
79. [to wite þe UTH₂] two V ; see ll. 73, 81, 88. weyes] werkes T.
80. eȝe were] eiȝen wern T.
81. whi þat] why T. þat—wolde] Begins l. 82 in U ; cf. l. 74.
83. Or] Er T. bitraye] betrayede T.
84. Iheried—þou] yworsshipid be þou T ; I-wyrchepid þou be U.
85. al] U om. [worþ TUH₂] beo V.
86. [my TH₂] me V.
87. nou] U om. daffe] defe TU.
88. [Siþen T] siþþe U ; sithen H₂ ;

V has Sire.
89. Bote—degre] But ȝif he lyue lely in þe last day U.
90. I] For I U. borw] bolde boruȝ TU. þat] TU omit. nul] wile TU.
93. He—confoundet] He becomeþ so confus T ; He come so confuse U. [mele TUH₂] medle V.
94. And as] Also T ; And also U. dore] dore-nayl and H₂.
95. Bote—þat] Ac for no carpinge T ; And for no carpyng U. to] to þe TU.
96. greyn] gayn T. [his TUH₂] hire V.
97. lauȝwhinge] lauȝinge T ; louryng U.
98. of] of his T ; of H₂.

¶ And whon I wuste of his wil · to his wyf con I knele,   I knelt to Study,
And seide, " Merci, Madame, ȝoure mon schal I   and asked her to teach me about
   [worþe],   Do-well.
To worchen ȝoure wille · while my lyf dureþ ;   101
[Kenne] me kuyndely · to knowen what Is Dowel."   [fol. 401 b. col. 2.]

¶ " For þi Mekenesse, Mon," quod heo · " and for þi   She said she would recommend
   Milde speche,   me to Clergy,
I schal [kenne] þe to my Cosyn · þat Clergye is I-hoten.   (Learning),
He haþ wedded a wyf · wiþ-Inne þis wikes sixe,   105   whose wife was Scripture
Is sib to þe seuen Ars · þat scripture is I-nempnet ;   (Writing).
Þei two, as Ich hope · after my be-sechyng,
Schul wisse þe to Dowel · I dar vndertake."

Þenne was I as Fayn · as Foul on feir morwen,   109
   Gladdore þen þe gleo-Mon is · of his grete ȝiftes,
And askede hire þe heiȝe wey · wher Clergye dwelleþ,
" And tel me sum tokne to him · for tyme is þat I
   wende."   112

¶ " I schal teche þe þe heiȝe wey," quod heo · " from   "The way thither is through
   hennes to soffre-   Suffer-weal-and-wo,
Boþe-weole-and-wo · ȝif þat þou wolt leorne,
And Ryd forþ bi Richesse · Reste þe nouȝt þer-Inne ;   passing by Riches
For ȝif þou Couple þe to him · to Clergie comestou   and Lechery,
   neuere.   116
And eke þe longe launde · þat Lecherie hette,
Leue him on þi luft half · A large myle or more,
Forte þou come to a Court · kep-wel-þi-tonge-   119   till thou come to the court called
From-lesynges-and-lyȝeres-speche- · and-lykerous-drinke.   Keep-thy-tongue.
¶ Þenne schaltou seo Sobre · And Symple-of-speche,   Then shalt thou

---

99. *wuste*] was war TU.
100. [*worþe* TUH₂] beo V ; see l. 85.
101. *while*] þer whiles T.
102. [*Kenne* TH₂] To kenne U ; Teche V.
104. [*kenne* TUH₂] teche V. *is I-hoten*] hoteþ U.
106. *Is*] þat is U.
107. *as*] TU omit.
108. *dar*] dar wel TU.
109. *on*] of TU.
110. *is—ȝiftes*] þat gold haþ to ȝifte TU.
111. *askede*] axide TU. *dwelleþ*] wonide T ; wonde U.
113. *I—teche þe*] Axe TU.
116. *ȝif*] U om. *to*] with UH₂.
119. *Forte*] Foor til U ; Til T.
120. *From*] For T ; fro U. *speche*] U om.
121. *sobre—symple*] sobirte & simplite T ; soberte of symplesse U.

128   SHE COMMENDS HIM TO CLERGY AND SCRIPTURE.   [PASS. XI.

see Sober and Simple.

Coming to Clergy, tell him it was I who put him to school.

Say I taught his wife the Psalter and Wisdom, logic and music.

I taught Plato and Aristotle.

I also taught masons the use of level and line.

But Theology has vexed me often; musing on it only makes it mistier.

But for the love that is in it, it

þat [eche wyȝt] beo in wil · his wit þe to schewe.
So schalt þou come to Clergye · þat con mony þinges ;
  Sei him þis [signe] · þat I sette him to scole,   124
And þat I grette wel his wyf · for I wrot hire a Bulle,
And sette hire to sapience · and to hire psauter I-gloset.
¶ Lo ! logyk I lered hire · and al þe lawe after,
And alle Musons In Musyk · I made hire to knowe.   128
Plato þe Poyete · I put him furste to Boke,
Aristotle and oþer mo · to Arguen I tauȝte ;
Gramer for [gurles] · I gon furste to write,
And Beot hem wiþ a Baleys · But ȝif þei wolde lernen.
¶ Of alle Maner Craftus · I con Counterfeten heor
  tooles,   133
Of Carpunters and keruers ; · I [kende] furst Masouns,
And lered hem liuel and lyne · þauȝ I loke dimme.
Bote Teologye haþ teoned me · ten score tymes ;   136
  For þe more I [muse] þeron · þe [mistiloker] hit
  semeþ,
And þe deppore I diuinede · þe [derkore] me þouȝte.
Hit is no science forsoþe · to sotilen þer-Inne,
Neore þe loue þat lyhþ þerinne · a lewed þing hit weore.
Bote for hit [let] best bi loue · I leeue hit þe betere ;   141

---

122. [*eche wyȝt* UTH₂] eueri mon V.
123. *þinges*] wyttes T.
124. [*signe* TUH₂] tokene V.   þat] TU *omit.*
125. U *omits. And—grette*] And þat þou grete T ; And if thou grete H₂.   *a Bulle*] þe bible T.
126. *to hire*] to þe U.
127. *Lo*] TUH₂ *omit.*
128. *alle—in*] alle þe musons of T ; alle þe musonys of U.   *to knowe*] knowe alse T.
130. *to—tauȝte*] I tawte ferst to argue U.
131. [*gurles* H₂TU] children V ; *see* P. X. l. 155.   *to*] TU omit.
133, 134. And alle kynne craftis · I contreuide here,
  Tolis of carpenteris & kerueris ·

& kende ferst masons T ;
And alle kynne craftis · I construed hure ferst to lere,
Tolis of carpenteris, & kerue · I tauþte (*sic*) ferst masouns U.
[*kende* TH₂] tauȝte V
135. *lered*] lernide TU.   *liuel—lyne*] lyne & leuel U.   *loke*] lokyd U.
137, 138. *The words* mistiloker *and* derkore *both occur in* V, *but in the wrong lines; see various readings.*
137. [*muse* TUH₂] studie V. [*mistiloker*] mistlokere TU ; derkore V.
138. [*derkore*] derkere T ; deppere U ; mistiloker V.   *me*] I U.
140. U *omits. lewed*] wel lewid T.
141. [*let*] lat T ; last U ; *see* l. 29. *leeue*] loue TU.

PASS. XI.]   ASTRONOMY AND GEOMETRY ARE DIFFICULT.   129

For þat loue is þe lord · þat lakkede neuer grace ;   *were a sorry thing.*
¶ Leef wel þer-vppon · ȝif þou þenke Dowel ;   *Believe in love, if thou think to Dowell.*
For Dobet and Dobest · beoþ drawen of [loue] scole.
In oþer science hit seiþ · seo hit in Catoun,   145
   Qui simulat verbis, nec corde est [fidus] Amicus,   *Cato (Dist. l. 20) says differently,*
   [*Tu quoque fac simile, sic ars deluditur arte.*]
But Theologie techeþ not so · hose takeþ kepe,   *but Theology bids us love*
He [kenneþ] us þe contrarie · aȝeyn Catons wordes,
And biddeþ [vs] ben as Breþeren ·and Blessen vr enemys,
And louen hem þat lyȝen on vs · lellyche at heor neode,
And do good aȝeyn vuel; · God him-self hoteþ,   150   *and return good for evil.*
And seide hit him-self · In ensaumple for þe beste,
   Necesse est vt veniant scandala.   *Mat. xviii. 7.*

¶ Bote Astronomye is hard þing · *and* vuel to knowe,   *Astronomy, geometry, and geomancy are three evil things,*
Gemetrie and Gemensye · is gynful of speche,   153
þat worcheþ wi*th* þeose þreo · þriueþ he late,
For sorcerye Is þe souereyn [bok · þ*at* to þat science   *and deal with sorcery.*
   longiþ,
Ȝet arn þere febicchis of Forellis] · of mony mennes
   wittes.   156   *Deal not with alchemy,*
¶ Exper*i*mentis of Alconomye · Of Alberdes makynge,   *nigromancy, or pyromancy;*
Nigromancye and p*er*imancie · þe pouke to Rise makeþ ;

142. For þere þat loue is lord · lakkiþ neue*r*e grace TU ; H₂ *the same, but with* lakkede *for* lakkiþ.
143. *vel þervppon*] lelly þeron TU.
144. [*loue scole* U] lore in scole V ; louis skile T ; loues skyle H₂ ; *see note.*
145. *seo*] I saiȝ T ; I saw U. [*fidus* TU] fidelis V. [*Tu—arte*] *Omitted in* VTUH₂, *but given in* D.
146. *techeþ*] techiþ vs TU ; techit it H₂. *hose*] who T ; who so U. *kepe*] heed TU.
147. [*kenneþ*] kenniþ T ; kennes U ; techeþ V. *us*] U *om.*
148. *biddeþ*] bit U ; bidditb H₂ ; T *omits.* [*vs* TUH₂] V *om.*
149. *hem*] U *om. lellyche*] & lenen he*m* TU.
151. *hit himself*] himself hit V ; TH₂

transpose *the words ; see* note. *Necesse —scandala*] Dilige dominum deum tuum ex toto corde tuo U (*see* l. 236).
152. *Bote*] Ac U ; T *omits.*
153. *Gemetrie*] Geometrie TU. *Gemensye*] geomesie T ; gemessie U. *gynful*] gryfful U. .
154. *worcheþ—þeose*] þinkeþ werche wiþ þo T ; þenkeþ to werche wi*th* þo U ; thynkist dele with tho H₂. *he*] wel T ; wol U.
155, 156. [*bok—forellis*] *From* T ; *also in* UH₂ ; V *omits. febicchis*] fibeches U ; febucches H₂.
156, 157. U *omits the last half of* l. 156, *and the first half of* l. 157. *alconomye*] alkenemye T ; alknamye H₂.
158. *Rise makeþ*] reisen TU ; a-reysen H₂.

9

I invented them to deceive men.

Farewell!"

So I went on till I met Clergy and his wife,

who received me gladly.

Clergy asked after Wit and Study,

And I said they had sent me to learn about Dowell, Do-bet, and Do-best.

'Do-well,' he said, "is an active life, such as that

3if þou þenche Dowel · dele with hem neuere.
Alle þeose sciences · siker, I my-seluen   160
Haue I-founded hem furst · folk to deceyue.
I be-take þe to crist," quod heo · " I con teche þe no
    betere."
I seide, "graunt Merci, Madame " · And Mekeliche hire
    grette,
And wente forþ on my wei · withouten more lettynge,
And fond as heo fore-tolde · and forþ gon I wende, 165
¶ And ar I coome to clergye · couþe I neuer stunte.
I grette þe goode mon · as þe gode wyf me tau3te,
And afterward his wyf · I worschupet hem boþe, 168
And tolde hire þe tokenes · þat me I-tau3t were.
Was neuer gome vppon grounde · seþþen God made
    heuene,
Feirore vndurfonge · ne frendloker maad at ese,
þen I my-self soþli · so sone as heo wuste   172
þat I was of wittes hous · and with his wif Dam Studie.
Curteisliche Clergye · Clupte me and Custe,
    And asked hou wit ferde · and eke his wyf Studie.
And I seide soþlyche · " þei sende me hider   176
To leorne at 3ou Dowel · and Dobet after,
And seþþen Afturward to seo · sumwhat of Dobest."
¶ " Hit is a wel feir lyf," quod heo · " Among þe lewed
    peple,

159. *with hem*] þerwith TU.
160. *siker*] sykerly U. *my-seluen*] my-self foundit TU.
161. Hem formest · folke for to desceyue T ; þurw hem formest · folk to deceyuen U (*see note to l.* 160).
162. *betake—to*] bekenne þe TU.
164. *forþ on*] wi3tly T ; wi3th in U.
165. *foretolde*] fayre tolde U.
167. *I*] And U.
168. *I*] & U. *hem*] T omits.
170. *gome vppon*] grom vpon þis TU.
171. *frendloker*] frendliere T ; frendlekere (*sic*) U ; frendloker H₂.
172. *I*] TU omit. *so*] as U. *as heo*] heo it T.
173. *with*] U om.
174. *Clergye*] clergise T ; clergie H₂. *Clupte*] collide H₂ ; callide T ; calde U.
175. *asked*] axide T ; asked me U. *ferde*] U *omits (by mistake)* ; *it also omits* wyf. *eke—wyf*] his wif T ; his wif dame H₂.
176. *seide*] sei3e T ; seide H₂ ; seyde hem U. *sende*] sente TU. *hider*] þeder U.
177. *leorne*] lere TU. *Dowel*] to dowel U. *after*] þere aftir TU.
179. *feir*] lelly T ; lely U.

PASS. XI.] FURTHER ACCOUNT OF DO-WEL, DO-BET, AND DO-BEST. 131

[Actif it] is I-hoten · hosebondes hit vsen; 180 *of husbandmen, tailors, cobblers.*
['Trewe tilieris on erþe · taillours & souteris, *[The rest is from T, fol. 50 b.]*
And alle kyne crafty men · þat cunne here foode wynne,
Wiþ any trewe trauaille · toille for here foode,
Diken or deluen · do-wel it hatte 184
To breke beggeris bred · & bakken hem with cloþis, *Do-bet is, to feed and clothe*
Counforte þe carful · þat in castel ben fetterid, *beggars, to comfort those in*
And seken out þe seke · & sende hem þat hem nediþ; *prison, and the sick;*
Obedient as breþeren · & sustren to oþere; 188
þus bed þe do-bet · so beriþ witnesse þe sauter;

 Ecce quam bonum et quam iocundum, habitare, *and to live in unity with all,*
 Fratres, in vnum. *Ps. cxxxii. 1 (Vulg.).*

Sike with þe sory · singe with þe glade,
 Gaudere cum gaudentibus; Et flere cum flentibus, *(Rom. xii. 15.)*
[Dredles, is dobet · dobest wot þe sothe!]
Sire dobest haþ benefices · so is he best worþi, 192 *Do-best is to teach*
be þat god in þe gospel · grauntiþ & techiþ; *the people by preaching, Matt.*
 Qui facit et docuerit, magnus vocabitur in regno *v. 19.*
 celorum.

Forþi is dobest · [a] bisshopis pere,
Prince ouer godis peple · to prechen or to chaste.
Dobet doþ ful wel · & dewid he is also, 196 [Fol. 51 a.]
And haþ possessions & pluralites · for pore menis sake. *Do-bet has possessions and*

---

180. [*Actif it* TUH₂D] A lyf V; (*by mere mistake*). *hosebondes*] lewide men T.
 OBS. *Here, most unfortunately, the Vernon text ceases; for the rest, the Trinity MS.* (T) *is taken to form the text, and it is collated with* UDH₂.
181. *taillours*] as taliours U. *&*] or D.
182. *here foode*] with here craft U.
183. *toille*] tilie U.
184. *hatte*] hyȝte U; hattith H₂.
185. *bakken hem*] bak hym D; bachem U.
186. *Counforte*] confortid H₂ (*wrongly*). *þat in*] þat in þe U; in D. *ben*] is U.

187. *seke*] D omits (*by mistake*).
188. *breþeren*] broþer D; brothren H₂. *sustren*] sistres U. *oþere*] alle othir H₂.
189. *þus—þe*] Thus byt D; Thus bad the H₂; þese ben þat U. *so*] þus U.
191. *From MS. Harl. 3954, fol. 122.* TH₂UD *have only a half-line, viz.* God wot, þis is dobet; *and they divide ll. 192, 193 wrongly.*
193. U *omits this line, and the Latin. docuerit*] docuit D.
194. For þis dobest is a bysschopis pere U. [*a* UD] TH₂ *omit.*
195. *ouer*] of U. *or—chaste*] & to techyn U.
196. *dewid*] dewyd H₂; dowel UD.

9 *

endowments to relieve the poor with.	For mendynauntȝ at mischiefe · þe men were dewid ;
	And þat is riȝtful religioun · none renneris aboute,
	Ne no leperis ouer lond · ladies to shryue. 200
Gregory the pope says,	Gregory þe grete clerke · a good pope in his tyme,
	Of religioun þe rewele · he reherside in his morals,
	And seide it in ensaumple · þat þei shulde do þe betere :
'as fish die out of water, so does Religion when out of a convent.'	'Whanne fisshes faile þe flood · or þe fresshe watir,
	þei diȝe for þe drouȝte · whanne þei dreiȝe lengen ; 205
	Riȝt so be religioun · it roileþ and steruiþ,
	þat out of couent & cloistre · coueiten to libben'.
But now Religion is a rider, a land-buyer, and wears a dagger.	Ac now is religioun a ridere · & a rennere aboute, 208
	A ledere of [louedayes] · and a lond biggere,
	Poperiþ on a palfrey · to toune & to toune,
	A bidowe or a baselard · he beriþ be his side ;
	Godis flessh & his fet · & hise fyue woundis 212
	Arn more in his mynde · þan þe memorie of his found-ours.
Such bad lives these lords lead.	þis is þe lif of þis lordis · þat lyuen shulde wiþ do-bet,
	And wel-a-wey wers · and I shulde al telle.
Kings and knights and earls ought to be very good men ;	I wende þat kinghed & kniȝthed · & caiseris wiþ Erlis
	Wern do-wel & do-bet · & do-best of hem alle; 217
	For I haue seiȝe it my-selfe · & siþþen red it aftir,
	How Crist counseilliþ þe comune · & kenneþ hem þis tale,
Mat. xxiii. 2.	*Super cathedram moisi sederunt principes.*
	For-þi I wende þat þo wyes · wern do-best of alle ! 220

198. *þe—dewid*] þo men were I-dued U ; þat men were sumtyme D.

203. *seide it*] seiþ hym U. þei] men U. *do þe*] do D.

204. *or þe*] of þe H₂.

205. *þei—lengen*] þey drye lyggyn D ; thei dreiȝe leggen H₁; it dryheþ longe U.

206. *it roileþ*] þat roxleþ, (*loosely written for* royleþ) U.

208. *aboute*] be strete D; be stretis U.

209. [*louedayes* H₂ ; lufdayes U] ladies TD; *see* l. 20. *lond biggere*] lond-beggere D.

210. *tv—to*] fro toun to H₂UD.

212. *fet*] feet H₂UD.

213. *Arn*] Buþ D. þan þe] þan UD.

215. *shulde*] wold D; *see* note.

216. D *transposes* kniȝthed *and* kinghed ; U *reads*, I wende kyngis & knythis · and kayseres and Erles.

217. *of*] ouer U.

218. *seiȝe it*] it sen U ; seyn it H₂D. *red it*] i-rad U.

219. *counseilliþ*] conseylede U. þis tale] þese lawes U. *In* U *a blank space is left for the Latin.*

I nile not scorne," quod scripture · "but scryueyns
   liȝe;
Kinghod & kniȝthod · for auȝt I can aspie,
Helpiþ nouȝt to heuene · at one ȝeris ende,
Ne richesse ne rentis · ne realte of lordis. 224
Poul prouiþ it is vnpossible · riche men in heuene,
Ac pore men in pacience · & penaunce togidere
Hauen eritage in heuene · ac riche men non."—
"Contra," quod I, "be Crist! · þat can I þe wisse, 228
And prouen it be þe pistil · þat petir is nempnid;
   Qui crediderit et baptizatus fuerit, saluus erit."
"Þat is *in extremis*," quod scripture · "as sarisines &
   Iewis
Mowe be sauid so · & so is oure beleue;
Þat [an] vncristene in þat cas · may cristene an heþene,
And for his lele beleue · whanne he his lif tyneþ, 233
Haue eritage in heuene · as an heiȝ cristene.
Ac cristene men, god wot · comiþ not so to heuene;
For cristene han a degre · & is þe comun speche,
   Dilige deum, etc., Et proximum tuum sicut teipsum.
Godis word witnessiþ we shuln ȝiue · & dele oure
   enemys, 237
And alle men þat arn nedy · [as] pore men & suche, [Fol. 51 b.]
   *Dum tempus est, operemur bonum ad omnes, maxime
   autem ad domesticos fidei.*
Alle kynne creatures · þat to crist beleuiþ

Where as kinghood and knighthood help not to heaven.

Paul says the rich cannot win heaven (1 Tim. vi. 9)."

"I deny it," I said, "I refer you to Peter" (Mark xvi. 16).

"That refers to Saracens and Jews," said she.

"The rule for Christians is given in Lu. x. 27;

and in Gal. vi. 10.

221. *nile*] nel D; wele U.
222. *auȝt*] nouȝt D.
223. *heuene*] hefne-ward U.
225. *it is*] U *om. is*] D *om. riche—heuene*] þe riche to comen in hefne U.
226. *men*] D *omits*. *penaunce*] U *repeats* pacience.
227. *Hauen*] han here U. *ac*] and U.
228. *þat—wisse*] i kan þe withseye U. *þe*] D *omits*.
229. *þe pistil*] apostil U. *is nempnid*] it nemnyþ D. *saluus erit*] U *omits*.

230. *is*] U *omits*. *as*] among U.
231. *so is*] þat U (*omitting* is).
232. *þat—cas*] þat oon cristen in cas U. [*an*] oon U; arn TH₂; buþ D; *see* note.
234. *Haue*] Haue an U.
236. *degre*] dirige U. *is þe*] our U. *Dilige, &c.*] Nemo, &c. U (*see* l. 255).
237. *we—ȝiue*] þat we schal þeue (l) U (*by error for* yeue).
238. [*as* H₂U] & T; D *omits. fidei*] H₂ *omits*.
239. Alle kynde creatours þat crist ben y-lyche U. *beleuiþ*] longen D.

We be holde hei3ly · to herie & honoure, 240
And 3iuen hem of oure good · as good as oure seluen,
And souereynliche to suche · þat sewen oure beleue ;

Christians ought to help each other.
þat is, iche cristene man · be kynde to oþer,
And siþen hem to helpe · in hope hem to amende. 244
To harme hem ne slen hem · god hi3te vs neuere ;
For he seiþ it hym-selfe · in his ten hestis,

See Lu. xviii. 20 ; and Rom. xii. 19."
[Non] mecaberis, ne sle nou3t · is þe kynde englissh,
For, Michi [vindicta], et ego retribuam ;
I shal punisshen in purcatory · or in þe put of helle
Eche man for his misdede · but mercy it make." 249

" But I am no nearer than I was," said I.
"3et am I neuere þe ner · for nou3t I haue walkid
To wyte what is do-wel · witterly in herte ;
For how so I werche in þis world · [wrong] oþer ellis,

" I am saved, if saved, by predestination.
I was markid, withoute mercy · & myn name entrid 253
In þe legende of lif · longe er I were ;
Or ellis vndir-writen for wykkid · as witnessiþ þe gospel,

John iii. 13.
 Nemo ascendet ad celum nisi qui de celo descendit.

Solomon, who wrote Wisdom—
And I leue on oure lord · & on no lettrure betere ; 256
For salamon þe sage · þat sapience made,
God 3af [hym] grace · & richesse to-gidere
For to reule his reaum · ri3t at his wille ;

did he not well ?
Dede he not wel & wisly · as holy chirche techiþ, 260
Boþe in werke & in woord · in world in his tyme ?

Yet he and
Aristotle & he · who wrou3te betere ?

240. *We—holde*] We ben I-holde U ; Ben holde D.
241. *oure*] here D. *oure seluen*] hem-seluen D.
242. *þat sewen*] as suen U.
243. *is*] U *omits*. *kynde*] kende U.
244. *to helpe*] helpyn D. *to*] D *omits*.
245. *ne*] ne to H₂ ; or to U.
246. *For*] U *omits*.
247. [*Non* UD] Ne TH₂. *mecaberis*] Sic ; (the mistake is the author's). *kynde*] D *om*. [*vindicta*] vindictam TH₂UD (*all wrong*).
248. *punisshen*] pyne U.

249. *Eche*] Euery U.
250. *nou3t*] nowth þat U.
252. *So the line stands in* D ; TH₂ *omit* wrong ; U *reads*, For how so I werche · wrong or ellis.
253. *withoute*] with U.
254. *þe*] H₂ *omits*. *were*] ded ware U.
255. *vndirwriten*] vnwrite U. *wykkid—gospel*] wiled · þus sciþ þe gospel U.
256. *And—on*] And I leue it, be D ; And beleue on H₂. *lettrure*] lettere U.
258. [*hym* UD] hem TH₂.
260. *& wisly*] ne wysly D.

And al holy chirche · holden hem in helle ! _{Aristotle are in hell!}
And was þere neuere in þis world · to wysere of werkis ;
For alle cunnynge clerkis · siþþe crist ȝede on erþe 265 _{All clerks follow their advice;}
Taken ensaumples of here sawis · in sarmonis þat þei maken,
And be here werkis & here wordis · wissen vs to dowel;
And ȝif I shal werke be here werkis · to wynne me heuene, 268 _{and were I to do the same, and yet go to hell, I were unwise indeed !}
And for here werkis & for here wyt · wende to pyne,
þanne wrouȝte I vnwisly · wiþ alle þe wyt þat I lere !
A goode friday, I fynde · a feloun was sauid _{But the thief on the cross was saved, because he shrove him to Christ;}
þat hadde lyued al his lyf · wiþ lesinges & þeftis ; 272
And for he kneuȝ on þe crois · & to crist shref hym,
Sonnere hadde he saluacion · þanne seint Ion þe baptist,
Or Adam or ysaye · or any of þe prophetis,
þat hadde leyn with lucifer · manye longe ȝeris ; 276 [Fol. 52 a.]
A robbere hadde remission · raþere þanne þei alle, _{and so a robber escaped purgatory.}
Withoute penaunce of purcatorie · to haue paradis for euere.
þanne marie þe maudeleyn · who miȝte do wers ? _{Who did worse than Mary Magdalen, or Paul?}
Or who dede wers þanne dauid · þat vrie destroyede ?
Or poule þe apostil · þat no pite ne hadde, 281
Cristene kynde · to kille to deþe ?
And arn [none] for soþe · souereynes in heuene, _{Yet they are now in heaven.}
As þise þat wrouȝte wykkidly · in world whanne þei were. 284
And ȝet I forget [ferþere] · of fyue wyttis techinge,

---

263. *al*] U *omits*. *hem*] hym D.
264. *þere*] U *omits*. *to*] two D; no U.
266. *ensaumples*] ensaumple H₂; exsample U. *maken*] maden H₂.
268. *werkis*] werk U; wordes D.
269. And I for here werkis · wende to pyne U.
270. *þanne—I*] þan wroutty U. *vnwisly*] vnwittily U. *þat*] D *om*.
272. U *omits this line*.
273. *And—on*] For he knelyd to U. *kneuȝ*] knew H₂D. *shref*] *so in* TDH₂; schrof U.
274. *he*] UD *omit*.
275. *þe*] þese U; those H₂.
276. *with*] be U.
278. *of*] in U.
279. *þe*] UD *omit*.
280. *who*] U *omits*.
281. *ne*] UD *omit*.
283. [*none* U; non DH₂] now T. *souereynes*] souereyn D. Arn none for sothe · so fer in hefne U.

136   CLERKS LOSE HEAVEN ; PLOUGHMEN WIN IT.   [PASS. XI.

Christ never commended clergy (learning); see Mark xiii. 9, 11,

þat clergie of cristis mouþ · comendite [was euer] ;
For he seide it hym-selfe · to summe of his disciplis,
  [*Cum*] *steteritis ante presides, nolite cogitare* [*quid loquamini*] ;

which says,

And is as muche to mene · to men þat ben lewid,   288

' When ye are brought before kings,' &c.

' Wheþer 3e ben aposid of princes · or of prestis of þe lawe,
For to answere hem · haue 3e no doute,
For I shal graunte 3ow grace · of god þat 3e seruen,
þe help of þe holy gost · to answere hem at wille.'   292
þe douʒtiest doctour · or dyuynour of þe trinite,

Augustine says,

þat Austyn þe olde · & hiʒeste of þe foure,
Seide þis for a sarmoun · (so me god helpe !)

(Confess. Lib. viii. c. 8),

Ecce ipsi [*ydiote*] *rapiunt celum, vbi nos sapientes in infernum mergemur ;*
And is to mene in oure mouþ · more ne lesse,   296
' Arn none raþere yrauisshid · fro þe riʒte beleue

' Wise clerks are often sunk in hell.

þanne arn þise grete clerkis · þat conne many bokis ;
Ne none sonnere ysauid · ne saddere of consience,

whilst poor ploughmen and shepherds attain heaven,'

þanne pore peple as plouʒmen · and pastours of bestis.'
Souteris & seweris · suche lewide iottis   301

by help of but one Pater-noster ! "

Percen wiþ a pater noster · þe paleis of heuene,
Wiþoute penaunce, at here partynge · in-to heiʒe blisse !
Breuis oracio penetrat celum."

285—287. U *omits.*
285, 286. *These two lines are corruptly given in all the* MSS. *See* Critical Note.
287. [*Cum* U] Dum TH₂D. [*quid loquamini*] *In* U *only.*
288. *And*] It U. *as*] H₂ *omits.*
289. *Wheþer*] Whar D ; Whan U. *or of*] othir of H₂ ; or UD.
290. *hem*] hym U.
292. *at wille*] alle UD.
293. *or—trinite*] dempnour of þe lawe U
294. *þat*] þat was U. *hiʒeste*] þe heist U.
295. *Seide þis*] And seide þus U.

[*ydiote* U] ydioti TH₂ ; Idioti D. *rapiunt*] rapuerunt H₂. *vbi—mergemur*] et nos cum doctrinis nostris demergemur in infernum U.
297. *Arn*] Buþ D.   *fro*] for D.
298. *þanne—þise*] þan þese U ; Than buþ D.
300. *and*] or D.
301. *suche*] and swiche U.   *iottis*] Iuttis U.
302. *Percen*] Pasen U.
303. *heiʒe*] þe heye U ; the heʒe H₂. *Breuis—celum*] UD *omit.*
OBS. *See* Critical Notes *as to this ending.*

(*To follow page* 136.)

SUPPLEMENT TO "PIERS PLOWMAN," PART I. TEXT A.

[*MS. Rawl. Poet.* 137. *Fol.* 40.]

PASSUS XII.

Passus tercius de dowel.

"Crist wot," qu*o*d clergie · "knowe hit ȝif þe lyke,   "Christ knows,"
I haue do my deu*er* · þe dowel to teche;   said Clergy, "I have tried to teach you Do-wel.
And who-so coueyteþ do*n* betere · þa*n* þe boke telleþ,
He passeþ þe apostolis lyf · and put hi*m* to au*n*gelys | 4
But I se now as I seye · as me soþ thinkytȝ,
þe were lef to lerne · but loþ for to stodie.
þou woldest konne þat I can · and carpe*n* hit after.   You want to learn in order to cavil."
P*re*sumptuowsly, p*ar*auenture · a-pose so manye,   8
That [hit] myȝthe turne me*n* to tene · & theologie boþe.
Ȝif I wiste witterly · þou woldest don þer-after,
Al þat þou askest · a-soylen I wolde."
Skornfully þo scripture · [set vp here] browes,   12   Scripture set up her brows,
And on clergie crieþ · on criste*s* holy name,   and told Clergy not to tell me more.
That he shewe me hit ne sholde · but ȝif [hit] stryf were
Of þe kynde cardinal wit · and cristned in a font;—
And seyde [hit] so loude · þat shame me thouȝthe,   16
"þat hit were boþe skaþe · and sklau*n*dre to holy cherche,   "Theology

[NOTE. See the account at the end of the Passus, shewing whence this Twelfth Passus is derived.]
Pass. XII. *Called* Passus tercius de dowel *in* MS. U *and* MS. Rawlinson 137. See the note to Pass. XI. l. 303, on p. 154.
1. þe] ye U; *but the* y *represents* þ.
3. *coueyteþ don*] coueite to don U.
4. þe] U *om.* him] hem U; *corruptly.*
6. U *omits.*
9. [*hit*] it U; MS. Rawlinson *omits.*

men] me U.
12. þo] *miswritten* þe *in* MS. Rawlinson; U *has* yo = þo. [*set vp here*] *So in* U; MS. Rawlinson *has* sherte vp his, *where at least* his *is wrong.*
13. crieþ] cryede U. cristes] godis U.
14. *shewe me hit*] schewiȝt U (*corruptly*). [*hit*] it U; MS. Rawl. *om.*
15. *kynde*] U *om.*
16. [*hit*] it U; MS. Rawl. *om.* me] me it U.
17. *boþe*] U *om.*

forbids me to teach sinners.	Sitthe theologie þe trewe · to tellen hit defendeþ;
	Dauid godes derling · defendyþ hit al-so:
Ps. cxviii. 158 (Vulg.).	*Vidi [preuaricantes] et tabescebam :*
	I saw synful, he seyde · þer-fore I seyde no-þing, 20
	Til þo wrecches ben in wil · here synne to lete.
	And poul precheþ hit often · prestes hit redyn,
2 Cor. xii. 4.	*Audiui archane que non licet homini loqui :*
	I am not hardy, quod he · þat I herde with erys,
	Telle hit with tounge · to synful wrecches. 24
	And god graunted hit neuere · þe gospel hit witnesseþ,
	In þe passioun, whan pilat · a-posed god al-myȝthi,
[Fol. 40 b.]	And asked Ihesu on hy · þat herden hit an hundred,
Jo. xviii. 38.	*Quid est ueritas ?* quod he · verilyche tel vs; 28
	God gaf him non answere · but gan his tounge holde.
So do not tell him any more"	Riȝt so I rede," quod she · " red þou no ferþer ;
	Of þat he wolde wite · wis him no betere.
	For he cam not by cause · to lerne to dowel, 32
	But as he seyþ, such I am · when he with me carpeþ."
At this, Clergy withdrew.	And when scripture þe skolde · hadde þus wyt y-sheued,
	Clergie in-to a caban · crepte anon after,
	And drow þe dore after him · and bad me go dowel, 36
But I prayed Scripture to tell me where her cousin Kind Wit (Common Sense) lived.	Or wycke, ȝif I wolde · wheþer me lyked !
	Þan held I vp myn handes · to scripture þe wise,
	To be hure man ȝif I most · for euere-more after,
	With þat she wolde me wisse · wher þe toun were, 40
	Kynde wit hure confessour · hure cosyn was Inne.
	Þat lady þan low · and lauȝthe me in here armes,
	And sayde, "my cosyn kynde wit · knowen is wel wide,
	And his loggyng is with lyf · þat lord is of erþe. 44
	And ȝif þou desyre · with him for to a-byde,

18. *Sitthe*] Scihoþ (*sic*) U. þe trewe] yat trewe is U. to] U om.
19. [*preuaricantes*] *So in* U; MS. Rawl. *corruptly has* preuaricationes.
20. MS. U *ends with* tabescebam; *and from this line to the end, we have only* MS. Rawl. *to trust to.* seyde no-þing] It is clear that the poet construes *tabescebam* as if it were *tacebam*.

The same idea recurs in ll. 23 and 29.
22. *Audiui*, &c. Quoted again in Text B. Pass. XVIII.
33. *such I am*] i. e. I am not to be commended; alluding to Pass. XI. l. 286.
41. *wit.*] The MS. *has* wt, *the usual contraction for* with; *but see* ll. 43 *and* 53; *and* hit *for* hit, l. 25.

[PASS. XII.] THE AUTHOR GOES TO SEEK OUT KIND WIT.

I shal þe wisse · where þat he dwelleþ."
And þanne I kneled on my knes · and kyste her wel sone,   *"I will tell you," she said.*
And þanked hure a þousand syþes · with þrobbant herte.   48
She called [to ken] me · a clerioun þat hyȝt   *She said to Omnia-probate,*
Omnia-probate · a pore þing with alle,   *"Go and show Will the way."*
" þou shalt wende with wil," quod she · " whiles þat him lykyþ,
Til ȝe come to þe burghe · quod-bonum-est-tenete.   52
Ken him to my cosenes hous · þat kinde wit hyȝth,
Sey I sente him þis segge · and þat he shewe hym dowel."
Þus we lauȝþe oure leue · lowtyng at onys,   *So we went to the court called Quod-bonum-est-tenete.*
And wente forþ on my way · with omnia-probate,   56
And ere I cam to þe court · quod-bonum-est-tenete,
Many ferlys me by-fel · in a fewe ȝeris.
The fyrste ferly I fond · a-fyngrid me made;   *[Fol. 41.]*
As I ȝede thurgh ȝouþe · a-ȝen prime dayes,   60   *As I went through Youth, I met a man and hailed him.*
I stode stille in a stodie · and stared a-bowte;
" Al hayl," quod on þo, and I answered " welcome · and with whom be ȝe?"
" I am dwellyng with deth · and hunger I hatte,   *He said he lived with Death, and his name was Hunger.*
To lyf in his lordshepe · longyt my weye,   64
I shal felle þat freke · in a fewe dayes!"
" I wolde folwe þe fayn · but fentesye me hendeþ,
Me folweþ such a fentyse · I may no ferþer walke."
" Go we forþ," quod þe gom · " I haue a gret boyste   68   *He offered me some scraps of bread.*
At my bak, of broke bred · þi bely for to fylle;

49, 50. *These two lines are written as one in the MS. Some such phrase as* to ken me *seems to have been lost; see* l. 53.

50. *Omnia probate*] *Compare Text B. Pass. III. l. 335.*

52. *burghe*] ? burgher *MS. But* burghe = borough *is meant; it is called* a court *in* l. 57.

58. *Cf. Prologue; l. 62. Here follows the catchword*—þe ferste ferly.

60. ȝouþe] *miswritten* ȝou · þe *in MS.; the metrical dot being inserted by mistake after the letter* u. *But the reading is certain; cf.* Text B. Pass. XI. 17, 34, 59; *and especially observe the whole drift of* Text B. Pass. XI.

62. *A half-line has probably been lost here.*

66. Cf. Pass. V. 5.

HE MEETS WITH HUNGER AND FEVER. [PASS. XII.

A bagge ful, of a beggere · I bouȝþe hit at onys."
Than maunged I wit · vp at þe fulle,
For þe myssyng of mete · no mesour I coude. 72
With þat cam a knaue · with a confessoures face,
He halsed me and I · asked him after,
Of when þat he were · and wheder þat he wolde.

Next I met one called Fever.
"With deþ I duelle," quod he · " dayes and nyȝtes ; 76
Mi name is feuere, on þe ferþe day · I am a-þrest euere ;
I am masager of deþ · men haue I tweyne,
þat on is called cotidian · a courour of oure hous,
Tercian þat oþer · trewe drinkeres boþe ! 80
We han letteres of lyf · he shal his lyf [tyne ;]
Fro deþ, þat is oure duk · swyche dedis we brynge."
" Myȝth I so, god wot · ȝoure gates wolde I holden."

"Do not follow me, Will," he said.
"Nay, wil !" quod þat wyȝth · " wend þou no ferther, 84
But lyue as þis lyf · is ordeyned for the,
þou tomblest wiþ a trepget · ȝif þou my tras folwe ;
And mannes merþe wrouȝþ no mor · þan he deseruyþ here,

"But do well while your days last."
Whil his lyf and his lykhame · lesten to-gedere. 88
And þer-fore do after do-wel · whil þi dayes duren,

[Fol. 41 b.]
þat þi play be plentevous · in paradys with aungelys.
þou shalt be lauȝth into lyȝth · with loking of an eye,
So þat þou werke þe word · þat holy wryt techeþ, 92
And be prest to preyeres · and profitable werkes."

So Will made haste to write his Do-wel; and he also wrote his Peres the Plowman.
Wille [wiste] þurgh in-wit— · þou wost wel þe soþe—
þat þis speche was spedelich · and sped him wel faste,
And wrouȝthe þat here is wryten · and oþer werkes boþe 96

---

70. *bouȝþe*] *cf.* wrouȝþ, l. 87 ; lauȝþe, l. 55 ; &c.

71. *Corrupt ; probably two half-lines lost.*

78. Fevers *and* Death *appear in* Text B. Pass. XX.

81. [*tyne*] *The* MS. *has* tyme, *corruptly. See* Pass. XI. 233.

86. *þou*] *miswritten* þe *in the* MS. ; the *being the preceding word.*

87. *wrouȝþ*] = wrouȝte. Cf. l. 70. *The reading* worþe *would make better sense.*

94. *The word* wiste *has evidently been dropped here, probably on account of* wost *following.*

96. *This means that, besides the* Vita de Do-wel, Do-bet, et Do-best, *the author wrote* Peres the Plowman.

THE AUTHOR'S WORKS AND DEATH.

Of per*es* þe plowma*n* · and mechel puple al-so;
And wha*n* þis werk was wrouȝt · er*e* wille myȝte a-spie,
Deþ delt hi*m* a dent · and drof hi*m* to þe erþe,   *Now he lies buried under the*
And is closed vnder clom · crist haue his soule!   100   *clay!*

And so bad Iohan but · busily wel ofte,   *John But added this ending.*
When he saw þes sawes · busyly a-legged
By Iames and by Ierom · by Iop and by oþer*e*,
And for he medleþ of makyng · he made þ*is* ende.   104
Now alle ke*n*ne creatur*es* · þat cristene were euere,
God for his goudnesse · gif he*m* swyche happes,
To lyue as þat lord lykyþ · þat lyf in he*m* putte.
Furst to rekne Richard · kyng of þ*is* rewme,   108   *God save King Richard, and al.*
And alle lord*es* þat louy*n* hi*m* · lely in herte,   *lords that love him!*
God saue he*m* sound · by se and by land;
Marie moder and may · for man þou by-seke;
þat barn bryng vs to blys · þat bled vp-on þe rode!
     Ame*n*.   112

𝕰𝖝𝖕𝖑𝖎𝖈𝖎𝖙 𝖉𝖔-𝖂𝖊𝖑.

Nomen scriptoris · tisot plenus amoris.

98—100. These are the author's own words; he kills himself off, by way of finishing his poem, but he lived to re-write it, nevertheless.

101—112. Obviously added, as stated, by another hand, viz. that of John But, who made a second "end," because he was accustomed to "meddle with makyng," i. e. to compose verses.

102. *busyly*] *Read* sothely? Busyly *is repeated from the line above.*

NOTE ON PASSUS XII.

THE discovery of the *unique* copy of the greater part of this Passus is due to Mr Geo. Parker, assistant in the Bodleian Library, from observation of my note at p. 154 of the volume containing Text A of Piers Plowman. It is a most important and satisfactory discovery, as offering the complete solution of the problem as to the true termination of Text A. I had made out this much ; (1) that there was once a Passus XII., or more strictly a *Passus tertius de dowel*, of which 18 lines were preserved in MS. U (belonging to University College, Oxford) ; (2) that this Passus must have been the *concluding* one of the Poem of *Dowel* in its earliest form ; (3) that it must have contained considerably less than 180 lines, as shown by the state of the Vernon MS.; (4) that it must, in fact, have consisted of less than 131 lines, as shown by the state of the University College MS. All these suppositions are now fulfilled ; the missing portion—100 lines long—was found by Mr Parker in MS. Rawl. Poet. 137, in the Bodleian Library, the very existence of which was unknown to me until the Rawlinsonian MSS. were recently catalogued. This is now here printed, with various readings of the first 19 lines, one of which, the sixth, is omitted in the University College copy. This Rawlinson MS. is corrupt in places; in fact, *every* MS. of Piers Plowman is corrupt occasionally ;—but it is sufficiently good to show us clearly how the poem ended. I here add a formal description of it, to supplement the descriptions on pp. xv—xxiv.

XI. MS. Rawlinson Poet. 137 ; on vellum ; of the early part of the fifteenth century. Size, about $9\frac{1}{2}$ in. by $5\frac{3}{4}$. It consists of 41 leaves bound together, containing the *whole* of Piers Plowman, Text A. The four loose leaves, mentioned below as forming part of the old cover, are numbered 42—45. It is very remarkable as being the *only perfect* copy of its kind. At the beginning is the important heading—" Hic incipit liber qui uocatur pers plowman. *Prologus* ; " and this is the *only* copy of any kind I have yet seen wherein the word *Prologus* occurs. See Page 1, first footnote. At the end is the very important colophon— Explicit Do-wel, shewing that the poem really *did* end here, in its earliest form. It is beyond a doubt copied from an earlier MS., viz. *the very same one that MS.* U (No. IV) *was copied from.* The text is in *precisely the same wrong order*, the misarrangement of which is explained at p. xx. It has nearly the same readings, such as *when I south wente* (Prol. l. 1)—*y wente wyde* (l. 4)—*I sweuenede* (l. 10)—*tryly ontyrid* (where MS. U has *a-tired;* l. 14); and so on. But it nevertheless varies slightly from that MS. occasionally, the most curious instance which I have noticed being in the Prologue, at l. 54, where MS. Rawl. has the lines—

  Schopyn hem ermytes · here ese to haue.
   on fele halue · fonden hem to done,
 Lederes þei be of louedayes · and *with* þe lawe medle.

All these MS. U omits, possibly on account of an undecipherable word in the second line, where MS. Rawl. has a blank space. But the most curious point about the two latter lines is their non-appearance in other copies. After Piers Plowman follow "Fragments of the old French Romance of Guy earl of Warwick, four leaves on vellum." ff. 42—45 (end of MS.)[1]

  Ces ciz li quice ad riame.
  Assez sur donc or e argent.
  Del son meint vesselment.
  Sire q̄s Jonas dit li rei.
  Entendez ore vers moi.
  Ma vie me auez ore garri
  Par ceo cher ke esta ici, &c.

On fol. 42 *b* is written in an old and large hand, *Hoc volumen conceditur ad vsum fratrum minorum de obseruantia cantuarie.* The name of the scribe was one Tisot.

I have not the slightest doubt of the entire *genuineness* of the new portion. It is Langland's beyond a doubt, every word of it, from line 1 down to the end of line 100. All these lines are not only in his manner, but contain his favourite words, phrases, and turns of expression, and have the same changes of rhythm as we find in his works elsewhere. We obtain also a new proof that the author's name was "Will;" as had been already ascertained by observing that Thought calls the author "Wille" in Pass. IX. l. 118, just after it had been noted (l. 62) that the same Thought was acquainted with the author's "kind" or Christian name. We learn further that the author's original idea was to conclude the poem in the following way. "I met," he says, "with a man named Fever, who was the messenger of Death." Fever brought a letter from Death, and was authorized to slay Life. "If I may"—says our author—"I would go with you on your way." But Fever tells him to live on, as God has ordained, to continue to *do well,* and to look for a reward

---

[1] These probably formed part of the old cover, the MS. having now a modern binding.

in Paradise, if he will only be regular at prayers, and ready to do profitable works. "Now William (i. e. the author) knew by his conscience that this speech required immediate attention, and so he made haste and completed the poem here written; and besides this Poem of Do-wel, he wrote the poem about Piers Plowman and many others;

> and when this work was wrought, ere Will might spy,
> Death dealt him a dint, and drove him to the earth;
> and he is enclosed under clay; now Christ have his soul!"

It is obvious that this notice of his own death is a mere flourish, introduced for the sake of winding up the poem at a moment when he had no idea of expanding and rewriting it; which, however, he certainly did, and even used again some of the phrases and thoughts contained in this very portion at the end of which he kills himself off. And with these words—"Christ have his soul!"—the poem, in its first form, truly ends. But in the present copy we have 12 superfluous lines, added by one "Johan But," who, having read the whole poem, and being satisfied that most of the ideas in it could be well supported by quotations from James, Jerome, Job, and others, was pleased to dignify it with an ending of his own, as he had been accustomed to metrical composition himself, having before then "meddled in making," i. e. dabbled in verse. But he has very little more to say than to hope that God will bless all men and teach them to do right; and so God save King Richard and all his lords, and may Mary, mother and maiden, beseech for man, and may Christ bring us all to bliss. The commonplaceness of these lines, and the smallness of their number, is of some importance. It shews us how men fared who attempted to add to the master-poet's words, and it affords some proof of the genuineness of the numerous additions which Langland made in his later versions, and which are not in the "Johan But" style by any means.

CRITICAL NOTES, ETC.

CRITICAL NOTES.

[The following notes explain a few things more at length with respect to the various readings of the MSS.; to have inserted them in the footnotes would have been inconvenient.]

PROLOGUE, l. 14. In the word *I-maket* in the text, the MS. has a short tag to the final *t* ; a similar tag occurs twice elsewhere, one instance being in the word *prechet* (Pass. I. l. 137). It has no significance.

I have altered *wonderliche* to *triȝely*, to preserve the alliteration, although MS. H supports the reading of V. The fuller alliterations found in the later copies were no doubt due, partly to corrections by the author himself, and partly to emendations (often ignorantly made) by copyists. Thus in l. 20, *Eringe* was soon changed (no doubt by the author) into *settyng*, but it does not follow that the alteration should be made in this early text. Nevertheless, I have ventured to write *triȝely* here, for the reason given by Mr Wright in making a similar change. "Though we find instances of irregularity in the sub-letters (or alliterative letters in the first [part of the] line) in Pierce Plowman, the chief-letter is not so often neglected." In other places, I have not always given my reason for making alterations in the text, but the footnotes will generally supply one; and besides, I have always had regard to Text B.

22. Alliteration is here at fault. Even if we write *And wonnen þat* for *þat monie of*, it is still imperfect.

28. This line is repeated at Pass. VII. l. 134.

39. The two parts of this line are (in V) written in separate lines.

41. See note to l. 14.

54. The omission of *hem* is a mere mistake; it is certainly required, and assists the alliteration.

63. The reading *and he* is perhaps the best; it improves both the sense and the alliteration, and it is supported by Pass. I. l. 55.

68. I have here missed noting a small, yet important variation; instead of "*and* Fastinge" MSS. T and U read "*of* Fastinge;" in the former case, *Falsnesse* and *Fastinge* are considered separately; but in the latter case, the phrase *Falsnesse of Fastinge* means the "breaking of vows made that they would fast."

71. Mr Morris (following Mr Wright) has printed *bouchede;* but the *u*'s

and *n*'s in this MS. are often distinguishable, and in this case the *n* is quite plain. Cf. the readings *bunchiþ* and *bunchid*, which are quite clear also. The reading *bonches* is open to doubt. "Bunchon, *tundo, trudo*." Prompt. Parv.

75. The reading of the text is supported by MS. H, but the alliteration is improved by the alteration, *His sel shulde not be sent*.

79. The chief-letter of the alliteration is wanting.

81. The word *tyme* should certainly be inserted, for even MS. V has the phrase *seþþe Pestilence tyme* elsewhere. *See* Pass. XI. l. 59.

108. For *and* the MS. has *ad*, by mistake; another form, *an*, is not uncommon. The mistake is repeated in Pass. II. l. 17.

PASSUS I. l. 1. For *derke* a great improvement is to read *merke*, as in Text B.

4. The reading *loft* is altogether wrong; even *toft* would have been better, as that would agree with Prol. l. 14, and Pass. I. l. 12.

8. The chief-letter of the alliteration is missing.

37. The same remark applies here. *Word* = world; there is no need of an *l*; we also find, in old English, the spellings *werd* and *ward*.

39. *Seo* = see, in the imperative mood, and the sentence means, "perceive it well inwardly;" but *set* is a simpler and perhaps better reading.

46. The alliteration is defective, as also in ll. 50, 58, 120.

69. For *hit wcore* MS. H has *þis was*.

79. Instead of *teche* we might with advantage read *kenne*, both here and in ll. 90 and 127, and the alteration would be supported by l. 130; but I have preferred leaving the text intact to making *three* alterations.

87. The second *doþ* seems repeated by mistake; I prefer *willeþ*, with which cf. Text B.

121. I am not sure that "wende" is required, and have therefore not inserted it.

122. There is no doubt about the reading of V, as *Corouneþ* is spelt with a capital letter; but *c* and *t* are hardly distinguishable in some MSS., so that *tronen* and *cronen* would look very much alike: still, MS. T has *tronen*, which suits the alliteration.

128. For *Corps* MS. H has *body*, written over an erasure.

135. For *techeþ* the true reading is probably *wisseþ*, and this would explain how such readings arose as *witnesseth* and *askiþ wytnesse*, the latter of which is not very intelligible. Cf. Pass. XI. l. 8.

137. The reading of V—*prechet þe þin harpe*—must surely be wrong, being meaningless; *prechet* seems to be a contraction of *preche it*.

139. The omission of the final *þ* in *Cumseþ* is probably due to the word *þer* following.

143. MS. U omits the word *wo*, evidently by mistake.

148. The wrong reading *by* (for *heiȝe*) is easily explained; the scribe must have been thinking of the mercy shewn by Christ to the penitent thief; but this idea does not agree with the statement that they "pierced his heart."

149, 150. Though V has only *one* line, it is so long as to suggest that it is made up of parts of two; it must have been originally,

Forþi I rede þe [riche · haue reuþe on þe pore,
þauȝ þou beo] Mihtful of Mayn · be Meke of þi wordes.
MS. H has,

þerfore I rede þee ryȝte · haue rewþe of þe pore,
þeiȝ þou be myȝtful of mayn   be meke of þi warkys.

152. For ȝe *schul* MS. H has þou *schalt*, and for ȝe *wenden* it has þou *wendest*, both variations being written over erased words. There are several erasures and alterations in MS. H hereabouts, and the alterations are all for the worse, judging by what can be traced, or guessed at by comparison with the present text.

155, 156. In the first of these lines it would improve the metre to write *lelly* for *trewely;* and in the second, to write *goodliche* for *Treweliche*. But there is a certain *propriety* in the continuous repetition of *trewe* and *treweliche,* which is destroyed by these alterations.

160. MS. V is here clearly wrong, but I have kept the word *Fey*, merely altering its place. *Fey* = faith, as in l. 14 of this Passus; *fait* or *feet* = feat, i.e. deeds or works.

175. MS. V abruptly ends the Passus here, but the remaining lines seem required, and are found in THUH₂D.

182, 183. These lines have occurred before; *see* ll. 123, 124, by help of which we might write them thus, according to the spelling adopted in V;

For-þi I sigge as I seide er · bi siht of þe textes,
Whon alle tresor is I-triȝet · Treuþe is þe beste.

PASSUS II. l. 5. I have altered the reading *heo* of MS. V to *he*, because the next line has the appearance of being added as an after-thought. The meaning of "heo stondeþ" would be "*they* stand;" but what seems to be intended is—"Look on thy left hand (quoth she) and see where *he* (i.e. Falsehood) stands; (there are) both, Falsehood and Flattery, and all *his* (i.e. Flattery's) whole company." The chief reason for supposing that *stondeþ* is here in the singular number is that the form of the question is such as to lead one to suppose so. *He* in MS. V means *he*, *heo* = *she* or *they*.

9. I since find that I omitted to insert that MS. T (as well as H₂) has the reading *pureste in;* this would certainly improve the alliteration, but MS. H supports the reading given, having *richest*. Still, the alteration should, perhaps, have been made.

21. Here the "chief-letter" is certainly lacking in *all* the MSS.; and this is what renders the propriety of altering such lines as line 9 so doubtful.

23. *Forgid* is only better than *brouȝt* because of the alliteration. In Mr Wright's edition we find

Favel thorugh his faire speche
Hath this folk enchaunted,

where the line is mended another way.

27. Here *wyte* is better than *seo* on every account.

28, 29. These lines must have been left out in V by mistake, because the lines as they stand,

"þat þou miht seo ʒif þou wolt · whuche þei ben alle,
Bote ʒif þow wilne to wone · wi*th* treuþe in his Blisse,"

hardly make sense. Line 31, on the contrary, being found in MS. H only, may be an interpolation; it is but a poor line.

34. This line, occurring in H only, may be an interpolation, but something of the sort is greatly wanted to make the sense clearer; and this is why I have inserted it, notwithstanding that it fails to be an alliterative line. I ought to have added that, in MS. H, the next line begins with

And sawe al þat ryche retenaunce, &c.

38. The reading *fyn* is supported by MS. V itself; for *see* l. 51;—"þe *fyn* was arered."

56. The reading of V—*schewen* (omitting *to*)—seems to be a mere error.

59. This line is much wanted; probably omitted in V accidentally.

64. Perhaps the words "of leccherie" should have been inserted; read

Wiþ alle þe lordschupe [of leccherie] · of lengþe and of brede.

76. It should have been added that MS. H inserts *and*, having the reading "and paulyns douʒter." It thus appears that "Pers þe pardoner" and "Paulynes doctor" were probably different persons.

87. Compare l. 101. All the various readings, in both lines, are clearly due to attempts at improving the alliteration.

88. In all the MSS. the chief-letter is wanting.

97. MS. T has the spelling "notories," but it is only the first *a* in "Nataries" that need be altered.

108. The reader will observe that I have *omitted* the word "on," as not needed any longer, when "counseil" is inserted.

118. This line (like ll. 136—139, and 141—143) is a sort of explanatory gloss, and is almost certainly spurious. It means that men cease to believe those who often deceive them; a remark which has nothing to do with the context.

121. Part of this line is written in a later hand, and the words are ill arranged; the true reading is probably,

Many comen to counforte · from care þe false.

129. For "Cuntre" we should probably read "Schires."

136—143. *See* note to l. 118.

160. *Tome*, meaning *leisure*, is no doubt the reading; *see* Text B.

175. The curious reading of T is easily explained; *any skynes* is there written for *anys kynes* or *anyskynys* (any kinds of); the forms *alleskynnes* (all kinds of) and *noskynnes* (no kind of) also sometimes occur in Early English, and these are instances of the genitives *anys* (of any), *alles* (of all), and *nones* (of none); *see* also the footnote to Passus X. l. 2.

183. The reading of V (*dune*) might stand, as it gives sense, viz. "and

the *din* heard." But the alteration to *dume* seems preferable, considering the various readings.

200. It would appear that *hem* was originally the reading in V, and that it was inconsiderately altered to *him*, owing to the frequent occurrence of *him*, as in ll. 199, 201, 202, 203, 204, &c.

206. The right reading is probably not *kepten*, but *copeden;* cf. Text B.

PASSUS III. l. 15. The reading "be clergie leue" suits the alliteration, and is supported by Text B.

19, 20. These lines are absolutely necessary to the sense, if the reading of V is to be retained in l. 18; they were probably omitted in V by mere mistake.

23. The chief-letter is wanting.

26. Here *lauȝten* is the past tense of *lacchen*, to take; thus V gives the right sense, but the wrong word; cf. Text B.

32. H supports V in the reading *tellen ;* but *callen* is better, and occurs in Text B.

43. In H this line ends a page, and the scribe has given two readings of the first half of the line, viz. "A-monge þese courteors & þe comyns," and "A-monge þese clerkes and knytȝtes" (*sic*).

45. Though V alone reads *schomeliche*, it should be retained as more forcible than *schameles ;* it is, of course, to be understood as ironical.

48. *Siþ* must be inserted, *metri gratiá;* it is in Text B.

51. The chief-letter is wanting.

67—72. This sentence is incomplete, having no principal verb; we should, for the sense, supply "I lere ȝou," from l. 61, before "As to punisschen;" i.e. "I instruct you to punish." Cf. ll. 91—94

80. H reads "presentes withoute pans." The sense is "other presents besides pence," or, "presents that are not given in actual money."

88. H supports the reading "brenne;" but "forbrenne" supplies the chief-letter *f*, though not at the beginning of a strongly accented syllable.

91. The chief-letter is wanting here, and also in l. 98; and in l. 93 it is badly placed.

100. The reading *melodyes* of the Vernon MS. can be thus accounted for; the *y* and þ are, throughout, only distinguishable by careful inspection; and thus *melodyes* is put for *melod þes*, i. e. spake these. Nevertheless, it seems better to use the *present* tense *meleþ* (as in the other MSS.), and to adopt the usual spelling þ*eose*.

105. It would greatly improve the alliteration to read *late com* instead of *com late ;* but the chief-letter is not unfrequently thus badly placed; see ll. 93, 124.

133, 134. *False* is here a plural adjective, but *trewe* is singular.

141. *Vre* means *our;* the sense requires *your*, spelt ȝ*oure* in l. 62. Another spelling of *your* is *oure* (*see* l. 64), and for this, *vre* is miswritten.

151. For the second *heo* H reads *& hem*, which improves the sense.

167. *Congeye* may be miswritten for *Conge þe*, the *y* and *þ* being so much alike; but Pass. IV. l. 4 is against this supposition.

174. I could hardly insert *hals* instead of *Nekke*, as the MSS. have *half;* but yet *hals* is probably the right reading, and occurs in MSS. of type B.

189, 224. The alliteration is defective.

243. This line does not run well, probably because the word *apert* is lost; read, Hit is *apert* permutacion.

244. *þou* is the reading of Text B.

245. The alliteration seems to be altogether lost.

260. I have since observed that the *m* in *Samuel* in MS. V is partly erased, thus leaving *Sauel*, i. e. Saul.

264. *clause;* in Text B we here find *cas* = case.

265. The reading of V—*munged*—is a mere mistake, and it has also caused the scribe to write *In Auenture* for *In Aunter* or *An Aunter;* the alliteration resides in the letter *n*, the words being run together, much as though it ran,

I *n*aunter hit *n*uyȝed me; a *n*ende wol I make; compare *nale* and *noke* for *ale* and *oke* after the article *þe*. Text B has, *An auenture it noyed men.*

266—269. I have little doubt that these lines ought to be put lower, having ll. 270, 271 above them, as in TUD and in Text B. But as H preserves the order of V (though it omits ll. 265, 266), I have not made the transposition. The sense is much the same either way.

274. No MS. has here the right reading; it should be, *or takeþ aȝeyn his wille*, as in Text B. V and H are right, except in putting *doþ* for *takeþ* (which spoils the alliteration); the other MSS. are right in suggesting *takeþ*, but wrong otherwise.

Passus IV. l. 11. I insert *Crist* for *god* on the sole authority of T, because it is the reading of Text B, and supplies the chief-letter.

15. For *sende* T has *sente*.

51. Text B resembles TUD; the words *And seide* do not count in scansion, but even then the line, as in TUD, is very long, and the best line would be made by reading,

And seide, "Hedde I loue of my lord · luite wolde I recche."

68. The word *ȝeorne* seems wanted; yet it does not occur in Text B, and only in MS. V of type A.

69. *catel* suits the alliteration, and is in Text B.

73. The note means that the quotation from U is written all in one long line; and so it is in D; clearly owing to the omission of the first half of l. 72.

91. The reading *Crist* is better for the alliteration, but only appears in U; Text B says, "so me Crist helpe."

94. *hynen* was probably omitted in V because of *myne* preceding; the scribe may have thought he had finished writing *hyne*, when he had only finished *myne;* Text B has "myne hewen;" cf. l. 42 above.

114. The misreading *do euere* in T and D is a mere corruption of the word *Dover*.

124. That *gold* in MS. V is an error is plain enough; the context shews that *gold* is the very last thing that "Reson" would swear by.

126. Whatever be the meaning of this line, *withouten* must be a misreading; Texts B and C have *with;* and *with-outen* seems peculiar to V.

151. The alliteration is defective; Text B shews that *quod* should be *seide*, and the leading letter of the line is an *S*.

158. This is a good example of the variations of spelling; *lyue* and *leue* are the same word, repeated.

Passus V. 1. 29. *wyuene*. Mr Wright prints *wynene*, and in several MSS. it is doubtful; but in MS. T the *u* is made with peculiar care, and so is the *n* following. The misreading in U is owing to the fact that the scribe first wrote *heuene*, and then drew the pen through it and substituted *wyuene*, which suggests a *similarity in sound* between the words *heuene* and *wyuene*. Again, the misreading in V in the line above, *stauenes* for *staues*, seems due to this same word *wyuene*, and to confusion between the endings of *staue* and *wyuene*, which also points to the probability of the letter being *u*. The *wyuene pyne*, or punishment for women, is intelligible, and may mean the cucking-stool (cf. *pynnyng-stoles*, Pass. III. 69); but *wynene pyne* is inexplicable.

58. *dynen;* so in Text B.

83. *As I his frend were* is the right order of words, and is used in Text B. For the syllable *I* gives the chief-letter of the alliteration, and we must lay a slight stress on it, as also on the first syllables of *heilede* and *hendely*.

100, 101. Text B also has these lines rightly arranged; hence it is certain that the arrangement in V and H is a mere mistake.

109, 110. I mark T as *faulty* because such a long line is inadmissible; and even the first line of H is somewhat of the longest. But the fact is that *all* the early MSS. seem here wrong, owing to the omission of a half line—(*as a blynde hagge*)—for which see Text B. The confusion arose from there being two lines following having the same rime-letter (*b*). The arrangement in the Vernon MS., though perhaps not really right, scans well and makes good sense.

114. Text B also gives this line rightly, in the same shape.

125. *lernde I* should perhaps have been *I rendrit*, as in T, U, and Text B; but I let it stand because H agrees with V, and my object is to avoid alteration as much as possible.

131. Here, however, the word *by* must be inserted because it is necessary to the sense. V seems to have *a quartrun more peisede*, but there are marks shewing that the words are to be transposed.

142. *sopely;* Text B, however, has *so the ik*, so thrive I.

165. The reading in V is absurd; the *ribibor* and *ratoner* are distinct personages.

182. Partly imitated from l. 177; not in Text B, and probably spurious.

188. *lotering*. It is to the credit of MS. V that it has preserved this word; for Text B, like T and H₂, has *louryng*, which is inferior. It is from the French *losterie*, badinage.

195. *I-wipet*. I suppose the true reading to be *wexed*, as in Text B, and in T, H, and U. Mr Wright guessed the meaning of *wexed* to be *washed*, but in that case it is unlikely that so many MSS. would have preserved the letter *x*. It probably means *waxed*, i.e. stopped up, as one would stop with wax, much as in the following:—

"But to ende the hole were stopped and faste made,
 A litell cloute cute he without delay,
 With *wax* melled, stopped the hole alway," &c.
    Romans of Partenay (E.E.T.S.), l. 2817.

The metaphor is rather a bold one, to talk of waxing a thing up with furze, but this seems to me the only way of getting any sense out of the passage. Cf. the spellings of the word in H and U.

199. *lacche*; so in Text B.

202—207. Though these lines are in U only, they appear in all later versions of the poem, and are certainly genuine.

232. *deore*, dear. There is no doubt about the reading; see Text B. V has *dore* miswriten for *deore*, for which spelling see Pass. VI. l. 83.

257. The meaning is, "that he should polish anew his pike named Penitence;" where a *pike* means a staff with a spike to it, such as is used by pilgrims. Compare Text B,

"þat *penitencia* his pyke · he shulde polsche newe."

If the word *him* be retained, it either means polish up *for himself, for his own use;* or it merely signifies *it*, the word *pyke* being masculine, as the next line clearly shews.

PASSUS VI. Passus V. and VI. are in most MSS. considered all as one Passus. It is one of the simplest and best tests of a MS. of the *earliest* form, that they are *separated*, and numbered as distinct. It is curious that only MS. H has preserved the first two lines, the first of which scans but poorly.

30. *kende*; Text B has *kenned*; the alliteration shews it is right.

57. Also in Text B.

73. Text B also inserts *se*, which is necessary to the sense.

98, 99. The alterations are authorized by Text B.

103. *kepe*; so in Text B, and required by the alliteration.

114 The curious readings in U, viz. *unwelcome* and *unfair*, instead of *welcome* and *fair*, can be explained by arranging the subject-matter in a different order, i.e. by altering the punctuation.

Lines 114, 115 are taken together, and stand thus:—

"He is wondirly vnwolcome · and vnfair vndirfongen
 But if he be sib to some of þese seuene."

This arrangement, however, is very awkward.

PASSUS VII. ll. 22, 25. *kennest, kenne.* So also in Text B.

29. I quoted here the various spellings of *labre,* from an idea that it was misspelt for *labore ;* but it seems to have been intentional, judging by ll. 221, 259 of this very Passus.

54. The reading *we fynde treuþe,* as in T and H, suits the alliteration better, and is the reading of Text B ; but the alteration seemed hardly worth making.

57. The alliteration of each half-line is kept separate, *h* being adopted in the first part of the line, and *s* in the second. A similar example occurs again very soon, at l. 69 ; and perhaps at l. 73. Cf. V. 125, and the note.

68. It should be noted that "Deleantur de libro viventium : et cum Justis non scribantur" is all one quotation.

71. The reader who consults MS. U must remember to turn back here some 18 folios to fol. 5 *b*, or he will not find ll. 71--215.

85. *heo ;* MSS. H and U have *Chirche* is properly feminine, so that *him* in l. 86 may mean the parson (*persona ecclesiæ*).

94. The chief-letter is wanting.

109. The reading of U, *dieu sa* (= *saue*) *dame emme,* is borrowed from the Prologue, l. 103.

124. The word *holde* may mean *faithful,* and it is very probable that the other reading *olde* is corrupt, but it is difficult to make sure of this, because *holde* may be written for *olde* in the same way that *heren* is for *eren* in ll. 60, 99. Text B has *olde.*

130. The word *brod* in T has a small *k* written over the *d* evidently by way of correction.

133. The word *gare* is uncommon in this version of the poem, but occurs in l. 289 below.

134. Repeated from Prol. l. 28.

140, 141. The reading given in the text is the only one that satisfies all the requirements of the case. It is better to put *wastours* in the *plural,* because of ll. 144, 149, 151 ; and at the same time the word *one* is wanted in the *singular,* to denote the particular ringleader who speaks again in l. 153, and of whom Hunger made a special example in l. 161, where V errs in using the plural number.

145. Faulty in scansion.

159. *hoped,* hopped : but none of the MSS. double the *p.*

181. *sonenday* may not mean Sunday ; the expression reminds us of the very first line of the Prologue—*whon softe was þe sonne ;* and a "*softe sonenday*" is a day when the sun is mild and warm.

182. *hot* may = *hote,* i. e. oaten ; cf. the various readings, and note to l. 124.

186. *Al* seems to make better sense, but the line is not in Text B.

197. The chief-letter seems wanting, unless we put a little stress on the word *to ;* but the MSS. all agree, and it is the same in Text B.

202. *mete*; I let this word stand, as it is in VHU, and we have *bred* twice in the next line; still Text B has *bred*, and T has *breed*.

204. *Bamme*; so in V; but I hardly understand it or the word *bane*. The reading of H—*a-bane*—seems to hint at *a-bate*, which is the actual reading of several MSS.; see Text B.

215. *Seint Matheu* is really St *Luke*, but it is the author's own mistake. The reading þer*myde* for þer*with* should be noticed; it gives a sort of alliteration to the line, (*M*ak, þer*m*yde, *M*atheu), which is otherwise wanting.

226, 228. The words in small print are written over the word *npnam* in V.

239. There is little alliteration here, except in the words *him*, and *his* (repeated).

241. The words *lyf, lif, leef* certainly end with *f* (very plainly written), not with a long *s* (ſ).

251. *I-ȝeten = eaten*, not *gotten*. The very soft *y* sound of the ȝ does not destroy the alliteration, which is made up of vowel-sounds.

287. The alliteration is obtained either by supposing each half-line complete in itself (the first half having *h* and the second *c*), or by adopting the reading in T and U, which is given in Text B.

311. At the end of the Passus, we find, in MS. T, the following entry in a later hand.

"Here is lefte oute v. versis w*hi*che is in the olde coppi, & ar set benethe.
and when you se the sune amisse · & to mvnkes heades,
and a mayde have the masteri · And mvltiply by (eight) hight, (*sic*)
than shall deathe withdraw · and derthe be Justice,
and da*v*i the diker · shall die for hu*n*ger,
But if god of his goodness · gravnte vs a trewe."

But the writer of this makes a slight mistake; for these lines belong to MSS. of Class B, and do not appear in any of Class A. *See* Text B.

PASSUS VIII. 1. We must lay a slight stress on *to*, for the alliteration's sake.

5, 6. *heren* has no *h* prefixed in any MS. but V; *see* Pass. VII. ll. 4, 60.

45, 46. This reading of MS. H is doubtless right; *see* l. 61 below. Text B gives little help, but Text C has the lines,

"Men of lawe hadden lest · þat loþ weren to plede
But þai *pre manibus* weren ipaid · for pledyng at þe barre,"
which gives the sense, and authorizes the word "loþ."

47. Ps. xiv. 5. "Qui pecuniam suam non dedit ad usuram, et munera super innocentem non accepit. Qui facit hæc, non movebitur in æternum." For the latter part of the quotation, *see* l. 55 below. The word *eorum* is from Text B. I cannot quite trace the quotation, *A Regibus, &c.* It seems to be a reminiscence of Ecclesiasticus xxxviii. 2—"A Deo est enim omnis medela, et a rege accipiet donationem."

58. *þriuen*, thriven; hence, *beo þriuen =* are thriven, i. e. thrive. But

though this seems quite right, it is proper to note that the reading is unsupported. Texts B and C vary from A here-abouts.

73. The reading given is quite satisfactory, and is in Text B.

75. *wo* here does not mean *woe*, but is equivalent to the *woo* of MS. H, and the *wehe* of MS. T, a word used to denote the sound made by animals; the usual reading of MSS. is *wehe*. See *whi, wey*, or *wehe* in IV. 21.

78. The misreading *Fautes* in V is merely owing to the omission of the mark of contraction for *n*; it should be "Faūtes;" *see* Pass. X. ll. 58, 64.

88. *loue of*. The omission of these words in V is a mere accident; the line is left far too short.

106. This reading is confirmed by Text B.

109. So in Text B; here the author, quoting Matthew, refers to Luke; just above (Pass. VII. l. 215) he makes the exactly reverse error.

114. *who fynt*, i. e. who findeth or provideth for them; so in Text B.

125, 126. These lines are of very doubtful authenticity, and may have been added by the scribe of MS. H to explain the Latin quotation. Most MSS. have *Ecce* for *Ejice*, owing probably to confusion between *Ecce* and the less common and curious-looking word *Eiice*, as it would be spelt.

128. *waitide*, looked; so in Text B.

136. The quotation as given in H is corrupt; the word *est* should not appear: *quod* (which seemed to me indistinct) is right, but *optat* should be *optans*.

"Somnia ne cures, nam mens humana quod optans,
Dum vigilat, sperat, per somnum cernit id ipsum."
Dionysius Cato; Distich. II. 31.

The English translation of it in H is almost certainly a spurious line.

136—139. MSS. T and U and Text B help us out here. V reads,
"Ac for the Bible bereþ witnesse · hou daniel deuynede
þe Dremels of a kyng · þat Nabugodonosor hette."

The confusion arose from the shortness of l. 137, which is lengthened in U by writing "how daniel þe prophete." And then, this line being once miswritten, the next line had to be shortened by cutting away part of it.

153. Not in Text B; hence *men* depends on MS. T only, but would suit the alliteration excellently.

177. A small cross is prefixed to this line in MS. T, no doubt as a mark that it is imperfect. A few other imperfect lines are marked in the same way, the marks being as old as the rest of the writing.

187. *Explicit, &c.* This important note, for which we have the authority not only of MSS. T, U, H₂, and D, but of many others, gives us the right titles of the poems, and shews that the first one, the "Vision of William concerning Piers the Plouȝman," ends here, and that the remaining verses form a second and distinct poem, which is, however, a sort of continuation of the former. This is very clearly pointed out even in MS. V; for we here meet with the only *title* which can be found in it; *see* Passus IX. l. 1.

It is pretty clear that Langland had intended to wind up his poem here by discoursing on the excellences of Doing Well; and in this concluding passage, the word *Do-wel* accordingly occurs four times, without any hint of Doing Better or Doing Best. But an afterthought suggested that Do-well, if supplemented by Do-bet and Do-best, deserved that much more should be said about it, and that, in fact, here was matter for a whole new poem. The opening lines of Passus IX. (which, it should be remembered, is only a *prologue*, and therefore, like the first prologue, much shorter than the other Passus) seem to indicate a short lapse of time between the conclusion of the one poem and the commencement of the other. The poet's adventure with the two Minorite friars may possibly have had some foundation in fact; at any rate, it is very naturally introduced, and serves admirably to introduce a new vision.

Passus IX. Observe that the Title to this Passus is given at the end of Pass. VIII. It is the Prologue to the Vita de Do-well, as has just been said above.

3, 4, 5. For the alterations here, and in ll. 11, 12, 24, 32, see Text B.

11. The change of place of *furre* and *passede* greatly improves the metre; it is amply authorized.

20. The reading of V—*a tom*—is very curious; it is an evident corruption of *at hom*. It is also curious that MSS. of class B omit these two words.

47. The alteration is necessary in order to obtain the chief-letter of the alliteration, which is the *s* in *self;* and there is no *s* in the latter half of the line, as given in V.

50. þe occurs also in Text B.

64. wiȝt occurs in Text B, and is needed for the alliteration.

65. The corrupt reading in V probably arose from taking *I-seide*, the past participle, to mean *I seide*. Text B has the same as I have given, which is certainly right. In MS. T, we find the word *seide*, and just over it and in front of it the letter .I., the alteration having been made by the scribe himself.

66. *seȝe þou*, sawest thou. It seems better to insert þou, as in Text B.

80 The expression, *Erl Auerous*, is in Text B.

83. The Vulgate has, "Libenter enim suffert*is* insipientes, cum sitis ipsi sapientes;" but it is clear by the next line that the poet took the reading to be *sufferte* in the imperative mood. But in Text B we find *suffertis*, and a corresponding alteration of the following line.

95. *puiten;* sic in MS. V, both here and elsewhere. The alteration of *him* into *hem* in this line and the next seems required; but it is just possible that the scribe of MS. V considered *him* as a *plural*. The alteration, however, would still be justified by the occurrence of *hem* in l. 94.

101. So in Text B.

107. þroly, quickly. This reading seems to be preserved in V only.

111. Also in Text B.

114. So in Text B.

118. *hym techen;* Text B has *teche hym.*

Passus X. Here the "Vita de Dowel" properly begins.

6—8. Miswritten in V after this manner;

A loueli lemmon lyk him-self · *Anima* heo hette,

To hire haþ Envye · A proud prikere of Fraunce, *Princeps huius mundi.*
This mistake arose (1) from the shortness of l. 6; (2) from the fulness of the stop in the middle of l. 7; and (3) from supposing *Princeps huius mundi* to be an independent quotation. In order to make these three lines into two, the scribe had to omit *to* after *lyk*, and to neglect the alliteration altogether.

9. *mihti; sic* in MS. V; so I let it stand.

11, 12. The missing words are also in Text B.

27. *Ceatour* in MS. V, by mistake.

30. The meaning of *lisse* and *Blisse* is the same, but *lisse* is required for the alliteration, and appears in very many MSS., although they give the word *Blisse* afterwards, in l. 36.

31. *arn*, not *ben*, must be the reading, and is supported by Text B.

50. The reading *kepeth* is also supported by ll. 10, 15, 24.

52. I have little doubt the reading given is right, but there is hardly any more evidence than that given, for this line does not appear in Text B. Still we have the evidence of MSS. TUH$_2$, and it is clear that V is corrupt, as *Bringeþ* spoils the alliteration, besides affording but little sense.

53. The reading in U, *goynge*, may have been suggested by mistaking *cunnynge* for *cumynge*, and it would then strike the scribe that *goynge* would suit the alliteration better than *cumynge.*

61. *ben* is wanted to complete the sense.

71. The reluctance of the scribe of V to write the word *wiȝt* is curious; a similar correction has been often made before; see, for example, Pass. IX. l. 64; and cf. XI. 122.

72. Either *of* or *ouer* must be inserted; the former suits the flow of the line better.

75. *wyte* (MS. U) means *blame.*

86. It may be doubted whether David really meant to praise the consolation to be found in a birch-rod!

89. I have not yet traced this quotation. MS. V has, *Intencio I hoïe.*

95. *kepe*, not *hede*, suits the alliteration.

106. I cannot yet trace this quotation.

107. The alliteration is defective; it is somewhat better preserved in MSS. T and U, but not so much better as to justify alteration.

124. *molde* is of course right; cf. Pass. III. l. 71.

135. The chief-letter is wanting.

143. The readings *a barn*, and *wrouȝte* are made certain by observing the line following, "Caym men cleped *him.*"

152. *Sem* was no doubt written for *Seth* as being a more familiar name; else it is obviously wrong.

154. *suster sed*, i. e. sister's seed ; *see* l. 173.

165. *banne* (not *curse*) suits the alliteration.

190. The misreading in V here was a necessary consequence of the misreading in l. 188. The scribe clearly did not understand the allusion to Dunmow.

193. The reading given is from T, slightly modified; for it is usual in MS. V to use -*eþ* as the plural ending of the imperative, and to write *ou* instead of *ȝow*, and it is better to adhere to a uniform system, where it can so easily be preserved.

197. The punctuation is difficult. In Text B, there seems to be almost a full stop in the middle of this line ; but then, the subsequent lines vary considerably.

204, 205. The alliteration and Text B both shew that these lines are rightly restored.

213. *werke ;* so also in Text B.

PASSUS XI. 2. In Text B we find,
"þat lenc was of lere · and of liche bothe."

13. The alliteration seems to be formed either by the initials of *hit, heo,* and *heore,* or by those of *sigge* and *schewen.*

18. *cardet ; carded* in Text B.

23. *bene est.* If the mark of interrogation be omitted, it is very natural that *bene* here should be turned into *ve,* as in MSS. TU. The Vulgate however (Jer. xii. 1) has "Quare via impiorum prosperatur : bene est omnibus qui prævaricantur et inique agunt ?" where the sentence is an interrogative one.

28. Observe how the voice is to be sustained at the end of this line ; i. e. as for *him,* he is but little loved.

30. *Daunseled* seems peculiar to MS. V ; cf. prov. Eng. *dawntled,* fondled, made much of. Text B has *daunted,* tamed, put down, made little of, which does not suit the context.

46. The alliteration is hardly perceptible ; it is probably formed by dwelling on the *f.* Thus, in Mr Wright's text, we find,
Bothe a-fyngred and a-furst · and for chele quake,
which is probably the correct reading, *afyngred* and *afurst* being a provincial pronunciation of *of-hungred* and *of-thurst,* i. e. afflicted by hunger and thirst.

71. *musen on,* &c. Text B ends the line with, " þat muse moche on her wordes."

79. *to wite ;* so in Text B ; cf. l. 81.

85. *worþ ;* so too in Text B ; it greatly improves the line. Cf. Pass. I. l. 26.

96. *his ;* so in Text B ; the reading *hire* is clearly wrong.

100. *worþe ;* see l. 85.

102, 104. This is another of the many instances where MS. V wrongly uses *teche* instead of *kenne.* Cf. Pass. VI. 30 ; VII. 22, 25.

111. The alliteration is defective.

131. *gurles.* It must be remembered that this means *boys* quite as much as *girls;* see Pass. X. l. 155.

134. *kende;* this surely must be the true reading, for *c* or *k* is required for the alliteration; it is supported by MS. T only, but we should compare ll. 102, 104, and the many passages where *kenne* is wrongly replaced by *teche;* see, e.g. Pass. I. 79; II. 4; VIII. 120. Text B varies, reading, "and *compassed* masouns."

137, 138. The alliteration helps us to restore these lines with certainty.

144. The word *loue* being feminine, the genitive may very well end in *e;* very numerous examples of this are given in Morris's "Specimens of Early English;" Introduction, p. lvii.

145. In some editions of Cato we find *simules* for *simile*, to the improvement of the prosody.

147. *See* note to ll. 102, 134.

151. The position of the words in V, viz. *himself hit*, makes the line halt instead of flowing smoothly.

155, 156. Text B has two lines very like these.

180. Text B varies here; but there is no doubt but that *Actif it is 1-hoten* is the true reading. The subject of the poem is *Vita* de Do-wel, the "wel feir lyf" as it is called in l. 179; and the poet is merely repeating what he has already said in Pass. VII. 234-236. A great deal more is said about *Activa Vita* in Pass. XIII. of Text B.

181. The reader will observe by this extract that the Trinity MS. presents an excellent text.

191, 192, 193. These lines stand thus in MS. T,

"God wot, þis is dobet · sire dobest haþ benefices,
So is he best worþi be þat god in the gospel · grauntiþ & techiþ."

The great length of the second line shews something wrong; next, the alliteration tells that *benefices* and *best* occur in the same line, and then only the words "God wot, þis is dobet" remain to form l. 191; whence it is plain that a half-line has here been lost. This has been recovered by help of the Ashmolean MS. and MS. Harl. 3954, and found to be —*dobest wot þe soþe;* for the readings there given are,

"Sekyrly, þis is dobet · dobest wot þe soþe;" (A.)
"Dredles, is dobet · dobest wot þe sothe (H.)

The omission of this half-line, and the confusion in the division of lines, arose from the fact of ll. 191 and 192 both having the same letter *b* as the rime-letter. The alliteration and rhythm also shew that the reading "Dredles" is the correct one, and it is a favourite word with Langland. "Sekyrly" is a mere gloss upon it.

215. *wolde* suits the alliteration, but *shulde* seems to be better grammar.

232. The reading of MS. T, "þat *arn* vncristene," &c., is a mere mistake of *arn* for *an*. But the reading *vncristene* is very curious, and is exactly contrary to what we should expect, viz. *cristene*. Yet MS. authority forbids alteration. Thus, we find in Harl. MS. 3954,

"þat vn-krysten in þat case · may cristenen a hethene,"
and the line occurs in Text B in the same shape.

247. *Mecaberis* seems to be the author's own mistake, the seventh commandment being put for the sixth. The words of which "ne sle nouȝt" is the "kynde englissh" are "*Non occides.*"[1] I have ventured to write *vindicta* (though all the MSS. seem to have *vindictam*), because *vindicta* is the actual reading of the Vulgate.

253. *murkid withoute mercy*, pre-ordained to life, without any need of a subsequent act of mercy; so most MSS.; but the reading of U, *markid with mercy*, is simpler.

273. *shrefe*, shrived. It ought to be *shref*, and the tag to the *f* can hardly mean a final *e*. It is another form of *shrof*, the more usual past tense of *shrive* or *shrieve*.

283. The misreading *now* probably arose from confusing *non* with *nou*.

285. The readings are,

And ȝet any I forget · for of fyue wyttis techinge
þat clergie of cristis mouþ · comendite what is neuere T;
And ȝet am (*or* ani) I forget · of fyue wittes techynge
That Clergie of Cristes mouþ · comonded hit neuere D;
And ȝit any I forget · for of fyue wittes techyng
That clergie of cristes mouȝt · comendite what is neuere H₂;
And ȝit I forgat ferþere · of fyue wittis techyng
Wat clergie of cristis mouth · comendid was   A(shmole);
And ȝet haue I forgete ferthere · of v wittys techynge
þat clergyȝe of crystys mowth · comandyd was neuer. Harl. 3954;

Text B has the single line,

Clergye þo of crystes mouþ · commonded was it litel.

MS. U omits both lines.

From all these the sense intended is plain enough, and as regards the former line, it is clear that   Ashmole and Harl. 3954 MSS. supply the word really wanted, viz. *ferþere*, owing to the absence of which TH absurdly introduce *any* and *for* to fill up the line. Again, as regards the latter line, the true form is shewn in Harl. 3954, only it is necessary to alter *neuer* to *euer* in order to preserve the sense. The reading *neuer* arose from considering the line as a simple statement instead of that which it really is, viz. a dependent clause. The reading *what is* in TH₂ is a curious and meaningless corruption of *was*. The lines, as given in the text, mean—"And yet I forget further—by help of the teaching of my five wits—that learning was ever commended by Christ's mouth;" i.e. "my five wits do not enable me to remember that Christ ever commended learning."

---

[1] Mr Wright says, "A mistake in the original MS. for *necaberis*, as it is rightly printed in Crowley's edition." But surely, *non necaberis* means—" thou shalt not be killed."

303. In the preface, abundant reason is given in support of the view that the early version must have ended here, as is actually the case with MSS. Douce, Harl. 3954, and Ashmole, 1468; and this is where the poem probably ended also in the Vernon MS. The only MSS. that go beyond this point are TH²U. Of these, the two former are supplemented by what is really a portion of the C-class of MSS., and there is a consequent jumble in the numbering of the subsequent Passus and a very abrupt transition in the sense, sufficient to shew clearly that the junction of the A and C texts is but clumsily effected after all. It ought also to be noted that the quotation "*Brevis oracio penetrat celum*" does *not* strictly belong to the A-class of MSS., but to the C-class. But I have introduced it for two reasons: (1) because it is very appropriate and makes an excellent concluding line, and is closely connected with the sense of the lines before it, and (2) because it is *useful* as indicating the point of junction of the A and C texts, as the reader will find when he consults Text C. If the poem *in its earliest form* was ever continued beyond this point, it was probably continued in the manner indicated by MS. U, which has 18 lines of a "passus tercius" which are, as far as I can make out, *unique*.[1] Perhaps the poet may really have begun a third passus in this manner, which he afterwards gave up, and turned his attention to re-casting and expanding the whole poem. The 18 lines in MS. U are as follows:

Passus tercius de dowel, &c.

"Cryst wot," quod clergie · know it[2] yif ye likeþ,
I haue don my deuer · ye[3] dowel to teche;
And who-so coueite to don betere · þan ye bok telleþ,
He pasith apostlis lif · and put hem in-to angelis!   4
But y se now as i seic · as me soþ þynkeþ,
you[4] woldist kunne yat[5] i can · and carpyn it after,
Presumptuously par auenture · appose so manye,
þat it myȝte turne me to tene · & theologie boþe.   8
ȝif i wiste witterly · you woldist don yer-after
Al yat you askest · assoilen I wolde."
Scornfulliche yo scripture · set vp here browes,
And on clergie cryede · on godis holy name,   12
yat he schewiȝt[6] ne schulde · but if it stryf were
Of ye cardynal wit · & cristenyd in a font;
And seide it so loude · yat schame me it þoute,
þat it were scathe & slaundre · to holy cherche,   16
Scihoþ[7] theologie yat trewe is · tellen it deffendeþ,

[1] If there exists any other copy of these lines, I should be glad to have it pointed out to me.
[2] MS. "knowit."   [3] "ye" for "þe."   [4] "you" for "þou."
[5] "yat" for "þat;" so too we have below "yer-after," "yo," for "þer-after" and "þo."
[6] Should we read "schew it?"   [7] Probably an error for "Siþ."

Dauyd godis derlyng · deffendeþ it also,
Vidi preuaricantes & thabescebam.

This may be thus briefly paraphrased:

"Christ knows," said Clergy, " I have done my duty in teaching you to do *well*; and to do *better* is for angels to attain to. But I fear you want to learn all I know merely in order to cavil and vex me and Theology. If I thought you were in earnest, I would grant all you ask." But Scripture scornfully told him to be quiet, and talked so loud that I thought it a slight upon holy church; as David says, "It grieveth me when I see the transgressors, because they keep not thy law."[1] What the exact meaning of lines 13 and 14 is, I can only dimly guess. Perhaps it is—"that he should not shew (declare it) unless it were considered as a dispute between supreme knowledge and one who is christened in a font." That is—in allusion to line 7, where Clergy thinks that the dreamer will perhaps, after being taught, become presumptuous and ask trying questions—Clergy ought not therefore to teach William anything at all unless he at the same time remembers that any discussion between them would but be a dispute between supreme knowledge (Clergy) and a mere infant (William). But the passage is certainly hazy.

It is pretty clear that this passage is supplanted in Text B by the first three lines of the Passus immediately following the passage with which Text A ends. The three lines are these:—

"Thanne scripture scorned me · and a skile tolde,
And lakked me in latyne · and liȝte by me she sette,
And seyde, *multi multa sciunt · et seipsos nesciunt.*"

And there are similar lines in Text C, in the middle of Passus 11. de Do-wel.

"Þanne scripture scornede me · and many skyles schewede,
And coutynaunce made to clergiȝe · to conge me, hit semede,
And lackede me in latyn · and lith bi me sette,
And seide, *multi multa sciunt,[2] et seipsos nesciunt.*"

---

[1] Ps. cxix. 158 (Prayer-Book version); but *preuaricantes* must here mean *scoffers*.
[2] MS. Vesp. B. xvi. reads *sapiunt.*

GENERAL COMPARISON OF TEXTS A AND B.

The following is a list of parallel passages, and shews also where the texts differ. A few minor variations are not noticed.

PROLOGUE. Lines 1—49. So in B.
Here B inserts three lines.
Lines 50—83. So in B.
Here B inserts about 120 *lines, containing the fable of the* Cat and Rattons.
Lines 84—89. So in B.
Lines 90—95. Peculiar to A, but the sense of them is found in B, differently expressed, and at an earlier place.
Lines 96—109. So in B, with an extra line after l. 101.
PASSUS I. So in B, for the most part. The chief variations are that B inserts two lines after l. 31, puts ll. 96, 97 after l. 101, expands ll. 112, 113 into about 10 lines, and ll. 135—138 into about 17 lines.
PASSUS II. Substantially the same as Passus II. of B. The chief variations are in ll. 11—14, 19—74, which are expanded in B, and somewhat differently expressed.
Lines 75—212 agree very closely, except that ll. 150, 151 are expanded in B into 5 lines, and B has two more lines after l. 183.
PASSUS III. Lines 1—51. So in B, but ll. 18—20 somewhat vary.
Lines 52—66. The variations here are worth remarking.
Lines 67—282. So in B, very nearly ; but ll. 228—231 have their place supplied by a longer passage ; also ll. 252—259 vary.
After l. 282 B *inserts more than* 50 *lines.*
PASSUS IV. Somewhat expanded in Text B, especially in the following passages, viz. ll. 16—30, ll. 105—108, ll. 134—136, ll. 141—145. Otherwise, the texts substantially agree.

Passus V. Lines 1—33. So in B; except at ll. 11, 12, and 31.
Here B *inserts about* 6 *lines.*
Lines 34—39. So in B, with a new line after l. 35.
Here B *inserts about* 8 *lines.*
Lines 40—69. So in B, nearly
Lines 70—73. Differently expressed in B; *the variation is worth notice.*
Lines 74—99. So in B, nearly.
Here B *inserts a couple of lines.*
Lines 100—106. So in B, nearly.
Here B *inserts a long and most important passage, descriptive of* Wrath; *altogether some* 60 *lines.*
Lines 107—145. So in B, nearly, but note ll. 109—113.
Here B *inserts a long and important passage, about the sins of* Covetousness, *and how he skinned the poor; more than* 70 *lines.*
Lines 146—221. So in B, nearly; but note that l. 215 is expanded in B into *fifteen* lines.
Here B *inserts another long and important passage, containing the confession of* Sloth, *and his regrets for his mis-spent youth; nearly* 60 *lines.*
Lines 222—259. So in B, nearly.
Here B *again inserts about* 40 *lines, concerning the* Crucifixion and Resurrection of Christ.
Lines 260—263. So in B, nearly. But note, that *Passus V. of text* B *does not terminate here.*

Passus VI. This forms, in B, the concluding portion of Passus V.; the agreement is pretty close. However, there are some variations about ll. 36—38, 82—84, and line 97, and B has an extra line after l. 112.
After l. 126, B *inserts four new lines.*

Passus VII. Agrees substantially with B, Passus VI., but *the occasional variations are very numerous.* Observe, e. g. ll. 9—20, and the insertion of two lines after l. 40, of four lines after l. 46, of a line after l. 59, and of two lines after l. 65. Observe also the slight variations and insertions at ll. 128—139, l. 149, ll. 167—172, ll. 178—188, l. 190, ll. 212—215, ll. 238, 239, and after l. 301.

At the end of the Passus B *adds* 5 *lines, containing a curious prophecy; see the* Critical Notes, p. 147.

Passus VIII. Called Passus VII. in B.
Lines 1—72. In B, but there are *numerous variations,* best observed by actual comparison. It is worth noting that ll. 13—17 and 38—44 seem to be fuller and better expressed in the earlier version.
After l. 72, B *inserts some* 20 *lines about* Beggars.
Lines 73—187. In B, but with a few variations, e. g. at ll. 132, 147, 151, and 153—155.

Passus IX., or Prologue to Dowel. Called Passus VIII. in B, and the two agree pretty closely.

B *has four extra lines after* l. 13, *and five extra lines after* l. 47, *one extra line after* l. 115, *and two more lines at the end of the Passus.*

PASSUS X., XI. Called in B Passus IX. and X. Here all close resemblance soon ceases, and the variations become numerous and important. Text B is far the fullest on the whole, but there are a few passages which are fuller and better expressed in the earlier version. Both versions are very good, and it would be a pity to lose or pass over either of them. Ll. 180—303 of Passus XI., for instance, are varied and expanded in B at great length, and it is here that we meet with the curious prophecy (a mere chance guess, but none the less notable) that a king should come, and amend monks and canons, and the abbot of Abingdon should have a knock of the king, and incurable should be the wound. Of all this there is, in Text A, no hint whatever.

Text C is much farther removed from Text A than B is, and as the variations between B and C will be pointed out hereafter, it is not necessary to say much about it here.

The manufacturer's authorised representative in the EU for product safety is Oxford University Press España S.A. of el Parque Empresarial San Fernando de Henares, Avenida de Castilla, 2 – 28830 Madrid (www.oup.es/en or product. safety@oup.com). OUP España S.A. also acts as importer into Spain of products made by the manufacturer.

www.ingramcontent.com/pod-product-compliance
Ingram Content Group UK Ltd.
Pitfield, Milton Keynes, MK11 3LW, UK
UKHW022151230426
12049UKWH00003BA/42